The Brainjac Paradox

Mark Cornillie

STEIN, KLAUBER & COMPANY

Published by Stein, Klauber & Company
Chicago • Detroit • Cincinnati
P.O. Box 15051, Detroit, MI 48230

Discounts are available for bulk purchase in the U.S. For more information,
contact the Group Sales Department at Stein, Klauber & Company, P.O. Box
15051, Detroit, MI, 48230 or email sales@steinandklauber.com.

Library of Congress Control Number: 2013943244

ISBN: 978-0-9891-8850-0

1 3 5 7 9 8 6 4 2 0

For Elizabeth, whose unwavering and
reckless support made this possible.

– Table of Contents –

SECTION I – THE ISSUE

SECTION II – THE ANSWER

SECTION III – THE FOIBLES

– Preface –

As I wrote this book, I envisioned a sample of past and present colleagues sitting in a circle around me as I explained what I have come to call the Brainiac Paradox. I selected these particular individuals because they represented a cross-section from the sciences, technology, engineering and mathematics (STEM) and because I had long observed in them the characteristics I have come to associate with this phenomenon. I hoped this exercise would help me anticipate and proactively address the questions, objections and preferences of readers. This approach, however, presented its own paradox.

Some common traits among this group were precision … but also impatience; self-reliance … but also a desire for prescriptive solutions. So as I described this issue, I imagined some stopping me frequently to contest details and ask for explanations and substantiations, even as others pushed me to get to the point. Then, when I offered potential remedies, I could hear some requesting that they be very specific and prescriptive, "Just tell me what to do, and I'll do it," while others preferred to do their own problem solving, "Just define the problem and I will figure it out myself."

Another challenge that became apparent as a result of having this virtual focus group accompany me through the writing process was the diversity of the assistance that would be needed. During the planning phase, I had been conceptualizing this as an abstract whole: an amalgamation of the various communication-related issues I had observed interfering with certain professionals' abilities to succeed in the workplace. However, as my mind's eye scanned the faces of these individuals, I was reminded of the great variation in form and magnitude of the contributing characteristics. Each of these colleagues exhibited different combinations of these and to different degrees. In fact, one might have weaknesses in some areas, yet strengths in others; while the next person might exhibit those strengths and weaknesses in reverse.

And, as if that did not complicate things enough, there was an entirely different audience I needed to consider: those *indirectly* affected by the Brainiac Paradox.

Over the years, I have encountered many managers who agonized over "what to do with" very talented subordinates who exhibited chronic communication or collaboration issues. Their technical skills and expertise would be difficult to replace, but they represented a net liability to the team.

Similarly, I had heard the rumblings of colleagues, project managers, customers, suppliers, etc., whose own work was hampered when it was necessary for them to interact with certain individuals or teams.

Finally, there was the affect on personal relationships. The work challenges and career setbacks of those affected would sometimes simmer into a stew of frustration that could not help but spill over into the lives of spouses, loved ones, and close friends. As Bruce Springsteen is purported to have said, "I have never met a man who hated his work, but who loved his life."

Thus, I assumed those indirectly affected would likely have a keen interest in understanding the Brainiac Paradox and a vested interest in seeing it overcome; in fact, they may play a key role. Noted psychologist and bestselling author, Tony Attwood suggested that because of denial, or a belief by those affected that they could "fix things themselves," it may only be through such colleagues, loved ones, and friends that this book would find its way to some of those who need it most. Furthermore, many of the remedies prescribed in this book call for second parties to provide assessments, feedback, and suggestions. In some cases, loved ones, and friends may be the ideal people to serve those roles.

I struggled to find a single elegant method that would satisfy these sometimes conflicting audience perspectives and requirements. In the end, I decided on a quasi-modular design that could work well for those approaching the book traditionally – reading sequentially and in full – as well as those preferring a custom path. This is described in the "How to Use This Book" section, starting on page 11.

— Introduction —

The Tower of Technobabel

Nothing in science has any value to society if it is not communicated.
— Anne Roe, The Making of a Scientist

T*he Tower of Babel* is the biblical tale of an ancient peoples' attempt to build a great tower "whose top will reach into heaven." God, however, is angered by their heresy and "confounds their language, that they may not understand one another's speech." No longer able to communicate, the ambitious project fails and is abandoned.

Though not the result of divine retribution, aspects of this primeval story are sometimes replayed on the most modern of stages: the offices and labs of today's science, technology, engineering, and math (STEM) professionals. In both cases, great aspirations are thwarted by difficulties with the most fundamental of human functions: communication.

Those who experience challenges as the result of aspects of communication are found in every segment of society, but they appear to be notably more common and pronounced among those who work in STEM professions. Many attribute this to the special terminology, jargon, and acronyms that pervade various technical fields, which create a language within a language. But even if such language could be magically abolished, significant communication issues would continue to plague some in these professions.

Others assert that this is the result of the reduced emphasis on the study of the humanities as necessitated by increasingly demanding and specialized technical curriculums. "We have added more and more technical content and subtracted more and more of the soft sciences and the arts and so we have effectively created a series of monsters – and those monsters are called technical people," says James Smith, a professor of mechanical and aerospace engineering at West Virginia University and former president of the Society of Automotive Engineers. "They have no communication capabilities and rely on people who have no expertise on the technical side to do their selling, which is a disastrous equation." While no doubt a major contributor, that cannot be the entire explanation. After all, there are many in these fields who are gifted writers and polished presenters, yet may still find their work hampered by other communication-related issues.

Still others believe that this is not so much a result of environmental factors, but instead of certain characteristics and aptitudes that are hardwired into some individuals. "One can make the argument that the genes of technological innovation are frequently in conflict with emotional intelligence," said Elliot Schrage, former Google vice president, in the book *Googled*, by Ken Auletta. But if this is solely related to an inherent characteristic, would not we expect to see more uniformity in the way people are affected?

Then there are those who contend the real problem lies with the non-technical people who are unable to operate on a higher cognitive plane. "Why should we have to dumb things down just so incompetent bosses can understand," one said to me. Granted, this may be a valid point for most technical professionals at certain times, and even for certain technical professionals most of the time, but it is not valid for most technical professionals most of the time. Keep in mind that technical professionals are among those most critical of the communication foibles of other technical professionals.

However one looks at it, it should be clear that **some** of the people who have been bestowed with the aptitudes necessary for success in demanding technical professions have been conspicuously less fortunate in terms of the aptitudes necessary for effective communication.

This is a common perception, one that both weaves through recorded history and spans contemporary society (it is the entire premise of the hit CBS television show *The Big Bang Theory*). But while this issue may be widely accepted, it has been little explored. It is as if people just dismiss it as one of the many social curiosities that populate our communal psyche – like the reputation of some great artists to be temperamental and some great actors to be narcissistic: unfortunate, yes, but just the way they are.

Such neglect, however, can come at enormous costs. Contemporary society is increasingly dependent upon technical professionals to provide the innovation critical to economic growth and the solutions needed to tackle rapidly evolving difficulties and threats. However, communication problems can significantly undermine the delivery of innovations and solutions. This results in important opportunities being lost ... and everyone pays the price.

Over the years I have encountered countless individuals with great minds and unique talents, yet who were confounded in their ability to capitalize on their gifts. What hampered one may be different than what hampered the next, but whatever the source of their troubles, they all traced back to aspects of communication.

Too often these people were cursed by continuingly-diminishing hopes and expectations. They may have started their careers brimming with confidence, ideas, and enthusiasm, but those were eroded over time by relentless frustrations and setbacks stemming from interpersonal and organizational dynamics. Some eventually gave up, even if they did not quit; they merely slogged along in their professions delivering a fraction of their potential. A sobering example is relayed by John Elder Robison in his 2008 memoir, *look me in the eye*, "I had come to accept what my annual performance reviews said. I was not a team player. I had trouble communicating with people. I was inconsiderate. I was rude. I was smart and creative, yes, but I was a misfit. I was thoroughly sick of all the criticism. I was sick of life …. I hated to get up and face another day at work." Even though few will feel this issue as acutely as Robison, there are many more who will be disheartened by less than fully-realized careers.

What a waste! Within these groups are some of our most brilliant people. They often represent the cream of our academic crops, a source of tremendous potential, yet too many become sub-optimized. They offer expertise that is essential to our economic wellbeing, yet society does not reap their full potential.

This book attempts to understand this issue, to explore its possible origins, and to provide practical and effective ways to address it. Its goal is to help affected STEM professionals mitigate the foibles that prevent their full contribution in the workplace.

Seeking Answers

Increasingly, facets of this phenomenon are alluded to in various social, psychological, and neurological research, but mostly as a byproduct, not the focus of the research. As ubiquitous and consequential as this issue is, it is surprising that it has not been studied more directly. This could be because the evidence comes from quite different arenas, obscuring the quest for a singular explanation. Another possible reason could be explained by the old saying, "The cobbler's children have no shoes." After all, the very people necessary to authoritatively research this issue would be within the group being studied.

I come to this subject through a circuitous route. I am not a scientist, psychologist, or similar specialist, but like Chrono's good-luck-piece in Kurt

Vonnegut's *The Sirens of Titan*, time and circumstances have uniquely shaped me for this purpose.

My degree and early career were in journalism and I approach the first half of this book – which defines and explores this issue – as a journalist: seeking out relevant information, interviewing those representing various perspectives, and attempting to provide a coherent, objective and balanced summary of the topic. I do not presume to fully explain the Brainiac Paradox, but I believe I have connected the dots in ways that provide useful insights. Moreover, my lack of scientific standing may be an advantage. I have been able to explore this topic as a neutral observer. I have no prior research to promote or scientific point of view to defend.

As for my credentials for the second half of the book – which offers solutions for mitigating this issue – my career eventually transitioned to corporate communications and, also possessing a keen technical aptitude, increasingly focused on technology communication. This led to more than 20 years working closely with, for, among, and on behalf of STEM professionals. Generally this entailed proactive work to bridge understanding between technical and non-technical audiences, but at times it also involved reactive work to address communication problems that arose among certain teams or individuals. From that work I developed various strategies, techniques and tools designed to help such individuals avoid repeated problems in the future.

Despite originally being a relatively small part of my responsibilities, I considered this developmental work to be very important. For while I had a gift for assimilating and distilling complex technical information in a way that could be understood and valued by any audience, the effect was never as great as when a true expert was able to communicate his or her work effectively and directly. Eventually, I was lobbying management for more opportunities to implement programs that would address common communication failure points and enhance overall communication effectiveness. I made it my stated goal to "eliminate the need for my services." To do this, though, would take a very different approach than what had been attempted before.

The Alternative
There have been numerous efforts (books, journal articles, college courses, organizational workshops, etc.) to address the type of communication issues discussed thus far, however, most have focused on communication mechanics – how to write and speak better. Alternatively, it has been addressed as a leadership issue: the challenge of managing technical teams.

While helpful, I belief these have missed much of what is needed to resolve this issue effectively. The former falls short: improving communication mechanics alone will only help some and even in those cases the improvements are likely to be fleeting. The latter relies too much on the wrong people: managers will be crucial to addressing this issue, but they can do only so much without the active participation of those directly affected. Note that despite relatively significant cumulative efforts over the years, the problem persists, and may be getting worse.

In the movie *The King's Speech*, Lionel Logue was portrayed as a frustrated stage actor turned speech therapist who used various techniques, some unorthodox, to alleviate King George VI's stuttering. The movie suggested that Logue succeeded – even after the most eminent speech therapists in Great Britain had failed – because his approach was predominantly based on his experience with the masses of WWI veterans (whose speech had been affected by injury or trauma), as opposed to a reliance on classroom and textbook study. In other words, the practical knowledge he attained through direct practice trumped those offered by the best theoretical offerings.

Like Logue, my approach is based on hands-on experience: more than two decades work with technical professionals *in the trenches*. Over that time, I have had the opportunity to work with some truly brilliant and talented people, but I repeatedly found myself thinking, "if only he didn't do this …" or, "if only she would do that …." Sometimes even the most basic aberrations would dramatically curtail their effectiveness and set them on a path of marginal careers.

I observed that the problematic characteristics fell into a relatively small set of behaviors, attitudes, and practices. Furthermore, I found that when I had a chance to work with these people in small groups or one-on-one, it was surprising what a difference it made. They were like machines with a couple binding parts. Remove the obstructions or just add a little lubricant in the right places and away they hummed. In this book, I refer to these obstructions or friction points as foibles and I identify and address nine of them. These are not the root causes of this phenomenon, merely a manifestation of them, but if they are resolved, those affected can contribute more closely to their full potential.

King George VI remained a stutterer, but the remedies provided by Logue allowed him to mitigate it enough to fulfill his public duties. Towards that end, I offer a handful of remedies that have been developed over my years dealing with this issue. Even those that are based on classic communication theory or common best practices have been modified and tempered by what I have encountered firsthand working with those affected. And like Logue's techniques, some of those offered within may at times seem very elementary and even a little inane if the particular foible being addressed is not among those applicable to the reader. However, what may be inane for one person, may be the key to success for another.

The Path of Moderate Resistance

In *StrengthsFinder 2.0*, Tom Rath, makes the case that it is a waste of time to focus on addressing our weaknesses, "the path of *most* resistance." He insists that if instead we focus on enhancing our strengths, and work with those who possess complementary strengths, we will achieve more and be happier. I applaud his sentiments, but unfortunately society is not yet so enlightened. If anything, it appears organizations are moving further away from that idea, with an ever-increasing emphasis on *well-rounded* employees. As such, they are willing to forgo the potential of creating synergetic teams comprised of people with special individual gifts in exchange for what may be described as low-maintenance employees.

This book strikes a balance with this reality. While it does focus on some common areas for improvement, it is not intended to *cure* them. This is not just because it would be unrealistic for everyone to write like Leo Tolstoy, present like Tony Robbins, or work organizational politics like Niccolò Machiavelli, but also because it is unnecessary. In fact, in most cases there is nothing to cure. If considered impartially, it is not so much a matter of certain people being deficient in terms of communication abilities, just different. "Our social norms stink," said Kathy Kolbe, founder of Kolbe Corporation and the Center for Conative Abilities, "because they pathologize perfectly healthy people and because they aggrandize a very narrow band of acceptable social behaviors."

Even if those working in technical fields encounter communication-related difficulties with certain non-technical groups, they might not with their peers. A friend of mine has a son who aspires to be an engineer. He is a quiet and reserved young man and likes to spend much of his free time working on his computer. However, when dropped off at a summer engineering camp hosted by a nearby university, my friend was surprised by the change in his son. "Almost immediately he became comfortable, outgoing, and engaged with his fellow campmates. He was now surrounded by people he *got* and who *got* him." The neural synchronizing and amplifying mechanisms that Psychologist Daniel Goleman says are key to social intelligence were now engaged for him.

It is as if different groups communicate and interact on different frequencies (neither of which is inherently superior to the other), and it is that mismatch that leads to communication problems.

Unfortunately, the onus still lies on those outside the mainstream to adjust *enough* to be able to work effectively with others. Even if they try to segregate themselves into like-minded groups, they still largely depend on outside groups (for employment, funding, resources, cooperation, etc.). It is similar to when we visit a country that has a language unfamiliar to us. If we cannot find some basic way to communicate, it will be we, and not they, who suffer.

Modest Change

Fortunately, mitigating the affects does not require outright conformity, but instead moderate accommodations. This book relies heavily on the 80/20 rule, where 80% of the problem may be related to only 20% of the behaviors; and 80% of the improvement can be achieved with 20% of the effort. If taken literally, this suggests that 64% of the problem can be addressed by 4% of the effort. There are reasons for this beyond what has already been said about not trying to transform those who experience the ill-effects of the Paradox into a Tolstoy, a Robbins, or a Machiavelli. Some are matters of practicality, and others of effectiveness.

First, it is very important to note that while nine foibles are addressed in this book, most people among those affected will exhibit only a handful of these to any significant extent, often just one or two. In addition, different people will exhibit different combinations. Thus, a one-size-fits-all solution would be ponderous and, ultimately, ineffective.

Next, many of the nine foibles are very involved topics in themselves. For example, Chapter 15 deals with the *aversion to selling* foible. A search on "sales techniques" in Amazon.com's book section returned over 12,000 entries. With a topic so extensive, it only makes sense to narrow the focus to the most relevant and productive topics.

Finally, providing an all-inclusive set of foibles, each addressed in great detail, might even hinder achievement of the book's goal: to help affected STEM professionals mitigate the foibles that prevent their full contribution in the workplace. It is like preparing a soldier for battle. If equipped for every conceivable contingency, they would be too weighed down to fight. Instead, it is better to focus on providing the equipment that is most likely to be needed, along with the consideration of which has the best effectiveness to weight/size ratio.

The methodology and remedies offered herein are not intended to be a detailed map, but more a compass and some guideposts. As Benjamin Franklin said, "Tell me and I forget. Teach me and I remember. Involve me and I learn." After all, if there is one characteristic that is almost universal among those in STEM fields, it is a gift for problem solving. By identifying and defining the problems, and setting the direction with the assistance of the provided explanations and remedies, I am confident resourceful professionals will achieve the right solution for their particular situation, and *learn* more in the process.

— How to Use This Book —

To accommodate the needs of different audiences as well as the different preferences within each audience type, this book offers the following content features and shortcuts.

I.   Content Segmentation
This book has been organized into sections according to tightly grouped and carefully-ordered topics:

- SECTION I – *The Issue*
  Defines the Brainiac Paradox and explores possible explanations.

- SECTION II – *The Answer*
  Offers a time-tested methodology for ensuring long-term success.

- SECTION II – *The Foibles*
  Introduces the nine foibles proposed to be the most common and/or detrimental to communication effectiveness and offers remedies for addressing them.

- SECTION IV – *The Alternative*
  Offers an alternative approach for dealing with the foibles.

As such, those only interested in better understanding the Brainiac Paradox may be satisfied by just reading Section I. Alternatively, those anxious to address it can jump directly to Section II. And those who feel certain they cannot overcome it may start at Section IV.

II.   Summaries
Summaries have been included at the end of most chapters. Those who only desire the gist of a chapter's content may use these to take shortcuts through the book. Others, who believe that one or more of the foibles (addressed in chapters 7 – 15) do not apply to them, may want to read the summaries of these chapters just in case. Moreover, for those who do read the entire chapter, reading the summary will facilitate memory retention.

III. **The *Problem Definition*, the *Remedy* or Both**

To address both the "figure it out myself" and the "just tell me how to do it" dichotomies discussed in the Preface, chapters 7 through 15 contain the following subsections:

- The Foible – Introduces and elaborates on the chapter's foible.

- Remedies – Describes various ways to address the foible.

- How To – Provides a prescriptive list of tasks that will help mitigate the foible.

Most will be better served by reading the chapters in whole, but those who prefer to figure it out themselves can instead focus on The Foible section, and those who prefer the prescriptive approach can jump to the How To section. Regardless, I urge all to also read the Remedies section. Even those who wish to figure out their own solutions may find value in some of the remedies offered, and at the very least, the remedies may serve as idea starters. What's more, those in the second group will likely need the information from the Remedies section to carry out the tasks in the How To section.

IV. **Other Book Elements**

While not necessarily intended to support charting a custom path through the book, following are additional elements provided to assist those striving to mitigate the foibles. The first two items are provided at the end of chapters 7-15.

- **Monitor, Assess and Log**
  The methodology proposed in this book calls for ongoing monitoring of progress towards overcoming each foible. Readers are encouraged to designate tracking metrics that make the most sense for them, but this section contains some initial suggestions.

- **You Will Know You Are Overcoming This When …**
  This section is offered as both a source of inspiration (the positive things likely to be experienced) as well as a potential measure of success with respect to the foible.

- **Toolbox**
  Located in the Appendix, the *Toolbox* serves as a source of additional detail for some of the remedies referenced in Chapters 7 through 15.

V.   **Additional Information Available at the Brainiac Paradox Website**

The site *www.brainiacparadox.com* is offered as a resource for additional information about the Brainiac Paradox, the foibles, remedies and other items related to this topic.

VI. **Shortcuts for STEM Professionals**

The following abridgement strategy is intended for those who may be directly affected by this issue. A shortcut for those indirectly affected (managers, colleagues, loved ones, etc.) are in item VII.

1.   If you have not done so already, read the Introduction, which starts on page 3. It provides a foundation, framework and context for best utilizing this book.

2.   Decide which approach you will take through this book, either a complete and sequential approach, or a customized approach.

   a.   The sequential approach is the most likely to provide significant and lasting improvements. If you choose this approach, advance to Chapter 1 now and proceed sequentially from there.

   b.   If you have limited time, only specific and minor needs, or are just anxious to start overcoming foibles, map out a customized approach with the following steps.

3.   If you seek long-term change, and are willing to commit the time to the prescribed methodology, but are not interested in the background information, go to Chapter 6 and proceed sequentially from there.

4.   For those whose priority is quick results, skip Chapter 6 and start work to determine which of the nine foibles you will be trying to mitigate.

   a.   If you have a strong sense of your areas of need, review the list of foibles on page 90.

   b.   If you do not have a strong sense of your areas of need, try reading the summaries of chapters 7-15.

   c.   Create a list of foibles upon which to focus.

   d.   Proceed to the appropriate chapters (chapters 7-15 correspond to the list of foibles on page 90).

5. As you work on individual foibles in chapters 7-15, you have additional options.

    a. If you want to get the most out of the chapter, read it sequentially and in full.

    b. If you are in a rush and desire the prescriptive approach ("Just tell me what to do and I will do it"), skip directly to the "How To ..." section of the chapter.

Note: The prescriptive instructions in this book are like recipes in a typical cookbook; they assume some basic background knowledge and skills of the reader. If some of the steps listed in the How To section of the chapter do not make sense as stated, refer to the preceding "Remedies" section where the various suggestions are discussed in narrative form.

    c. If you are in a rush and prefer the independent approach ("Just define the problem and I will figure it out myself"), start at the beginning of the chapter and stop when you get to the remedies. However, you still might want to read through the remedies for idea starters.

6. Once you are done with chapters 7-15, read chapter 16 to determine whether you may benefit from partnering with someone who possesses complementary characteristics or aptitudes.

7. If you take the minimalist's route through the book, consider returning to read the first section, which explains the Brainiac Paradox, or to returning to Chapter 6 and following the methodology provided. Doing so will increase the chance that any progress you have made is maintained and increased.

VII. **Shortcuts for Managers, Colleagues, Loved Ones, and Others**
Those seeking to support others working through this issue have an important, possibly even crucial, role to play. If you will not be reading the book sequentially and in full, following are important sections to read:

1. If you have not done so already, read the Introduction, which starts on page 3. It provides a foundation, framework and context for best utilizing this book.

2. Chapter 1, *Achilles' Heel,* which defines the Brainiac Paradox and explains its many nuances.

3. Chapter 2, *Great Minds Think Differently*, which explores possible explanations and provides the context for its proper understanding.

4. Chapter 6, *The Brainiac Paradox Methodology*, which outlines the process prescribed for delivering long-term results. It also lists the roles that you and others may play as well as introduces the nine foibles.

5. Read the summaries of Chapters 7 through 15. If one or more of the foibles seems pertinent to the person for whom you are reading this, you may wish to read the entire chapter(s).

6. Chapter 16, *If You Can't Be Them, Join Them*, which provides a complimentary, or alternative, strategy for those who need additional help overcoming the foibles that impeded their success.

Section I

The Issue

This section focuses on the Brainiac Paradox itself:
defining it, exploring possible explanations, and discussing
its implications.

Author's Note: If you are as I am, you usually skip past the front material of a book. While you are welcome to do so in this book, you may end up wishing you had first read the previous section, "How to Use This Book." It describes special elements, conventions and directions designed to facilitate an abridged path through this book based on reader type or preferences.

– Chapter 1 –

Achilles' Heel

As the technical content of engineering has grown,
so has the need for engineers to verbalize – to speak and write clearly –
and work with other people on a non-numerical plane—
to listen, understand, explain, persuade and empathize.

– Samuel G. Florman, *The Civilized Engineer* (1988)

Had I not known what I did about Paul, his unfortunate circumstances may have been perplexing. A stranger reviewing his resume would find much of what many employers are eagerly seeking: advanced degree from a top-tier university; impressive background in engineering and information technology; employment history with various notable organizations; track record of progressively-increasing responsibilities; and experience with seemingly all the process-improvement methodologies that have come and gone over the last 25 years. Yet, after more than a year without work, Paul was becoming increasingly more desperate.

I, however, did know Paul, and as regrettable as it was, his dilemma was not only unsurprising, it was predictable. In fact, long before I knew of his employment woes, I observed in him several of the telltale characteristics common among the "working wounded" in technical fields.

I met Paul through a professional organization. When he learned of my background, he shared his resume with me, requesting some feedback or suggestions. He may have hoped that I would catch a glaring flaw he had somehow overlooked, or recommend some content changes that would make his resume sparkle. Just as likely, he thought that I would recognize an unclaimed jewel and forward his resume to all I knew who might be looking for someone with his credentials. Regardless, what Paul had failed to realize – and would later be reluctant to accept – was that his problem was not the content of his resume or how it was organized and presented; it was with him or, more precisely, the way he communicated and interacted with others.

It was not that he did not write or speak well, nor do I mean that he was unpleasant. His problem was that he possessed certain traits, habits, and attitudes that limited his ability to make personal connections, create mutual interest, convey understanding, and appeal to the logic and emotions of disparate audiences – ultimately, the ability to influence the perceptions and behaviors of key audiences. These in turn impeded his ability to collaborate and contribute professionally. All are important to getting work done in the communal workplace.

Several examples of his unfortunate characteristics were on full display when the two of us met to plan an upcoming event. What first struck me was his utter lack of urgency about addressing the very issues we were meeting to discuss. Despite what I believed to be his sincere, even passionate, interest in the project, he would continually launch off on tangents, droning on with countless ideas and opinions that had little if any relevance. Then, when I was able to steer him back to a pertinent topic, it was clear that he was impervious to any point that did not conform to his pre-existing views. Then there was the matter of his delivery. His remarkably monotone voice – reminiscent of a computer voice simulator – and singular facial expression made it difficult to tell when he was serious, indifferent, or even kidding. Not only did this impede his ability to convey his thoughts, but it strained my listening endurance.

Despite our long discussion, little was accomplished. Unfortunately, such would also be the case in subsequent meetings with him.

Achilles' Heel

Communication is the Achilles' heel of some Science, Technology, Engineering, and Math (STEM) professionals. Like the mighty Achilles, who was brought down by a comparatively insignificant injury, these cognitive warriors are sometimes crippled by something that may seem equally trivial: communication.

This, however, is far from trivial. Our ability to communicate effectively is a key determinant of the type of work we are assigned, who will choose to work with us, whether our projects get funded, how smoothly our projects are executed, how much credit we get for our successes (or blame for failures) and ultimately likelihood of our career success.

In 2006 the Accreditation Board for Engineering and Technology (ABET) published the results of an extensive study to evaluate the effects of changes in their accreditation requirements. As part of the study, engineering employers were surveyed to determine, among other things, what was important to them in new hires. They were asked to rate 11 competencies — such as "Engineering Problem Solving," "Use Modern Engineering Tools," and "Apply Math, Science and Engineering."

So what was the competency employers most sought in new hires? The ability to "Communicate Effectively." Of the 1,600 engineering employers who responded to the survey, 98% indicated that it was at least *moderately important* and 91% thought it was *highly important or essential*. "Teamwork" was the fifth most important item. By comparison, only 66% indicated "Design System to Meet Needs" was *highly important* or *essential*.

Does that mean that communication skills were actually the most important thing? Of course not. But what the employers seem to have been saying was, "Good engineers I can find – engineers who can communicate effectively, I can't."

Motors without Couplings

"Great engineers who can't communicate are like powerful motors without a coupling," says engineer and business entrepreneur Bruce Burton. "They may be capable of doing great work, but it is not harnessed." And it is not just that they negatively affect themselves; like a stalled car in the middle of the highway, they impede others.

Although I do not know the stated reason for the loss of Paul's most recent position – probably a reorganization or downsizing – I strongly suspect his personal characteristics played a significant role in determining why he was dismissed, while some of his peers were retained.

And now, even as he endlessly tweaks his resume in search of the perfect pitch, he is oblivious to the traits he is broadcasting and which any skilled interviewer will quickly perceive. In fact, communication abilities are one of the key competencies focused on when hiring for STEM positions; it is an easy way of separating the top candidates from those who merely possess the requisite technical qualifications.

A Common Ailment

Engineers are not alone. They represent just one of a class of professions (information technology, the sciences, mathematics, and others) that have long been disproportionately challenged by communication issues. In fact, such issues are more commonly found among just about any field that requires significant aptitudes in math, science, analytics, and related cognitive abilities. In *Effective Project Management,* author Robert Wysocki notes that surveys within the technology field over the past decade "have found that the lack of timely and clear people-to-people communications is the most frequent root cause for project failure." In research conducted by the Pew Research Center in partnership with the American Association for the Advancement of Science, 71% of scientists identified public communication as a significant scientific failure of the past 20 years. And, according to one senior HR expert, "improved communication abilities" is by far the most commonly-cited developmental goal stated in annual work performance appraisals across STEM professions.

The Brainiac Paradox

Communication is one of the first things we learn to do in life and we do it extensively thereafter, yet some do it so much better than others. It is ironic that some of those among the most intelligent segments of society struggle with something that those at the other end of the cognitive spectrum may handle with ease: communicating effectively with other people. This is the Brainiac Paradox.

STEM IQs

Robert M. Hauser analyzed data from The Wisconsin Longitudinal Study, which contained IQ measurements for various occupations, and ranked the professions based on median IQ. Seven of the top nine occupations were technical professions, including those related to engineering, IT, and science.

The Brainiac Paradox holds that among those who possess superior aptitudes in science, technology, engineering, and mathematics (STEM), there is a *tendency* for diminished aptitudes in areas that facilitate effective communication. In addition, these aptitudes *tend* to range inversely, so that the greater the technical aptitudes, the fewer the others.

It is important to note that while Paul is an example, he is not *the* example. The Paradox is not a specific thing. There is no single characteristic or measurement that defines whether someone is affected by it. Different people may exhibit it in very different ways; the sole common denominator is that it is related to aspects of how we interact with others.

   Marilyn, for example, was an extreme introvert and loner. She became a software engineer not so much because she loved that specific field, but because she had heard that it required the least amount of teamwork or human interaction. Unfortunately she could not avoid all interactions. During team sessions, she would not speak unless forced. She grudgingly participated with various collaborative efforts, but was always anxious to get back to her office and work alone. Despite extraordinary talent and effort, her career has remained stagnant.

Randy, on the other hand, was an extravert, but his speech was so laden with jargon, acronyms, and obscure references, that there was only a small circle of people who could follow his technobabel. His inability to avoid undecipherable language frustrated his leadership and eventually they no longer let him meet with external clients.

Craig's problem was that he had to weigh in on every meeting topic. He constantly interrupted others and often launched off on tangents that would derail meeting objectives. Furthermore, when others tried to corral him, he would become belligerent.

Another outspoken person was Barbara. Unlike Craig, she could stay focused on the desired topic, but her problem was that it took her 100 words to say what should have taken 10. In a conversation, she would drone on endlessly. It was said that if you asked her what time it was, she would tell you how to build a clock. Her documents were equally long. Others groaned when they needed to meet with her or read her reports.

For Robert, communication was always an afterthought. He had such an extreme focus on his work that he consistently overlooked when it was necessary, even crucial, to share information with other members of his team or organization. Nor did he respond to others requests for information in a timely manner. As the fallout from such lapses accumulated, animosity from team members mounted. Others suspected ulterior motives for his lack of sharing or responding, and ultimately Robert found himself in a poisonous work environment.

Then there was Megan. She represented what many people might think of when they hear that someone has a communication problem. She just was not good with words, spoken or written. She could not organize her thoughts or convey them clearly. You would have to ask her a series of follow-up questions to make sure you understood what she was saying.

The examples could go on.

Communication? Collaboration? Social Intelligence? Interpersonal Interaction?

The concepts of communicate and socialize are often used interchangeably in this book. While these words can mean distinctive things, they are intrinsically linked. The only way we can socialize is through some type of communication, and every communication is a form of socializing. Hence, communicating is socializing and socializing is communicating.

To the extent I do distinguish them, I will generally use variations of the word *communication* when I am referring to a conscious effort to share information with others towards a purpose, variations of the words *social* or *interpersonal interactions* when referring to more common aspects of interacting with others, and variations of the words *collaboration* or *team* when referring to interpersonal interactions with a common objective. However, when no specific distinction is needed, or when all are implied, I will generally use the term *communication*.

An alternative approach could be to use the term social intelligence as shorthand for all of these. For those unfamiliar with it, social intelligence is a concept introduced by psychologist Edward Thorndike in the 1920's, which he defined as, "The ability to understand and manage men and women, boys and girls, to act wisely in human relations." In his 2007 book, *Social Intelligence*, psychologist Daniel Goleman proposes that social intelligence is made up of social awareness (including empathy, attunement, empathic accuracy, and social cognition) and social facility (including synchrony, self-presentation, influence, and concern). Social intelligence is definitely relevant to this discussion, and the use of a single term in lieu of a spattering of the other terms is desirable, but in practical terms the concept is at times too confining, and other times too encompassing. More to the point, using the term social intelligence would suggest that the solution to this issue is to improve social intelligence, and that is not the aim of this book (though a possible outcome). Instead, the book takes a more surgical approach, aiming to help individuals avoid the specific behaviors that most interfere with their success in the workplace. For those familiar with Lean concepts, it is like an Exceptions Management approach. Rather than spending potentially endless energy trying to identify, quantify, and optimize all aspects of a system, it can be far more productive to focus on the leading constraints.

Communication is an amazingly complex process, requiring a significant amount of our brain activity as well as all our senses and indeed, our entire bodies. However, it has only been recently – aided by such tools as Functional Magnetic Resonance Imaging and other developments – that researchers have come to better appreciate how much of our neural real estate is consumed by it. As Goleman puts it, we are wired to connect. "Neuroscience has discovered that our brain's very design makes it sociable, inexorably drawn into an intimate brain-to-brain linkup whenever we engage with another person."

Such complexity frustrates the ability to provide precise diagnosis criteria. Any attempt would likely encounter examples of people whose evaluation would seem to exonerate them, yet they may still exhibit communication-related issues that impair their performance, or conversely, people whose score would seem to implicate them despite little evidence of professional impairment.

As I struggled with how to best define and frame the Brainiac Paradox, I was reminded of training I received in college in preparation for an assignment as a resident assistant. As part of the weeklong session, a specialist was brought in to lead a workshop about alcohol abuse. At the end of the session one of my fellow participants asked, "How much drinking indicates a drinking problem?" The presenter responded that the numbers are not as important as the effect. For example, he said, one person may have a drink or two daily, but that behavior does not impair her school performance, her relationships, her health, or other important aspects of her life. On the other hand, another person may drink only once a month, but during those episodes, he drinks to great excess, leading to fights, driving while impaired, blacking out, or countless other dangerous results of excessive drinking. The former drinks much more than the latter, but it is the latter who more clearly has a drinking *problem*.

Likewise, the Brainiac Paradox is more easily understood and addressed by focusing on the specific problems it may create for each individual.

All STEM Profession*s*?

Even if this provides more clarity regarding the *effects* portion of the equation, there will be those who may balk at the way a broad range of quite different STEM professions are heaped into a communal pile. Let me address this with a sports analogy.

The concept of "athlete" is easily understood and conveys little ambiguity for most, at least at first. However, consider what happens when you dissect the term. What does it take to be a competent athlete? Is it strength, speed, endurance, hand-eye coordination or something else? There is a long list of abilities that can be important to athletics, and the more one possesses the better, but athletes do not have to be exceptional in all to be an exceptional athlete. For example, the world's greatest weightlifter may be a slow runner and the world's greatest marathoner may not be able to lift much weight. Weightlifting and running are two very different sports, but those proficient in them are still understood as athletes. The common denominator is the effort and achievement in a physical competition. Moreover,

STEM or Technical Professional
Just as I will be using *communication, interpersonal interaction, collaboration* and similar terms interchangeably, I will sometimes substitute the term *technical professional* for *STEM professional*. While the acronym may be more precise, its repeated use can grow tiresome. In general, I will utilize *STEM* as a first reference in each chapter or section as well as when the explicit meaning may be more important, and then interject *technical* when the more generic descriptor may be acceptable. Similarly, *Paradox* may be used in place of *Brainiac Paradox* upon second reference within a section.

despite the vast differences between a weightlifter and marathon runner, they may share many of the same keys to success: proper nutrition, regular training, mental toughness, adequate rest, and so on.

The same is true for STEM professionals. Prerequisites may be aptitudes in math, science, technology, or related areas, and the more strengths one has the better. Nevertheless, based on an individual's portfolio of these, they may be drawn to and excel in quite different fields. A marine biologist and an astrophysicist may conjure up images of two very different people, yet they both can be equally considered STEM professionals. Here the common denominator is the effort and achievement in science, technology, engineering, or math. And, just as disparate athletes share certain keys to success, so may those related to success among individuals grouped under the umbrella of the term STEM professional: analytics, precision, systemizing, problem solving, and so on.

Defining Effective Communication

Just as the defining characteristics of "athlete" or "technical professional" relate more to outcome than requisite abilities, communication is better defined by its outcome or results than by its component pieces. Individual aptitudes such as extroverting, empathizing, asserting, intuiting, networking, selling, and the like, play an important part in one's ability to communicate effectively and, once again, the more the better. Likewise, different people can be equally effective communicators despite vastly different communication aptitudes. Thomas Jefferson, for example, was *not* a great public speaker. He stuttered, had a weak voice, and was reluctant to speak in groups. However, Jefferson understood others' hearts and minds, and was a gifted writer. The common denominator that defines **effective communication is the ability to influence others' perceptions and behaviors constructively**, (i.e., communication that delivers the desired effect). Few can argue Jefferson did not do that.

A Matter of Degrees

There is no such thing as a perfectly effective communicator. Based on the definition used in this book, even the very best communicator would not be able to always influence others' perceptions and behaviors as desired. As such, *everyone has communication challenges*; it is just a matter of the extent of those challenges.

All STEM Profession*als*?

Just in case it has not been abundantly clear, I am *not* asserting that all, or even a majority, of those in STEM professions will exhibit the type of paradoxical characteristics thus far noted in this book. In fact, I would estimate that the percentage would be rather small. Nor am I suggesting that those in such fields cannot be very effective communicators. Many are. The Rubik's Cube that is human aptitudes and characteristics offers seemingly limitless combinations. However, there is increasing evidence to suggest that strengths in these two areas *tend* to relate inversely, similar to the way certain color sets on a Rubik's Cube inherently oppose each other.

The inverse relationship will be discussed in more detail in the next chapter, *Great Minds Think Differently*, but in the mean time, what about those in between? If such characteristics are not binary – and which human characteristics are – what about those for whom certain communication characteristics are not necessarily an obvious hindrance, but nor are they a strength?

The reality is that in many professional settings, if communication is not a relative strength, it is a relative weakness. Even seemingly minor communication issues can have profound implications for one's career success and fulfillment. Thus the Brainiac Paradox has implications for many more than might seem obvious.

Considering the range of those possibly affected, from obviously to stealthily so, it can be difficult to get one's arms around an actionable understanding. In other words, "Where do I fit within this rather nebulas grouping and what should I do about it."

To address this I have created a series of descriptive categorizes that may make the Brainiac Paradox easier to conceptualize. These *do not* account for the vastly different ways it is manifested; they are only intended to represent the degree to which technical and communication assets may present themselves. Not everyone will fit neatly into one of these groups.

1. Eccentric Geniuses

Evidence of the more pronounced cases of the Brainiac Paradox is found throughout history and across the globe. Albert Einstein, Isaac Newton, and Nikola Tesla were all high-profile technical individuals who exhibited signs of social aberrations (these will be expounded upon in the next chapter), as did ancient Greek mathematicians Pythagoras and the contemporary Russian mathematician, Grigori Perelman (solver of the "unsolvable" Poincaré conjecture), to name just a few. In fact, the greater challenge is to find the exceptions; what great geniuses have there been who did not display noticeable characteristics that affected their ability to interact effectively with others?

2. STEM Whizzes

A step below the Eccentric Geniuses are what I will call STEM Whizzes, those whose technical gifts are quite notable, but not to the extent of genius, nor likely are their deviations from communication norms. For example, one executive told me about a former colleague who was the sole person at his organization who understood complex algorithms used in one of their key products, yet who appeared to wear the exact same clothes every day (as will be discussed later, our appearance is part of how we communicate with others). Another described a colleague who was extraordinary with system architecture, but who would only smile and mumble a barely audible response when queried.

There are many more STEM Whizzes than there are geniuses and as a result, it is quite likely the average person can conjure up an example from their own lives. I, myself, am reminded of a brilliant and engaging college physics professor – one of my favorites because of his infectious passion for his subject and for teaching – who could never seem to properly interpret the questions posed to him in the classroom. A student would ask about one thing, but his answer would address something else.

The prevalence and sometimes colorful characteristics of STEM Whizzes explain their frequent references in popular culture: these include fictional characters such as those in *The Girl with the Dragon Tattoo* (Lisbeth Salander), *The Big Bang Theory* (Sheldon Cooper), and *Star Trek* (Mister Spock). These examples reinforce the disparity that can exist. Each of these characters is equally identifiable as being socially atypical in some way, yet they are quite different from one another, just as were the athletes in the previous analogy. It is also interesting to note that, while atypical, these characters are not portrayed negatively; in fact, they are usually endearing heroes and heroines in their stories.

This demonstrates the "different not less" aspect of this issue. It is discussed in more length in the next chapter but, in short, it holds that atypical neural characteristics create the specialists necessary for the "human team," just as a center, a guard and a forward represent different specialties on a basketball team. None is less; they just contribute in different ways.

3. The STEM Masses

Beyond the geniuses and whizzes is a third tier: one that dwarves the previous two combined in terms of numbers. These I will refer to as the STEM Masses. Among this group are those whose technical aptitudes are significant enough to avail themselves of various challenging technical fields, and whose communication abilities may or may not be affected, but if they are, they are usually not obviously so. The latter may be thought of as just having less social intuition or fluency. It is among these more subtly-affected individuals that this issue becomes more consequential, not just because of the greater numbers, but because the aberrations are easier for affected individuals to overlook, ignore or deny. However, while employers may excuse certain shortcomings in Eccentric Geniuses and STEM Whizzes – because of their unique technical gifts – they are less likely to do so for the STEM Masses, whose offerings are perceived as more easily replaced.

4. STEM Mercenaries

There are two other groups that require some explanation if one is to fully understand the Brainiac Paradox: The first I call STEM Mercenaries. These are people who enter technical professions but might not fit the same profile of those discussed above.

A common trait among individuals associated with the Paradox is their almost preordination for their fields. Their particular interests might trace back to their very early years, and some may have been interested in little else since. However, among STEM Mercenaries those interests may not be so pervasive and technical aptitudes may be more balanced with those important for other fields. Some only decide to pursue technical fields in their late teens or even later. They are not compelled towards technical fields but choose them for other reasons, most likely because of greater demand and starting salaries (hence mercenaries).

If, however, there was no "STEM premium," those in this group may have pursued other fields, while those in the previous three categories would likely have pursued a STEM field anyway.

STEM Mercenaries generally are marked by having some level of technical and communication strengths, and are often found in leadership positions because

The STEM Premium

According to the Bureau of Labor Statistics, technically-oriented occupations exceeded the median for all workers in 2004. In six of those, earnings exceeded three times the median and in 34 more, earnings were twice the median. Such premiums may constitute an irresistible draw to those with ability to succeed in both technical and non-technical fields.

of their diverse abilities. However, they are not necessarily immune either. Those who fit into this category may still find one or two of the communication foibles sometimes impede their effectiveness.

5. Polymaths

Finally, there are the polymaths. They have striking aptitudes in a broad array of fields, and seemingly very few weaknesses. These people often rise to the top ranks of their respective organizations.

If displayed graphically, with the area representing the population associated with each of the five groups, it may look something like the following figure. This should not be read literally (i.e., that there are the same number of Geniuses and Polymaths, or Whizzes and Mercenaries); it is merely intended to provide an approximation of the relative size of each group, with the bulk of individuals falling into the STEM Masses category and very few at either ends of the chart.

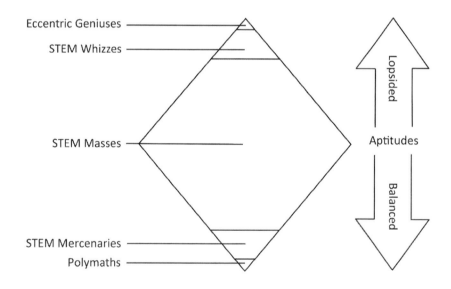

The Chronic Curse

Industry and academic leaders in various technical arenas have long lamented communication and collaboration problems among their technical teams and many have attempted various things to resolve them. For example, after alumni complaints that the university was churning out graduates who could not communicate effectively, Massachusetts Institute of Technology (MIT) instituted a program in 2001 that requires all students take four communication-intensive courses, paced over four years, before graduating. Robert Scott, a former vice president at P&G, tells of a program offered by the corporate giant – internally referred to as "Charm School" – intended to help the IT team interact more effectively with other organizational functions. And Stony Brook University, on Long Island in New York, recently created a specific program, the Center for Communicating Science. In addition, self-help resources like the book *Effective Communication Skills for Scientific and Technical Professionals* and college textbooks like *Technical Communication* have been published. The *Journal of Science Communication* is an online publication dedicated to improving the communication of science to the general public. These are but a few examples. Most universities and large organizations have in place, or at least have tried, their own remedies.

Despite these efforts, progress seems to have been elusive. A fundamental problem is that many of these programs limit their attention to the development of skills related to communication mechanics. These are important, but recall that effective communication, as defined in this book, is what one is able to achieve – influencing others – not just the skills of writing and speaking.

In order to overcome the Brainiac Paradox, it is helpful to start with a fundamental understanding of the problem:

- Why is it that those with technical aptitudes more commonly face some level of challenges in communicating, collaborating, and interpersonal interactions?
- What are underlying barriers that impede their ability to influence others constructively?

Its origins, which are the focus of the next chapter, can be traced to a combination of innate characteristics and environmental conditioning, which result in deep-rooted attitudes, thought processes, behaviors and habits. These are resistant to the type of one-off courses or limited programs implemented at various schools and organizations.

Who Is Affected?

If this only affects some, and is not the same for those it does affect, who needs to be concerned with it? This is examined in more detail in Chapter 7, but the easiest and possibly best approach is for technical professionals to start with the assumption that it does affect them, at least to some degree, and then consider some questions that may rule that out. Towards that end, the following is provided. Read and consider each question carefully, and answer *yes* or *no* in the space provided. Try not to hedge your answers based on what you believe are extenuating circumstances or possible alternative interpretations of the question: do your best to respond with what *most* accurately answers the question as stated.

_____ Do you prefer to tackle an initiative as part of a team (rather than individually)?

_____ Do you feel adequately recognized and rewarded for your contributions?

_____ Are you good at maintaining the attention of a broad cross-section of people?

_____ Do you have difficulties getting people to agree with you or at least see your point of view?

_____ Do you (individually and as a team member) have a good track record for delivering work as expected, on time, and within budget?

_____ Are you adept at reading non-verbal communications such as body language and facial expressions?

_____ Do your audiences usually understand you the first time, i.e., without follow-up questions, etc.?

_____ Do you make acquaintances easily?

_____ Do your communication plans usually deliver the desired results?

_____ Do others eagerly include you in discussions, projects or interpersonal interactions?

In Addition

_____ Does the topic of "communication issues" commonly arise in project discussions (not necessarily directed at you)?

_____ Do you dislike small talk?

_____ Do you struggle getting the support you need from others?

_____ Do others sometime receive credit for your contributions?

_____ Are you sometimes blamed for others' mistakes?

_____ Do the motivations and actions of others often puzzle you?

_____ Do you suspect others of not fully reading your communications (emails, reports, etc.)?

_____ Do others seem easily offended by your words or actions?

_____ Are your (or your team's) recommendations too often ignored or disregarded?

_____ Has communication or teamwork been cited in your performance appraisals as areas for improvement?

_____ Do you struggle to get approval or funding for new initiatives?

_____ Do you find yourself frequently hampered by personality conflicts?

_____ Have peers of lesser ability or qualifications been promoted ahead of, or above you?

If you answered "yes" to all of the question in the first series, and "no" to all in the second series, congratulations! You may be among the fortunate individuals who combine strong technical abilities and communication effectiveness. Before reaching that conclusion, though, confer with a spouse, friend or trusted work associate on these questions, as they may see things you do not. If you still believe this does not apply to you, read Chapter 7, before putting aside this book.

On the other hand, answering "no" to a few in the first series and "yes" to a few in the second series, does not necessarily indicate an issue (almost all people experience some of these), but at the very least this may indicate that effective communication is not one of your strengths and thus career success, fulfillment, and enjoyment are likely to be more elusive.

However, if you answered "no" to several in the first series and "yes" to several in the second series, then there is a reasonable likelihood that the Brainiac Paradox is impeding your career success.

Summary – Chapter 1
Achilles' Heel

Communication is the Achilles' Heel of some science, technology, engineering, and math (STEM) professionals. Even extremely talented professionals with advanced degrees can be hindered by seemingly much less important characteristics related to communication. The reality, however, is that these abilities are key factors in determining career success.

The Brainiac Paradox holds that among those who possess superior aptitudes in science, technology, engineering, and math (STEM), there is a tendency for diminished aptitudes in aspects of communication. Furthermore, these aptitudes tend to range inversely so that the greater the technical aptitudes one possesses, the less adept they are likely to be in terms of communication.

The Paradox, however, is not a specific thing. There is no single characteristic or measurement that defines whether someone is affected by it. Different people may exhibit it in very different ways; the common denominator is merely elevated technical aptitudes that are accompanied by challenges related to aspects of communication.

While this book attempts to better understand the Brainiac Paradox, its parameters, causes, implications, etc., when it comes to addressing it, the focus is on its effects. Likewise, effective communication is not a matter of just writing or speaking well. In this book, effective communication is defined as the ability to influence others' perceptions and behaviors constructively (i.e., communication that delivers the desired effect).

Another thing to understand about the Paradox is that it comes in various degrees, ranging from people who have pronounced cognitive abilities coupled with noted challenges achieving desired perceptions and behaviors among others, to those with modest characteristics in these areas. So, while there *tends* to be an inverse relationship of these characteristics, that is by no means always the case. There are those who have both strong technical abilities as well as a gift for effective communication, just as there are those with gifts for neither.

Following are some subjective categories created to facilitate an understanding of the how certain individuals may be associated with the Brainiac Paradox.

Eccentric Geniuses
These are the Albert Einsteins, Isaac Newtons, and Nikola Teslas. Exceptional talents but also known for some pronounced social

idiosyncrasies. In fact, it can be difficult to find examples of history's great geniuses that did not display noticeable characteristics that affected their ability to interact with others.

STEM Whizzes

These are a notch down from the first group, both in their cognitive abilities and their communication challenges. While there may only be a handful of prominent geniuses at any point in history, there are many more brilliant scientists, technologists, engineers, and mathematicians who have corresponding challenges in terms of communications.

The STEM Masses

The STEM masses can be defined as all the remaining people who have varying degrees of elevated technical abilities as well as some challenges in terms of communications. It is among these more subtly-affected individuals that the Brainiac Paradox becomes more consequential, not just because of the greater numbers, but because the aberrations are easier for affected individuals to overlook, ignore or deny. And, while employers may excuse certain shortcomings in Eccentric Geniuses and STEM Whizzes – because of their unique technical gifts – they are less likely to do so for the STEM Masses, whose offerings are perceived as more easily replaced.

STEM Mercenaries

These are the people blessed with both elevated technical aptitudes as well as those conducive to effective communications. They are referred to as mercenaries because their broad range of abilities may allow them to excel in a wide variety of fields – as opposed to many above who have always been focused on STEM subjects – but may choose technical fields because of the high employer demand and/or potential income premiums.

Polymaths

Polymaths are those who have exceptional abilities in a wide range of areas. Like the eccentric geniuses, there may only be a handful of true polymaths in existence at any point in history. That said, these categories are arbitrarily drawn and there will be people who span the entire length of this spectrum.

– Chapter 2 –

Great Minds Think *Differently*

In this world people have to pay an extortionate price for any exceptional gift whatever.
—Willa Cather: *The Old Beauty and Others*

Some called him a walking Google. He memorized – yes memorized – thousands of books and to prove it he would defy packed auditoriums to stump him on history or sports trivia questions. His correct responses to obscure questions would draw gasps of astonishment that would be the envy of any illusionist. No less amazing was his musical memory. Not only could he remember every piece of music he ever heard, but he could identify the composer of a new piece of music just by comparing style patterns against the vast database of music in his head. What's more, he could instantly calculate the day of the week for any calendar date over the last several hundred years. He may have been hailed as one of history's greatest minds … if not for an IQ of 73.

Kim Peek was a savant. He could perform mental feats that were inconceivable to even the most intelligent individuals, like reading books two pages at a time – one page per eye – at the rate of 10 seconds per set of pages, and yet he could not perform some of the most basic tasks, like dressing himself or operating a light switch.

Then there is Matt Savage. He has been dubbed the "Mozart of Jazz." Savage exhibited a number of profound developmental challenges as a young child and was diagnosed with a form of autism and hyperlexia. But Savage has a mind for music. He taught himself to play the piano at the age of six and by seven was composing jazz music. By eight he was jamming with Chick Corea and being described as "amazing" by Dave Brubeck. By his late teens he had already released eight albums.

Stephen Wiltshire has also been diagnosed with autism and has difficulty speaking, but he has an incredible visual memory and the ability to transfer his mental images to paper. In the documentary *Expedition ins Gehirn* (*Beautiful Minds: A Voyage Into the Brain*) he was challenged with a seemingly impossible task: to create an accurate drawing of the entire city of Rome after seeing it for the first time via a 45 minute helicopter ride. Over the next three days he created a 10-foot panorama of the city from memory alone. Wiltshire was able to draw details of buildings from memory with more precision than many people could if they were working from a photograph.

The abilities of these savants are astounding in themselves, but it is the contrast of their extraordinary gifts with their challenges that fascinate us. These examples confront our traditional notion of intelligence: that of a group of core cognitive abilities (analytical, verbal, memory, etc.) that, for the most part, range as a group, like hand and feet sizes do with height.

Such prodigious savants are exceedingly rare, but it is this scarcity that can draw our attention to things that may otherwise be lost among the everyday complexity of human diversity, just as the pronounced aspects of the species Charles Darwin encountered in the Galapagos Islands helped him recognize evolutionary clues that surrounded him in the British Isles.

The Peek, Savage, and Wiltshire examples suggest that maybe it is not a case of them possessing these great abilities despite cognitive handicaps … *but because of them.* If so, what about the larger population? Do certain pairs of cognitive characteristics relate to each other in a type of neural seesaw, where the ascendancy of one corresponds to the decline of another? Such would seem to be the case of history's great geniuses, and not just scientists and mathematicians. In *The Price of Greatness,* Arnold Ludwig points out that Walt Whitman, Cole Porter, Vincent Van Gogh, Gustav Mahler, Edgar Allen Poe, Earnest Hemingway, and Georgia O'Keefe are but a few of the creative geniuses from art, music, and literature who have been said to have suffered from bi-polar disorder.

This book focuses on one specific cognitive contrast: what appears to be an inverse relationship between the aptitudes necessary for success in the fields of science, engineering, technology, and math and those necessary for effective communication.

Brainiacs

The word Brainiac appears to have originated in the DC Comics' Superman series as the name of an arch-villain who possessed super-human intelligence. The word has subsequently entered common American English usage meaning a highly-intelligent person, usually in areas of science, technology, engineering, math, and other areas that require prodigious analytical powers. Albert Einstein, Alan Turing, Nikola Tesla, Isaac Newton, and Bobby Fischer are some preeminent "brainiacs" related to these, respectively, and in each case, these individuals exhibited atypical social characteristics.

Consider the most iconic brainiac of all, Albert Einstein. His name has become synonymous with genius, as evidenced by the popular phrase, "He's no Einstein" and the use of his name to sell products to parents eager to foster early cognitive development in their children. The latter is ironic because Einstein's own parents were so worried about his early development that they sought the help of experts. He was late to begin speaking, and toilet training, and was delayed in other areas of social development[1]. The family maid referred to him as the "dopey one." His first teachers shared similar opinions, and when Einstein's father consulted the headmaster of the school about an occupation for which Albert should prepare, he infamously responded, "It doesn't matter; he'll never make a success of anything."

Isaac Newton, easily one of the greatest scientists and mathematicians of all time, was known for being extremely introverted, insecure, and humorless. He was even known to give lectures to empty classrooms.

Nikola Tesla was an amazing innovator and visionary, and many consider him the greatest engineer of all time, but he was notoriously eccentric.

Alan Turing was a British mathematician, logician, cryptanalyst, and computer scientist. He is probably best known – to the extent he is known at all – for his revolutionary work at Bletchley Park during World War II, helping the Allies break the code of Germany's formidable enigma machine. It was an incredible feat, critical to winning the war, but it was his creation of what is now called the Turing Machine that most changed the world. While purely theoretical, the Turing Machine introduced the logic and processes on which all of today's computer central processing units depend. Turing, though, was notoriously idiosyncratic, a poster boy for the absent-minded professor.

The Brainiac Threshold
Relevant to our discussion is the relative nature of the term Brainiac. To some, anyone who can perform a calculus equation or program a computer is a brainiac. By that standard, almost anyone who matriculates to a STEM profession is a brainiac to some extent.

[1] These characteristics, along with strong puzzle-solving and memory abilities, have come to be labeled Einstein Syndrome. Physicists Edward Teller and Richard Feynman shared similar developmental characteristics.

Finally, Fischer, who some consider the greatest chess genius of all time, is the archetype for the genius recluse. At the near-height of his abilities, he disappeared from public view, refusing to defend his title and espousing ever-increasing anti-Semitic views, despite being half-Jewish himself.

The Socially-Gifted Paradox

As the Brainiac Paradox holds that those with greater technical aptitudes are likely to be disadvantaged in ways that limit their ability to influence others' perceptions and behaviors (i.e., effective communication), it may be useful to look at the other end of the spectrum. It would make sense that if there is something about having elevated technical abilities that inhibit effective communication abilities, should not the possession of significant communication gifts inhibit technical abilities?

In one study – an extensive poll of PR practitioners conducted by *PRWeek* – Abraham Lincoln, Winston Churchill, and Franklin D. Roosevelt were cited as among the top 10 communicators of all time (most of the others were religious figures). While these three may have been great politicians, writers, and speakers, it was more precisely their tremendous ability to influence others' perceptions and behaviors that set them apart. They overcame seemingly insurmountable leadership obstacles: maintaining the Union during the U.S. Civil War; rallying the British people during the most hopeless hours of World War II; and leading the American government and people out of the Great Depression. The ability to influence others is crucial to effectiveness in the workplace. Those who can do this well can, and likely will, succeed even if they lack in other cognitive areas. Conversely, those without it will likely struggle, despite other significant cognitive assets.

And what of these great communicators' technical abilities? Churchill failed the math portion of the Sandhurst entrance exam three times before barely passing, and in a personal letter Roosevelt wrote of his challenges with math. Unfortunately, Lincoln had so

The Popularity Premium

Recent research published by the National Bureau of Economic Research, found that students in the 80th percentile of high-school popularity experienced a 10% wage premium (after 40 years) over those in the bottom 20th percentile. While high-school popularity cannot be attributed solely to communication and social aptitudes (i.e., physical attractiveness and athletic prowess play a significant role at that age), these must be considered important contributors.

little formal education that no objective measure of early math or science abilities exist, but no technical gifts are prominently associated with him either.

This is not to say that all powerful communicators are challenged in math and science, just as not all those gifted in math and science are challenged in their ability to constructively influence others, but as sports writer and author Damon Runyon said, "The race is not always to the swift nor the battle to the strong, but that's the way to bet."

Why?

While authors, academics, and various organizations have touched on and around the effects of the Brainiac Paradox, there is a dearth of work to explain the underling *why* of this phenomenon. Why is there a pattern of people so accomplished in one area, yet challenged in another?

In Kim Peek's case, the answer was straightforward. His unique abilities and disabilities were believed to be caused by agenesis of the corpus callosum, a condition in which the bundle of nerves that connects the two hemispheres of the brain is missing. In his case, secondary connectors, such as the anterior commissure, were also missing.

When it comes to the characteristics described by the Brainiac Paradox, though, there is no single, simple answer. I have found no studies that have focused *specifically* on whether those with the aptitudes necessary to succeed in technical fields have disproportionately more communication challenges, let alone trying to answer why, but there is existing research, theories, and findings that appear to parallel, overlap or substantiate this concept. They fall into two main categories, those that attribute this to nature and those that attribute it to nurture.

Nature
Asperger Syndrome

Of the potential biological explanations, Asperger syndrome (AS), seems to be quite relevant, at least as a contributor. AS is part of the autism spectrum and is sometimes referred to as high-functioning autism. Those with it tend to exhibit significant difficulties in social interaction, along with the tendency for restricted and repetitive patterns of behavior and interests, but without the same effects on linguistic and other areas of cognitive development associated with autism.

AS is believed to be inheritable, and there are clues that the genes for AS are linked to those that confer a talent for grasping complex systems — anything from computer programs to music. Noted AS expert and author, Psychologist Tony Attwood said, "If you look at the characteristics of Asperger syndrome, it is almost like the job description requirements for a person in [technical] fields." Attwood stressed that, "It is not a defective way of thinking but a different way of thinking. The brain is wired differently. You come from a different culture in a sense ... one that values knowledge, perfection, truth, and understanding over feelings and interpersonal experiences. This can lead to valued attributes, but also liabilities." In an effort to explain this, he offers the following analogy:

Imagine a clearing in a forest, and in that clearing are many saplings, struggling for light [nurture], *nutrients* [nature], *etc. Each of these saplings represents a structure in the brain. For most children, one sapling quickly becomes a tree that dominates the clearing in the sense of the canopy of leaves that produce shade and a deep root structure that takes most of the nutrients, inhibiting the growth of the other saplings. For the typical child, that is the social structure in the brain, and it requires a lot of brainpower. But what if that sapling does not grow to dominate? Other structures are able to thrive and these may represent mechanical, mathematical, musical, and imagination abilities.*

Various studies have shown that a disproportionate number of people with AS become engineers, information technologists, and scientists. In *American Nerd* Benjamin Nugent notes that "Silicon Valley's unusually high rates of disorders on the autism spectrum are the most famous, but there are also off-the-chart numbers in the Route 128 tech company zone near Boston and the 'Silicon Fen' area of England."

And those are only the known cases. Experts believe that there

Tradeoffs

Even if it were possible to 'cure' those affected by the Brainiac Paradox, there is another reason not to attempt it: anecdotal evidence suggests doing so might simultaneously diminish the person's special positive gifts.

There is the case of a severely autistic girl named Nadia, a savant who at the age of six could draw a galloping horse with great accuracy from memory alone. However, by the age of 12, after intense therapy provided her speech abilities, she lost her special artistic abilities.

Then there is the case of John Elder Robison. In *look me in the eye: my life with asperger's,* he describes savant-like abilities in his youth that he seemed to lose after working to "re-wire" his brain to be more socially successful. "There was a trade-off for that increased emotional intelligence. I look at [electronic] circuits I designed 20 years ago and it is as if someone else did them. Some of my designs were true masterpieces of economy and functionality. Many people told me that they were expressions of a creative genius. And today, I don't understand them at all."

are many with undiagnosed AS within technical fields. Asperger syndrome was not included in the World Health Organization's diagnostic manual until 1991 and not in the American Psychiatric Association's manual until 1994. As such, adults born before then, and presenting with the associated symptoms, may not have been diagnosed or at least not diagnosed correctly. Attwood says that every time he provides TV or Radio interviews about AS, people call in to say in astonishment, "You have just described me!"

If AS is indeed relevant to an explanation of the Brainiac Paradox, then Attwood's sapling analogy can also provide a useful way to understand the more subtle manifestations. For example, if the development of social abilities were only slightly hindered, then we would expect a more modest elevation of the relevant cognitive abilities: i.e., the STEM Masses. It can also be extended to explain the exceptions to the Brainiac Paradox – individuals gifted in both technical and social aptitudes – with the scenario in which these individuals have grey matter that is so optimal (fertile) and an environment so nurturing (plentiful light) that all functional abilities may develop extensively, just as in other cases, the conditions are so poor that neither can thrive.

Empathizing and Systemizing

Another way to understand the Paradox is in terms of the E-S Theory. While not spelling out the Brainiac Paradox and its relevance to those in technical professions, it closely parallels it and could even be said to predict it.

It was developed by Cambridge University researcher Simon Baron-Cohen, one of the world's foremost experts on autism. He was the lead author of a 1985 paper introducing the Mind-Blindness Theory, which addressed the social and communication challenges faced by those with Asperger syndrome (AS). It described their difficulty to think and perceive in terms of another's perspective.

It did not, however, explain the tendency of AS people to focus on relatively narrow areas of interest. Subsequently, he developed the Empathizing–Systemizing (E-S) Theory, which classifies people according to their relative strengths in two areas, Empathizing and Systemizing. Empathizing is extremely advantageous to effective communication, and Systemizing, the drive to analyze or construct systems, is advantageous to most technical professionals. According to Baron-Cohen, those who have a significantly higher empathizing quotient are Type E. Those who have a significantly higher systemizing quotient are Type S, and those who are relatively balanced are Type B. These types range throughout the general population but those who are extreme S (thus low E) are believed to have AS or autism.

It is clear that there is an AS association for *some* who exhibit characteristics of the Brainiac Paradox, but it is certainly not implied that this is the entire explanation. If it were, we would expect all those diagnosed with AS to have elevated aptitudes for the qualities important to technical fields, and that is not the case. Nonetheless, AS provides an important insight to the Paradox both because it documents the *tendency* for such abilities to range inversely and because of studies that show it is more common among those in STEM professions.

Brain Hemisphericity

Another interesting possible explanation for the Brainiac Paradox lies in Brain Hemisphericity.

In the mid-20th century, doctors noted that physical damage to one side of the brain would affect certain abilities while leaving others intact, suggesting the two sides of the brain function asymmetrically. From these early observations, for example, researchers found that in virtually all right-handed people, the left hemisphere of the brain controlled the right side of the body, as well as their speech facility. Building on these finding, Dr. Roger Sperry conducted a series of experiments on split-brain patients. These were individuals whose connective tissue between the two hemispheres of the brain (among the tissue missing in Kim Peek's brain) was severed as a means of treating severe epilepsy.

Sperry's experiments involved providing information through various physical senses to only one side of these split-brain patients. For example, participants were asked to reach into a closed container with their right hand and identify a common object by touch; they could do so easily. However, when the experiment was repeated with their left hand, they could not name it; they said they knew what it was, but just could not find the word. From additional studies, Sperry concluded that the left side of the brain was necessary for speech.

Similar experiments were done in which different visual images were fed to each eye. When asked to *say* what they saw, participants named the item whose image had been fed to their right eye. But when asked to *pick up* the item they saw from among various items placed in front of them, they selected the item whose image had been fed to their left eye. Therefore, they were verbalizing in their left-brain, but conceptualizing in their right-brain. Sperry's groundbreaking work in brain hemisphericity earned him the Nobel Prize in 1981.

Sperry believed that people have dominant brain hemispheres, just as they have dominant hands, sometimes left and sometimes right, though the level of dominance varies, and some people are rather balanced (the neural equivalent of being ambidextrous). Through continued research, Sperry and others suggested that there were certain cognitive attributes that seemed to be related to dominance in each hemisphere.

Left Hemisphere	Right Hemisphere
Speech/verbal	Spatial/musical
Logical, mathematical	Holistic
Linear, detailed	Artistic, symbolic
Sequential	Simultaneous
Controlled	Emotional
Intellectual	Intuitive, creative
Dominant	Minor (quiet)
Worldly	Spiritual
Active	Receptive
Analytical	Synthetic, gestalt
Reading, writing, naming	Facial recognition
Sequential ordering	Simultaneous comprehension
Perception of significant order	Perception of abstract patterns
Complex motor sequence	Recognition of complex figures

A review of the attributes in the left column will find many characteristics most typically associated with technical professionals, including logical/mathematical, linear, detailed, sequential, controlled, and analytical. Conversely, many of the items in the right column may be associated with communication and interpersonal interactions: holistic, artistic/symbolic, emotional, intuitive/creative, receptive, facial recognition, and simultaneous comprehension.

So for some, the Brainiac Paradox may simply be the result of someone with a distinct left-brain dominance, a brain configuration that provides them abundant qualities useful when pursuing technical fields, but wanting in qualities that are helpful when interacting with others.

The Whole Brain

In recent years a more refined understanding of left/right brain dominance has emerged. It confirms that certain characteristics do relate to left or right hemispheres of the brain, but not always solely. Instead, they are usually the result of complex interrelations of various neural regions that may be located throughout the brain. In other words, while left/right brain dominance can be referred to as a description of certain people's characteristics; it should not be seen as a literal description of how the brain works.

Brain Anomalies

Kim Peek was an example of a severe anomaly of the brain structure that led to unique capabilities and disabilities. There are other brain anomalies, however, that are more subtle and that may provide clues for the Brainiac Paradox.

When researchers first physically studied Albert Einstein's brain after his death, they found nothing remarkable; it was roughly the same size and weight of the average person's. Since then, though, researchers have discovered that the inferior parietal region of his brain – important for processing visual and spatial thought, mathematical thought, and imagery of movement – was 15% larger than that of the average person. They also noticed that his brain lacked a groove, called the Sulcus, which normally runs through this same region. More recently they found his brain had more astrocytes and oligodendrocytes, two types of glial cells, especially in a part of the brain involved in imagery and complex thinking. These factors may help explain his prodigious gifts ... or maybe not. Undoubtedly such questions will be answered down the road, but for now they remain just intriguing possibilities.

Mirror and Spindle Neurons

Relatively recently, researchers discovered a new type of brain cell called a mirror neuron, which has a unique function. Mirror neurons fire in locations of our brains associated with what we witness in others. For example, if we see someone pound their finger with a hammer, the mirror neurons associated with that finger in our brains will fire. We will not feel the pain, but we may respond as if we did, and immediately grab our own finger in empathy. Likewise, if we see someone smile, the mirror neurons located with the parts of our brain associated with smiling will fire. Hence, mirror neurons seem to serve to immediately and non-verbally synchronize us with those around us and thus they are considered an important part of the "social brain."

There have also been recent discoveries regarding the roles another newly discovered brain cell type, spindle neurons, plays in socialization. These are comparatively large brain cells that are located in only a few parts of the brain, primarily at the interfaces between cognitive and emotional processing. They are said to facilitate rapid communication across different brain components and to play an important role in rapidly assessing social situations.

Perhaps one or both of these neurons equate to the "social saplings" in Attwood's metaphor that, when atypical in some way, allow other cognitive abilities to flourish.

The Social Brain

One part of Attwood's metaphor that would seem to have been physically demonstrated is the extent of neural activity consumed by social activity. For some time, researchers have been using functional magnetic resonant imaging (fMRI) to study how the brain functions under certain circumstances or when performing specific tasks. Solving a math problem may cause heightened activity in one or more areas of the brain and speaking a foreign language may trigger others. More recently, they have expanded such research to study brain activity when people are socializing, and what they found was that the brain lit up! It appears the brain is hardwired to socialize. As such, a person making small talk with a new acquaintance at a party may be using more neural real estate than a Ph.D. student working on her thesis.

However, rather than decreased social abilities making way for increased cognitive abilities, it could be the other way around. Maybe the elevated cognitive abilities related STEM professions edge out the resource-hungry social abilities. When researchers from the Centre for the Mind, at the University of Sydney, used low-frequency magnetic pulses to impair temporarily the left fronto-temporal lobe, they found that participants demonstrated significant stylistic improvements in their drawing abilities as well as enhanced proofreading abilities. While these changes were not specific to the characteristics negatively affected by the Paradox, they demonstrate yet again that certain characteristics or aptitudes relate to others inversely.

Root Cause?

As intriguing as these possibilities may be, multiple potential explanations may only muddy the waters of determining a root cause. Are all of these fully relevant or are their similarities to the Paradox mere coincidences? Maybe some are relevant and others are red herrings. Maybe all are relevant, but only to certain characteristics; recall that different people are affected in different ways with the sole commonality that the negative effects are related to aspects of communication. So maybe for some people the explanation lies with Asperger syndrome, for others it is left-brain dominance, and so on.

Then again, maybe some or all are woven together in a yet undiscovered way. Some researchers have found correlations between autism and left-brain dominance as well as atypical mirror and spindle neural characteristics. Autism itself is not fully understood and may only be describing similar yet different underlying conditions.

Trying to sort these out is complicated by the fact that the experts themselves do not always agree on many aspects of mind sciences, and on some topics they passionately disagree. The deeper I explored this issue, the more elusive a cohesive explanation seemed to be. When I expressed my frustration about this to psychologist Rich Thompson he replied, "There is still a lot that physicists don't understand about their field, but they can still make [nuclear] bombs go off." And so I suppose it is the same with the Brainiac Paradox; a precise and absolute scientific explanation does not yet exist but, looking at the glass half full, there is much productive use we can make of what we do know. If it is Asperger syndrome, there are ever-improving therapies available. If it is left/right brain dominance, the landscape is relatively well known and there are techniques for developing more balanced brain processing. The same is likely true if the Paradox relates to some aspect of brain structure and composition.

Whatever the ultimate explanation, it is hard to escape the conclusion that there is *something about the way the brain functions that tends to impose a tradeoff between technical aptitudes and social aptitudes.*

Neural Diversity
As natural selection works solely by and for the good of each being, all corporeal and mental endowments will tend to progress towards perfection.
— Charles Darwin *On the Origin of Species by Means of Natural Selection*

Before moving on to consider the potential environmental explanations for the Paradox – the nurture explanation – there is one other aspect of the nature explanation that begs answering: the philosophical question of why?

If social interactions are so important, why would such aberrations remain so relatively common? Is it just a case of the technical aptitudes being so valuable that they offset the social anomalies, or is it the relationship between the two that constitutes the greatest value from an evolutionary standpoint? After all, if evolution progresses towards perfection, we would expect those who possess special technical gifts to fall mainly into the "STEM Mercenaries" and "Polymaths" categories.

Consider, however, whether Newton and Tesla would have made their greatest discoveries if they were more socially typical. Would Turing have been able to tackle the immense challenge of deciphering the German codes? A case can be made that they would not have. Recall what was said earlier about the amount of brain activity consumed by socializing. Less social abilities presumably leads to less socializing, which frees up valuable cognitive capacity.

In 1944, Hans Asperger, after whom Asperger syndrome is named, said, "Able autistic individuals can rise to eminent positions and perform with such outstanding success that one may even conclude that only such people are capable of certain achievements …. Their unswerving determination and penetrating intellectual powers, part of their spontaneous and original mental activity, their narrowness and single-mindedness, as manifested in their special interests, can be immensely valuable and can lead to outstanding achievements in their chosen areas."

However, possibly it is more than that. The fact is that socially-typical people do not just have a *preference* for socializing; they have an intense *need* for it. It might be hard for us to appreciate this need because it is almost impossible for us to experience social isolation in our evermore crowded and connected world, but prisoners of war report that long periods of social isolation were as torturous as any physical abuse they endured. Likewise, solitary confinement is said to be the most powerful behavioral deterrent for even the most hardened prison inmates. Thus, maybe less of a need to be social serves as an advantage for some people.

Historically, there have been some tasks that required long periods of social isolation. In fission-fusion societies, for example, shepherds might be denied human interactions for extended periods. Those who require less social interaction would have an advantage (sanity).

And ever since the monetization of Internet technologies, there has been a breed of programmers who literally live at their computers in the quest for the next instant billionaire innovation. Some will spend nearly all their waking hours at the keyboard, sustained by energy drinks and pizza. They may even sleep under their desks. Most people could not do this. It is not so much a matter of the physical or mental stamina, which in itself would be a challenge, but the absence of social interaction that would eventually defeat them. For these programmers, however, it is not only possible, it is often fun.

As such, in the future, when human space travel reaches to Mars or beyond, perhaps those with high-functioning autism might make good candidates, considering the extended periods of isolation.

Hence, both aspects of the Paradox may represent the magic formula necessary to do some truly extraordinary things. As educator and author Temple Grandin, herself autistic, said, "The really social people did not invent the first stone spear. It was probably invented by [someone with Asperger syndrome] who chipped away at rocks while the other people socialized around the campfire. Without autism traits we might still be living in caves."

Nikola Tesla said, "I do not think there is any thrill that can go through the human heart like that felt by the inventor as he sees some creation of the brain unfolding to success …. Such emotions make a man forget food, sleep, friends, love, everything." He also said, "I do not think you can name many great inventions that have been made by married men." Tesla was asexual and celibate, and according to Clifford Pickover, in *Strange Brains and Genius,* that was true of an unusually high number of great scientific geniuses, including Leonardo Di Vinci, Galilei Galileo, and Rene Descartes.

This is not meant to indicate that everyone who can be claimed to fall under the broad umbrella of the Brainiac Paradox is less social and/or have less of a need to be. As already said, the Paradox may relate to different people in very different ways. As such, there will be those who are outgoing and very interactive, yet still suffer other challenges. For example, one of the more common problems I have observed is a tendency to be one-sided in social exchanges. Yes, certain technical professionals have a need to be social, but only so they can express their thoughts and ideas. On the other hand, they have little patience for listening to others. As such, they are not likely to develop the type of rapport and relationships that are important to influencing others. In fact, others learn to avoid them. Indeed, one engineering professor protested that when he encounters people at social events and they ask what type of work he does, "They make an excuse and walk away when they hear I am an engineer."

Additional insights may be gained by, once again, considering the opposite end of the Brainiac Paradox spectrum: those with strong social aptitudes but diminished technical aptitudes. It has been proposed that the driving force behind the evolution of social intelligence is the need to socially outwit competitors, the Machiavellian Intelligence Hypothesis. Just as aspects of being social may detract from the pursuits of the technical mind, maybe aspects of technical thinking detract from the pursuit of social achievement.

Thus, maybe both extremes of technical and social aptitudes might be necessary from a Darwinian standpoint. John Nash, Nobel mathematician and subject of the book and movie, *A Beautiful Mind,* focused on the issue of neural diversity in a speech he provided at the American Psychological Association 2007 annual meeting, stating that some mental aberrations may be essential to the diversity necessary for the survival of the species.

> *This is a topic that has been studied in game theory .... If species are considered as players in a game that continually repeats, and if the species are provided with the possibility of change through mutation of their playing behavior, ... then the effect is that the players or species can be shown to naturally evolve so as to get better payoffs from the game.*

Nurture

Even if such inherent characteristics may explain aspects of the Brainiac Paradox, the effect of environment should not be overlooked or underestimated.

The developmental paths of those who become STEM professionals can be very different from those who pursue other fields. In early education, children who exhibit special abilities or interests – especially in math and science – are often treated differently. Depending on the degree of precociousness and the school system, these children may be clustered into advanced classes, grouped with other high performers in an accelerated (magnet) class, or sent to special schools. Even if they are not segregated physically they may be virtually, and the children themselves may be the main culprits. One of the first ways children segment themselves is based on those who easily understand class subjects and those who do not. This can create a reinforcing cycle, as children focus more on what is rewarded, often at the expense of other developmental areas (sports, social, arts, etc.).

As the school years progress, more prominent opportunities to distinguish such students may arise (e.g., science fairs, Math Olympics), but correspondingly require even deeper commitments of focus, time, and energy on a narrow area of study while social and other abilities atrophy. The cycle of achievement and recognition continues until their special academic gifts become an integral sense of who they are, just as other students might be primarily seen as athletes, musicians or artists.

As the middle school years arrive, social posturing becomes more apparent and important. The social pecking order is usually determined by aesthetic rather than intellectual attributes. Those who combine good looks, athletics, and social skills rise to the apex of the social order and jealously guard it. As such, what was before an informal segregation becomes entrenched as these students progress through their teenage years. The labels placed on children at this time – the jocks, the nerds, the artists, etc. – are social brands that can be difficult to later remove.

The social order determines not just how individual children are seen, but with whom they can associate; so, whether they would be naturally inclined to or not, they end up socializing predominantly with others similar to themselves. These cognitively-oriented children have a tendency to focus

Multiple Exposures

For those with kids who may seem to fit this pattern, it is not necessary to avoid special academic programs or certain extracurricular activities in order that they avoid the affects of the Brainiac Paradox in later years. Such programs serve valuable purposes. The key, it would seem, is to augment them so that the children are exposed to significant additional and different social groups, situations, and priorities. This will help them strengthen their social brains while still honing their technical abilities.

on narrow areas of interest, and communicate more through their work and less through words. As a result, their ability to interact outside of their circles languishes even further.

Not all such children follow this path, but even those who do not, may experience enough of this to undermine their social fluency.

Academia

College curriculums in technical fields have become increasingly specialized over the last century, and as they have, the more mind-broadening liberal arts courses have been squeezed out.

However, it may not be just the curriculum influencing the students, it could also be the culture. In research conducted by professors Monika and Edward Lumsdaine, engineering students at the University of Toledo were assessed and monitored over time using the Herrmann Brain Dominance Instrument (HBDI) tool. The HBDI takes the work of Dr. Sperry one step further, associating cognitive types to quadrants of the brain, summarized as, A. Analytical thinking; B. Sequential thinking; C. Interpersonal thinking; and D. Imaginative thinking.

According to the database of HBDI assessments, the typical engineer profile is associated with the left-brain, with emphasis on the upper left quadrant (Type A or Analytical thinking). Among the freshman tested in the first year of the four-year study, typical "Left-Brain thinking" was found, but their average results were a little more towards the right (conceptual, emotional, etc.) than was found among practicing engineers. The faculty, however, had profiles that were further to the left than practicing engineers. Sadly, despite newly introduced academic programs intended to encourage creativity and teamwork (intended to shift the students towards the right and more balanced thinking) the average engineering students in this study shifted to the left by the time they graduated, becoming almost clones of their professors (as measured by the HBDI). What's more, of incoming freshmen whose profiles placed them in the center, or to the right of center (10% of the students), several switched majors after their first year. It was not that they could not perform academically. Instead, they said that they did not feel comfortable within the programs because they did not conform to the majority. Rather than valuing different perspectives and thinking styles, the programs (certainly unintentionally) discouraged them. Therefore, it can be more than a case of people with certain cognitive profiles being attracted to a particular field; it can be certain fields filtering out those who do not match the prevailing cognitive profile.

Workplace

By the time some technical professionals enter the workplace, the majority of their lives may have been spent in circumstances that emphasized narrow cognitive development over broad social development. But it does not stop there. Their first work environments are often solitary and segregated: writing code, small engineering projects, lab work, etc. The problem is compounded when they are in functions that are themselves physically set apart. In large organizations, IT, Engineering, R&D, and other similar departments, are sometimes located physically apart from the rest of the organization, even in different buildings or cities altogether.

They may work this way for years, even decades, becoming more professionally specialized and socially isolated. One is not just a biologist anymore, but an industrial microbiologist or a bioinformatician, and not a computer technologist, but a SQL server system administrator or a J2EE web developer.

Other organizational departments, however, may emphasize, recognize, and reward those with strong interpersonal abilities. So, as some in technical fields become more specialized and isolated, their peers in non-technical areas may be strengthening their ability to influence others. This sets the stage for potentially volatile clashes when these groups are eventually brought together to collaborate.

Bottom Line

For those it affects, the Brainiac Paradox is most likely the result of a combination of both nature and nurture: neurological factors that tend to allot certain people technical advantages but also interpersonal disadvantages, which are then amplified by a series of environmental developmental factors. This can be compared to how rivers form: a naturally occurring low path between two points that is then deepened by erosion. Nevertheless, even rivers can be redirected along more desirable paths, and once established, those paths strengthen over time. The same is true for the Brainiac Paradox.

Neuroplasticity

Until relatively recently, experts believed that the brain did not change after a certain stage of early childhood, but researchers have demonstrated that environment and experience can physically rewire the brain. This is referred to as Neuroplasticity. This concept has led to improved therapies for stroke victims and as well as other techniques that have been introduced to help with various learning disabilities, such as dyslexia.

Though brain dominance profiles are believed to be congenital, Herrmann International, administrators of the Herrmann Brain Dominance

Instrument (HBDI) assessment tool, report success in helping people shift them. CEO Ann Herrmann-Nehdi says it is not easy and takes time, but it can be done if people are motivated enough to stretch their thinking, adding, "The greater the pain of the status quo, the greater the motivation to change."

Likewise, therapy has been shown to be effective with people who have Asperger syndrome. Note, though students or those early in their careers may lack the angst that fuels the motivation to change, their attitudes and behaviors are not likely as fully entrenched, and thus easier to overcome.

Whatever the initial cause, it takes repetition and time to rewire the brain. Thus, just taking a class, reading a book, or simply willing oneself to change is not likely to work. And while this book proposes that the amount of change necessary to mitigate the foibles that hinder success is minimal in most cases, even that requires a methodology that drives and maintains progress. Moreover, if participants have others to support them, even prod them along the way, so much the better. The next chapter makes the case for change and Chapter 6 provides a methodology that will be helpful in achieving it.

Summary – Chapter 2
Great Minds Think Differently

The cognitive contrasts of both contemporary savants as well as history's greatest geniuses suggest that some special aptitudes are possessed not *despite* limitations in other aptitudes, but possibly *because* of them. This book focuses on the seemingly inverse relationship between aptitudes that support success in math, the sciences, etc., and those that support communication effectiveness.

Several areas of scientific study would seem to support a congenital explanation for this. Theories resulting from the study of brain hemisphericity suggest that characteristics associated with left-hemisphere dominance are remarkably consistent with those beneficial to the pursuit of STEM professions, while those associated with the right hemisphere are associated with those helpful to communication.

In addition, those with Asperger syndrome or high-functioning autism tend to exhibit characteristics beneficial in technical professions (summarized as systemizing) and deficiencies associated with socializing (summarized as empathizing). Demographic studies have found a relatively high incident rate of Asperger syndrome among those in technical fields.

Anomalies in brain structure or composition may also be a factor, but this is not as well understood. For example, in recent years scientists have discovered neuron types (mirror and spindle) that have special roles in supporting social interaction. One could speculate that a relative deficiency in these may inhibit a person's social abilities, but free up cognitive potential in other areas.

The Brainiac Paradox could be a result of all of these, different combinations of these for different people, or possibly none of these at all.

Instead, it could be explained by environmental factors. Those born with pronounced aptitudes in math, science, and related cognitive abilities are often identified early, treated differently, and experience a diverging path throughout their educational development and into their careers. For them, individual cognitive achievement is stressed and rewarded even as some other career paths emphasize communication and collaboration. As a result, they may struggle to navigate the intricate social mazes of complex organizations, while others thrive.

Most likely it is a result of a combination of both nature and nurture: neurological factors that tend to allot certain people technical advantages but also social disadvantages, which are then amplified by a series of environmental developmental factors.

This, however, is not a fait accompli. Recent findings related to neuroplasticity have found remarkable ways the brain can be rewired at any age. It is not easily done, and there are limits on what can be achieved, but change is possible for those willing to do what is necessary.

– Chapter 3 –

Cassandra's Curse

The first man to see an illusion by which men have flourished for centuries surely stands in a lonely place. In that moment of insight, he and he alone, sees the obvious which to the uninitiated (the rest of the world) yet appears as nonsense or, worse, as madness and heresy.
Gary Zukav – *The Dancing Wu Li Masters*

When it comes to tragic irony, no one has done it better than the ancient Greeks, and perhaps nowhere did they do it better than in the story of Cassandra.

Cassandra was the daughter of King Priam of Troy. So great was her beauty that she aroused the desires of the Greek God Apollo. In an intended exchange for her virtues, he gave her the power of prophecy, but when Cassandra spurned him, his revenge was poetically simple; he merely made it so no one would believe her. Thereafter, her tremendous gift became a tragic curse: she foretold the Trojan Horse and the fall of Troy, but her people dismissed her as mad; and she envisioned her ensuing rape, capture into slavery, and death, but was powerless to avert them.

The lives of *some* STEM professionals share tragic similarities to Cassandra's. They possess a vision for future solutions and innovations, and yet the "gods" have confounded their ability to be heard.

• • •

"I meet these guys because they are depressed, and they talk about their job failures," says psychologist Tony Attwood, "and you realize why they failed, and it wasn't because of a lack of ability. In fact, they are often very conscientious workers with great attention to detail, etcetera, but their problem was on the interpersonal, the social, and communication side. Employers would not spend the time to understand them; they thought it was much easier to just get rid of them."

The Brainiac Paradox can exact a dear personal cost from those it affects.

Even with impressive cognitive abilities, education, and skills, those who lack the natural social and communication abilities necessary to constructively influence others are likely to experience less rewarding and satisfying careers at a minimum, and extreme frustration and outright failure in some cases.

Those in technical fields usually start their careers with higher salaries than their liberal arts peers and may experience more early advancement as well. However, those who are not adept in their interactions with others are likely to peak early, stall, and possibly decline, as their special technical skills are supplanted by the next generation of desired skills, and as difficulties interacting become an increasing liability.

"These guys don't even see it. They have been straight-A students in school and told they were great. And now, after they have had all these great technical reviews, you're going to tell them they are poor communicators!" says engineer and entrepreneur Bruce Burton. "I have to explain to them, 'you are not going to get as far as you could because you have a real communication problem. This will be very career limiting. We are not going to fire you over it, unless we cannot get the results we need, but you are never going to be a manager, you are never going to move up the economic ladder here unless you can communicate better.'"

Conversely, those who possess strong people skills, but possibly more modest technical abilities, will likely start in fields that initially offer less standing and compensation, but then may thrive in the world of office dynamics and more quickly ascend the organizational and economic ladder.

In what can be a particularly indignant reversal of fortunes, those who were academic heavyweights in school all too often find themselves lagging behind and eventually working for the B and C students they previously towered above.

According to statistics from National Occupational Mortality Surveillance, provided by the National Institute for Occupational Safety and Health, engineers, scientists, and computer programmers committed suicide at higher rates than that of the general public (31%, 32% and 11% higher respectively)[2]. Considering the source of these figures, it can be assumed that career dissatisfaction was at least a likely contributing factor. And recall

---

[2] The rate for mathematicians was actually lower than the average (by 12%); however the sample size was very small.

the earlier-cited Bruce Springsteen quote, "I have never met a man who hated his work, but who loved his life."

Ask Not for Whom the Bell Tolls

Those who struggle professionally despite exceptional cognitive gifts, ambition, and hard work may cite this as evidence of a deeply flawed system, one where style wins out over substance, but there are legitimate and practical reasons for an emphasis on effective communication. Organizations are complex entities that require their various employees to work together, like parts of a machine. In a machine, if any part, no matter its individual importance, does not work with or, worse yet, interferes with the workings of other parts, it must be fixed, replaced or bypassed.

Furthermore, while the tendency is to attribute career frustrations and setbacks to office politics, the truth is that these reversals of fortune often have less to do with someone else's Machiavellian talents than they do with self-inflicted wounds. Some people just fail to do the basic blocking and tackling necessary to propel their careers: successfully pitching ideas, attracting tactical support for their work and, ultimately, drawing positive attention to their contributions.

This neglect may be driven by an idealistic belief that their work, their tangible contributions to the organization, should be the sole, or at least primary, determinant of value, and that competent leadership should be able to recognize such contributions without individuals having to promote themselves. The reality, though, is that people skills are almost always essential to achieving organizational success.

Gary Erickson, managing partner of Executive Search Partners, says he regularly sees people who are so upset at not being able to make the next career breakthrough, that they become eaten away by frustration. They get more and more bitter, asking, "'Why can't people see how valuable I am to the organization?' They fail to see that the problem is their communication style, their inability to listen to and understand the positions of other people, and then respond back to those people appropriately."

Psychologist and author Daniel Goleman popularized the concept of Emotional Intelligence and more recently Social Intelligence, both of which are extremely relevant to this issue. To determine the role these play in the success of climbing organizational ranks, he analyzed 181 competency models drawn from 121 companies and organizations worldwide. For those unfamiliar with them, competency models are tools designed to predict which qualities are likely to be important to a job candidate's success in a particular position. They are created by the quantitative analysis of the qualities and attributes possessed by those with proven success in those positions.

What he found was that factors related to emotional intelligence were two to one more important to success than those related to intelligence or expertise, and that ratio increased for higher-level positions. For the top position in organizations, 80-90% of the determinant factors for success were related to emotional intelligence.

Of course, those with extremely rare abilities or who can prodigiously produce (e.g., patents), may be excused from even the most egregious communication shortcomings, but they are few. The vast majority will have to find a way to interact more effectively if they are to achieve career success and satisfaction. Otherwise they may find themselves sliding into a negatively-reinforcing cycle: frustration, resentment, withdrawal, performance problems, reduced responsibilities, frustration ....

Emotional/Social Intelligence
The difference between Emotional Intelligence and Social Intelligence, according to Goleman is that emotional intelligence has to do with self-mastery, how one handles him or herself. Those with great self-mastery are more likely to be strong individual performers. However, when it comes to leadership, one's success depends on everyone else being effective; so one needs to be successful by influencing, persuading, developing, growing, inspiring, and motivating other people. That is the social intelligence ability. It requires empathy and skilled interaction.

It is this that helps explain the popularity and longevity of the comic strip "Dilbert," created by Scott Adams, himself a former technical professional. In the strip, Adams takes a cynical look at the workplace through the eyes of an engineer, Dilbert. Its core theme is the alienation and annoyance Dilbert and his technical colleagues feel in relation to the non-technical world. Adams says many if not most of his ideas come from his fans and despite 20 years of daily cartoons, he stays weeks ahead in the preparation of comics. "I'll never run out of material," writes Adams, "I get at least two hundred e-mail messages a day, mostly from people who are complaining about their own clueless managers."

Dilbert provides some needed comic relief to what are often emotionally exasperating circumstances. It also provides the reassurance that it is *they*, and not *we*. But in doing so, there is a danger. If we believe that *they* are the cause for our woes, does that effectively absolve us from the need to attempt change? Does it doom us to the status quo?

Success Must be Seized

Despite the difficulties that many face in being rewarded for their contributions, there are some glaring exceptions. Bill Gates and Steve Jobs are the most notable, and more recently there has been Mark Zuckerberg, but there have been a slew of people in the technology arena who have achieved phenomenal wealth at a young age, despite being socially atypical. Thanks to them, and others like them, *geeks* are hip. Nevertheless, that does not mean that the average person can ignore communication issues.

Years ago MIT conducted a retrospective analysis of the students who later went on to be their most generous donors – and thus by deduction the most financially successful. What they found initially surprised them. Those who would go on to become the most successful were typically not the students who entered with the best test scores, or who got the highest grades while at MIT. Instead, it was those who just barely got in and survived, but who had participated in other aspects of the school environment such as clubs and teams. Whether such social interaction is a cause or an effect, it is still safe to say that those who broaden their social interactions will likely find they are best armed to achieve success in society.

For every Gates, Jobs or Zuckerberg, there are countless more whose lives continue to more closely resemble Dilbert's. And it is not just because Gates and those like him were lucky, though I do not discount the importance of luck. An important factor they had going for them – and one that likely differentiates them from those who would like to follow – is the ability, even the zeal, to sell and exploit their ideas as well as, some would argue, the unexploited ideas of others.

Success

There is a lot more to defining success than job titles and financial compensation, but these are the two primary measures used here precisely because there are so many alternatives. Whatever our personal measures, there is a good chance that they can be more easily achieved by overcoming whichever foibles may afflict us.

The phenomenal success of Facebook has been marred by highly publicized accusations, accompanied by successful lawsuits, that Mark Zuckerberg took advantage of the ideas of others. As for Gates, consider the case made by Jeff Jarvis in his blog posting, *The Meaning of Bill.*

His first product was another version of the Basic programming language. His master stroke was taking the essence of a now-forgotten operating system called CP/M and turning it into MS-DOS, the neurology of the personal-computer revolution. He took the tool that truly created the technology age, VisiCalc – the spreadsheet that let business people ask "what if?" which is what put computers on every office desk in the world – and turned it into Excel, part of his Office suite that also included Word, which itself was really just an adaptation of WordStar. He took the art of the Apple Lisa and Mac and turned it into the clumsy painting-on-velvet, Windows. Gates took others' innovations and turned them into products and profits. Every great invention needs a business genius to bring it to market. For software, that was Gates.

Not everyone has the drive, ability or even desire (Russian mathematician Grigori Perelman even went so far as to refuse the accolades and $1 million prize for solving the Poincaré conjecture) to seize the recognition and rewards for their contributions. Unfortunately, if they do not, someone else likely will. Consider the *innovators* Gates was alleged to have exploited. Some of them had exploited earlier innovators themselves. The Apple Lisa and Mac system, utilized innovations from the Alto created by Xerox at its Palo Alto Research Center (PARC), which borrowed ideas and innovations from the Stanford Research Institute (SRI), and many of those innovations trace back to Doug Engelbart.

Doug Engelbart

In many ways, Engelbart is a dramatic contrast to Gates or Jobs. He may have been one of the most influential innovators of the 20th century, yet few have ever heard of him. Engelbart's lab at the Stanford Research Institute (SRI) was the birthplace of an astounding number of computer innovations. Most notably, he invented the computer mouse (with the assistance of colleague Bill English), but he led the introduction of numerous other technologies which are now equally ubiquitous. His work in the 1960's presaged the personal computer, networking, the Web and even cloud computing, which the industry has only recently begun to fully embrace. What has since become known as the "Mother of All Demos" provides a 45-year-old snapshot of his visionary contributions.

To appreciate fully the magnitude of this demonstration, you need to suspend your knowledge of the enormous explosion of technology that has occurred over the last four decades, and imagine yourself in 1968, when this demonstration took place: computers are still largely automobile-sized machines requiring special climate-controlled rooms. In most cases, you interface with them through individually-created punch cards that are gathered into a batch and fed into the computer through a special reader. The output is in the form of dot-matrix printed text on large fan-fold sheets of paper. Computing is laborious, slow and often frustrating.

Now, imagine taking an afternoon off from such a work environment to attend a demonstration in which Engelbart introduces a host of futuristic technologies. The demonstration featured mind-blowing examples of on-screen editing, a computer mouse, multiple windows, hypermedia, context-sensitive help, distributed collaboration and shared-screen video teleconferencing. Never before had there been such a concentrated demonstration of so much tremendous new technology, nor has there been since. It is as if while the Wright brothers were tinkering with their first aircraft, someone demonstrated crude, but working versions of the Saturn V Rocket, the Apollo Spacecraft, and the Lunar Lander. A link to a video of the demonstration is provide at *www.brainiacparadox.com.*

At the end of the presentation, nearly a thousand technical peers – normally inclined to greet such presentations with a skeptical eye and an attitude of, "Well, that's interesting, but I think I can do better" – leapt to their feet and cheered.[3]

While these technologies were the result of a collaborative effort – as of course were Microsoft, Apple, and Facebook – Engelbart was the visionary and mastermind. The current economic impact of these technologies and the industries they have spawned is incalculable. And what was Engelbart's recognition and reward? At the time of this writing, a Google search on "Bill Gates" returns more that 45 million results; a search on "Steve Jobs" returns 121 million; and a search on "Douglas Engelbart" returns 290 thousand (even Rin Tin Tin, the star canine of pre-1960's radio and TV returned more at 1.2 million). Gates' net worth is over $50 billion dollars. At his death, Steve Jobs' was about $30 billion. And when Engelbart died in 2013, his was, well … considerably less. Engelbart never received royalty payments on his mouse patent, but in a payout of the hypothetical, "If I had a nickel for every …" exercise, he would have earned over $50 million if he had received a measly five cents for every mouse sold. Imagine if he would have fully monetized all his innovations.

By no means was he left destitute and forgotten. Engelbart received many of the top honors from his peers: National Medal of Technology, Lemelson-MIT Prize, Turing Award, Lovelace Medal, Norbert Wiener Award for Social and Professional Responsibility, and a Fellow Award from the Computer History Museum.

But why did Engelbart not achieve anything near the wealth of Gates, Jobs, or Zuckerberg? Numerous factors likely played a role: too far ahead of his time, the idiosyncrasies of academia and fickle nature of government funding, luck, maybe he was not even interested in great wealth – but Engelbart himself provided some clues in a 1986 interview with Judy Adams and Henry Lowood for Stanford University: "I was immersed in my

---

[3] From *Innovation: The Five Disciplines for Creating What Customers Want,* by Curtis Ray Carlson and William W. Wilmot

own dream about things … I really didn't pay enough attention to the communications and to the basic everyday politics of trying to make sure that people understood, or that you were putting on a good image. There was a lot, I'm sure, that I could have done to forestall and improve a lot of situations."

Engelbart's comments reflect some of organizational communication challenges referenced by the Brainiac Paradox: the inability to make personal connections, create mutual interest, convey understanding, and appeal to the logic and emotions of disparate audiences – ultimately, the ability to influence the perceptions and behaviors of key audiences. If Englebart had done those more effectively, his story may have been much different.

Engelbart is just one of countless individuals throughout history whose innovations were eventually exploited by others. A book dedicated to the story of those unrewarded for their contributions to the Information Age would be massive.

Alan Turing

As mentioned in the previous chapter, Alan Turing was a critical part of Britain's code breaking program in World War II, and his creation of what is now called the Turing Machine provided the logic essential to modern computers. However, his contributions were not enough to overcome his idiosyncrasies and social ineptness. Less than 10 years after the war's end, he met a sad death, believed to be a suicide. This outcome was preceded by prosecution by the British government based on their laws against homosexuality.

While Turing was not alone in being prosecuted for homosexuality at the time (in the early 50's as many as 1,000 men were imprisoned for homosexuality each year), powerful and influential men were often able to escape prosecution. As such, it is hard to imagine that the government would have pursued prosecution of a man who had made such great contributions to the war effort and would be later listed among the "100 Greatest Britons" by the BBC and one of the "100 Most Important People of the 20th Century" by *Time Magazine*, had he only been more socially typical.

He was only 41 at the time of his death. It is chilling to think what his mind might have contributed had he lived longer.

Altogether Forgotten

It is a shame that such monumental contributions are not appropriately rewarded. At least Engelbart and Turing are referenced in history books and recognized in knowledgeable circles. How many more there must be who have broken significant new ground and made great contributions but, either because they failed outright to capitalize on them or because others usurped them, received neither financial reward or a place in history books? How many could tell similar, if more modest, stories? Of course, we cannot know that which by definition is not known, but without a doubt there have been multitudes. Maybe there are some among readers of this book.

Societal Costs

While the careers of countless others may share unfortunate similarities with Cassandra's tragic story, it is among the greater society that the repercussions of the Brainiac Paradox are most felt.

Gary Erickson, president and chief operating officer of Cybernoor Corporation tells the story of a former colleague, "A brilliant guy, one of the smartest guys I have known, ever!" He did quite well in the early part of his career as an engineer but was frustrated by what it would take to make it to the top. He had made great contributions and still had many more ideas, but got so fed up that he dropped out midway in his career. "He and his wife bought a boat and started sailing and the last anyone heard of him he was doing artwork in Nantucket," said Erickson. Here again we must wonder what great technical contributions went unfulfilled.

Modern civilization is increasingly dependent upon technical professionals to provide the innovation critical to economic growth and the solutions needed to address rapidly evolving societal challenges and threats.

An ever-increasing portion of our GDP is related to technology. Various studies have estimated that technology accounts for more than one-half of economic growth. While three-quarters of U.S. industries contributed to the acceleration in economic growth in the late 1990s, the four IT-producing industries were responsible for a quarter of that acceleration, while only accounting for 3% of the GDP[4]. In 2006, the information technology and communication industries by themselves were estimated to contribute over $1 trillion to the U.S. GDP. Incidentally, U.S. spending on research and development in 2006 was estimated to be $343 billion. Possibly most telling, the chief economist of J.P. Morgan estimated that the launch of the iPhone 5 would contribute as much as half a percentage point to the annualized GDP for the fourth quarter of 2012. All that from a single product!

Furthermore, technology has a tremendous multiplying factor. It affects almost all industries and on multiple levels. One of the things that has

---

[4] Jorgenson, Dale (2001), "U.S. Economic Growth In the Information Age", *Issues in Science and Technology* (Fall): 42–50.

helped U.S. industries remain competitive, or at least slow their rate of decline, has been huge productivity increases due to technology. According to a paper published by the National Bureau of Economic Research, the acceleration in productivity growth in the last half of the 1990s was due entirely to investments in information technology.

Technological products and services are also frequently the key differentiators for more traditional product segments. Automobiles have largely become commodities; what increasingly differentiate them are their technological bells and whistles.

Possibly less obvious is our tremendous reliance on technological innovation to resolve social and environmental issues. The world's explosive population growth is only supported by technology – such as those that improve crop yields – and medical advancements that are necessary to confront mounting health risks created by an increasingly mobile and congested world. New technologies often provide societal benefits that are far removed from their original intentions. Cell phones were merely the extension of an existing technology – land line phones – driven by the public's desire for ever-increasing convenience, but there is no doubt they have become an incredibly valuable tool in terms of personal safety. They allow those who are injured in remote areas or who are threatened by a dangerous situation to reach help. They are even used to locate people who are unable to place a call themselves. Evolving technology has also had an enormous affect on politics and human rights, as evidenced by the role social media (Twitter, Facebook, and YouTube) played in the Arab Spring of 2012.

Each major technical innovation translates into economic growth or quality-of-life improvements, usually both, and even though technological innovation can have some unanticipated negative consequences, those too are usually overcome with evermore technological solutions and innovations.

The tentacles of technology touch all aspects of our lives. And all along the innovation value chain, from pure research to final manufacturing and distribution, those in technical fields play a crucial role. As such, there is an enormous opportunity cost for everyone when talented professionals do not achieve their full potential or worse yet, become discouraged, demoralized, and disengaged.

Charles Babbage

Engelbart and Touring tell the unfortunate tales of those who were successful in making great contributions, but who were not commensurately recognized and rewarded.

Charles Babbage's story reveals a different facet of this issue: the potential opportunity costs when the Brainiac Paradox prevents a genius from achieving his potential.

Babbage (1791 to 1871) was an English mathematician, philosopher, inventor and mechanical engineer who originated the concept of a programmable computer. His first design was called the Difference Engine, which later was supplanted by the even more capable Analytical Engine.

These were large, complicated machines of gears and cams, but elegant in their design and sophisticated in their functionality. The Analytical Engine included many innovations that were not actually used until more than a century later: operations-based instructions, conditional logic, and separate input and output. The accompanying printer Babbage designed was itself a marvel of capabilities and practicality.

While working on these devices, Babbage came in contact with Ada Lovelace (officially Augusta Ada King, Countess of Lovelace and the daughter of Lord Byron), and while later translating a description of his work, she developed a vision of how such devices could be used for more than just crunching numbers. Her ideas presage modern computing and her innovations distinguish her as the first computer programmer (the computer language Ada was named in her honor).

Thus, the fundamental components of the modern information age were in place during the first half of the 19th century, but Babbage was never able to complete his machines, though he did develop limited prototypes that proved his concepts. What stopped him were not flaws in his ideas or even the crudity of prevailing supporting technologies – recently engineers have been able to build working versions of his machine using only his plans, and the materials and processes available in his time. It was Babbage's failure to collaborate and communicate effectively with those on whom he depended for funding that resulted in the forestallment of the Information Age by more than 100 years. For those who enjoy pondering the "what ifs" of history, there can be few more fascinating scenarios than the very plausible, "What if Babbage had succeeded in starting the computer revolution in the early 19th century?"

While Babbage's story poses an intriguing hypothetical case for the enormous potential opportunity costs of the Brainiac Paradox, the implications of this phenomenon do not depend on the theoretical. The BP Deepwater Horizon Oil Spill in the Gulf of Mexico is an all-too-real case where a thorough investigation cited communication problems as a root cause for a disaster of epic proportions.

Deepwater Horizon

On April 20, 2010, the Deepwater Horizon oil-drilling platform erupted into a searing ball of flame, killing 11 oil workers, injuring 16 others and setting off a chain reaction that would result in history's largest water-based oil spill. By the time the well could be capped 120 days later, almost five million barrels of oil would flow into the clear blue waters of the Gulf of Mexico, devastating its ecosystem and creating great economic hardship for those in the region. Its long-term effects are still unknown.

Long before the well was capped, a presidential commission was organized to investigate the cause of the incident and to make recommendations on how a similar disaster could be avoided in the future. In the final report, the commission stated, "Most, if not all, of the failures at [Deepwater Horizon] can be traced back to underlying failures of management and communication. Better management of decision making processes within BP and other companies, better communication within and between BP and its contractors … would have prevented the [Deepwater Horizon] incident."

A review of the details of the report show that the communication failures referenced were primarily among the technical staff of the various companies involved with the well: BP, Halliburton and Transocean.

When viewed in isolation, the failures cited often appear to be relatively innocent mistakes – ones anyone might make – and yet they were made by individuals who understood the enormous consequences at stake. When considered as a whole, the many mistakes suggest the subtle hands of the Brainiac Paradox at play.

For example, several weeks before the blowout, Halliburton engineers passed to BP the results of early tests of the cement slurry, which was essential to the well's integrity. However, they only passed on the raw results, not their interpretation that the mixture was unstable. Giving these engineers the benefit of the doubt, they probably assumed that those on the receiving end would study the findings and realize the dangerous implications. Halliburton, however, was the acknowledged expert in this tricky and crucial drilling step and the failure to include a summary suggested that the results were unremarkable. In addition, there were several other failed cement tests and there is no evidence these were communicated at all. While some may see a conspiracy in this – an example of management's push to make deadlines at all costs – keep in mind that it was not in Halliburton's interest to fail to communicate. It was BP that would shoulder the costs of any delays in cementing the well.

By the time Halliburton finally changed the test parameters and achieved, arguably, satisfactory results, the BP well had already been cemented.

Communication also played a part in BP's use of only six centralizers when 16 were called for (one computer simulation suggested 21 were needed). Centralizers are devices that ensure that the well is cemented evenly around its parameter for a prescribed length, thus preventing any weak points for the oil and gas to leak. Those who objected to so few centralizers either failed to share the information or were unable to influence management's decision.

Even after the blowout, communication failures were a problem. The report noted it took nearly 10 days for someone to realize they had been using the wrong hydraulic panel on the Blowout Preventer (BOP), in the attempt to manually shut off the flow of oil. By that time, the flow of oil and sand continued to wear down the BOP's parts, making closure more difficult. When they finally attempted a shutdown at the correct panel, they were unable. Communication continued to be a problem as they attempted other approaches such as the Containment Dome, Top Kill and Junk Shot.

I reiterate that this analysis is not intended to blame the technical staff for this disaster – overwhelming evidence points toward management pressure to avoid delays as the root cause. It does, however, suggest that communication shortcomings among the technical teams contributed to the *failure to prevent* the disaster at the numerous stages where it could and should have been.

Interestingly, similar issues – management pressure and technical staff's communication weaknesses – were listed as prime contributors in the report issued after the Challenger Space Shuttle disaster.

One does not need to have blatant communication shortcomings for it to pose a problem. Simple communication lapses can have enormous consequences.

Common Cause

It is in everyone's interest that technical professionals succeed and that their contributions are recognized and rewarded. It is especially true in the United States.

Long the undisputed leader in technological development, the United States has become a net importer of high-technology products. Its trade balance in high-technology manufactured goods shifted from plus $54 billion in 1990 to negative $50 billion in 2001. And, in 2005, only four American companies ranked among the top 10 corporate recipients of patents granted by the United States Patent and Trademark Office.

According to a recent survey, 86% of U.S. voters believe that the United States must increase the number of workers with a background in science and mathematics or America's ability to compete in the global economy will be diminished. The reality is that the numbers are decreasing.

In South Korea, 38% of all undergraduates receive their degrees in STEM fields. In France, the figure is 47%, in China, 50%, and in Singapore, 67%. In the United States, the corresponding figure is 15%.

What's more, federal funding of research in the physical sciences, as a percentage of GDP, was 45% less in FY 2004 than in FY 1976. At the time of this writing, the amount invested annually by the U.S. federal government in research in the physical sciences, mathematics, and engineering combined equals the annual increase in U.S. health care costs incurred every 20 days.

Unless there are dramatic changes in some of these metrics, an important element in a strategy to stay competitive in an ultracompetitive technological world has to be getting the most out of existing STEM professionals.

Summary – Chapter 3
Cassandra's Curse

The Brainiac Paradox presents a tragic irony: some of the most valuable innovations and solutions exist inside the minds of people who have a difficult time conveying them.

The reality of contemporary society is that few things can be accomplished as a lone effort, and indeed most ideas cannot be brought to fruition without the involvement of many people representing different areas of functional expertise. If one is unable to work effectively with others, his or her contributions likely will not be realized or, worse yet, will be usurped by others.

The chasm created between what could or should be and what is, can at times lead to a negatively reinforcing cycle – of frustration, resentment, withdrawal, performance problems, reduced responsibilities, frustration and so on. Before long, those who may have been stars during the academic phase of their lives are surpassed by those whose most prominent gifts lay in their people smarts.

On the other hand, the vast majority does not face such extreme fates (though possibly shades of this). In fact, some are among the wealthiest and most powerful people in the world, despite certain atypical characteristics (e.g., Bill Gates, Steve Jobs and Mark Zuckerberg). Nevertheless, using Gates, Jobs and Zuckerberg as rationale for ignoring the possible applicability of the Brainiac Paradox is like ignoring the management of one's personal finances because there are ongoing examples of lottery winners.

And, it is not just that these three, and others like them, got lucky. The biographies of such people usually reveal characteristics beyond their own personal brilliance that were essential to their success: maybe they were natural salesmen; maybe they were ruthless when engaging competitors; maybe they even exploited the work of others; maybe it was a combination of these or something else extraordinary altogether. The point is that if we depend upon intelligence, hard work, and great contributions alone to trump everything else, we are likely to be disappointed.

The stories of Charles Babbage and Doug Engelbart demonstrate that even the greatest work can go unrealized or unrewarded, and the story of Alan Turing is a cautionary tale for those who expect their genius to offset their social differences.

In such cases, however, it is not just technical professionals who suffer; the costs to society as a whole can be enormous. The world depends on these people for their innovations and solutions and when their efforts are hindered, everyone pays the opportunity costs: fuel is withheld from the economic engine; solutions to social, health, and environmental issues are delayed or unrealized; and other societal calamites are created.

The repercussions of marginalized professionals are even more acute in countries, like the U.S., which graduate a smaller percentage in STEM fields than those of most other developed countries. There is a direct relationship between such professionals' ability to communicate effectively and the overall prosperity of the nation. Everyone has a stake in this issue.

Section II

The Answer

This section shifts the discussion from the problem to the solution. It explains why this phenomenon is not as daunting as it might seem and introduces a methodology for mitigating the ill effects of the Brainiac Paradox.

– Chapter 4 –

The Best Revenge
Is Communicating Well

Everything that irritates us about others
can lead us to an understanding of ourselves.
– Carl Jung

The disheartening conclusion one might logically reach having read the preceding chapters is that for some, careers burdened by degrees of frustrations and setbacks related to communication issues are the price they must pay for their other gifts. This, however, is not inevitable – far from it.

In some ways, communication is like food. Communication is necessary for us to sustain ourselves socially and food is necessary to sustain ourselves physically. Communication comes in different mediums just as food is derived from various raw ingredients. And just as different types of food can be combined and presented in such ways that they are more likely to be consumed, so can communication.

Prime Ingredients

Top chefs always say that the key to a great meal is to start with top quality ingredients. Likewise, there are certain basic elements that serve as quality ingredients for effective communication, and several of those are frequently attributed to those in technical professions.

Passion

Many have a great passion for their fields. When they are on the topic of their choice, their eyes light up and the words pour out. This kind of passion is often contagious and can make a tremendous difference in the effectiveness of communication. The most effective communicators are usually the ones who feel most passionate about their subject.

Intelligence
Credibility is one of the most important ingredients in effective communication – and among the hardest to acquire – and an audience's perception of the communicator's intelligence has a significant impact on credibility.

Knowledge
Perceived depth of knowledge on a topic, like intelligence, is an important credibility factor, though they are not the same thing. Someone can be intelligent without a great depth of knowledge, and someone else can acquire a great depth of knowledge on a subject without being particularly intelligent. Few fields require the level of knowledge or education as those associated with technical professions.

Verbal Reasoning
When discussing the Brainiac Paradox, most people initially assume the communication issues referenced stem from difficulties with the mechanics: writing a clear sentence, using correct grammar, spelling or speaking articulately. While these are sometimes an issue, they rank fairly low on the list of things that most negatively affect such professionals. In fact, verbal reasoning is often a relative strength for them. Robert Oppenheimer was a poet, as was Nikola Tesla, and many others have impressive literary accomplishments. Recall that verbal abilities were one of the characteristics associated with left-brain dominant people. Strong verbal reasoning abilities do not automatically equate to effective communication abilities – just as having a good tractor does not necessarily make someone a good farmer – but it does provide the foundation upon which effective communication can be built.

Verbal
In her 1952 book, *The Making of a Scientist*, Anne Roe tells of enlisting 62 of some of the greatest science geniuses of her time into taking the Stanford-Binet IQ test. As one would expect, the participants achieved exceptional scores in the math and spatial portions of the test, but they also excelled in the verbal portion.

Topical Relevancy

Science, technology, and innovation – the currency of technical professions – are among the things people are most interested in today. They are both consequential to our lives and they often have the ability to invoke that childlike gee whiz factor that delights us. As such, they are a staple topic of the news and entertainment media.

Goodwill

While at times it may not seem like it, most technical professionals start out with the goodwill of others in their organization. After all, if they are successful, others are usually successful: corporations profit; universities gain prestige; government is more effective; and so on. They are the fountains of innovations and solutions and it is important for everyone that such contributions keep flowing.

Then What?

So, with so much seeming to favor STEM professionals in terms of communications, why the problems? Why is it that so many encounter MEGO (my eyes glass over) when trying to engage their audiences? Why don't others read, let alone respond to their messages? Why are their worthwhile requests for support or funding denied? Why don't they receive more acknowledgment or rewards for their contributions? Why is it that "weasels" (as Scott Adams calls the parasites that thrive in a corporate environment) prosper while those who work ethically languish?

An answer can be found in extending the food analogy used above. Even when cooking with the best of ingredients, the final food product can be inedible. They can be combined with the uncomplimentary ingredients, in the wrong proportions, undercooked, overcooked, or maybe they are fine, but are counter to the tastes of the consumer. Similarly, even someone with passion, intelligence, depth of knowledge, strong verbal skills, a relevant topic and goodwill can fail to connect with their audience. For example, intelligence is an asset, but can be presented in ways that make someone incomprehensible to all but their peers, or to come across as condescending.

Social Naturals

The reverse of the food analogy also works. There are those who may have a gift for connecting with and influencing others even without great intelligence, knowledge, passion, etc., just as a great chef can make something appealing out of mediocre ingredients. It comes naturally to these people just as the understanding of mathematics may to others.

Intelligence attracts, while arrogance repels, just as pepper seasons, but too much spoils the dish. Passion is important, but can lead to overwhelming the audience with excessive information or one-sided conversations.

The real magic, though, is when the best of both can be combined. In my experience, the most compelling individuals are often those in STEM fields who have found the way to connect with their audiences and express themselves effectively. Stephen Hawking, Neil deGrasse Tyson and Carl Sagan are like top chefs. They combine their attributes in a way that not only reaches, but also captivates non-technical audiences. Almost everyone has some Hawking, Tyson or Sagan in them; he or she only needs a way to channel it properly.

The fallacy is that it takes some special social and communication abilities to influence audiences. It is not a matter of matching the performance of those who have a natural gift for connecting with others. One just needs to avoid the things that restrict his or her own natural gifts from radiating. We just have to get out of our own way!

Exemplars

Such is the contentious nature of science that some may object to the use of one or more of Hawking, Tyson or Sagan as examples to spotlight. Whatever the critics' reasons, they do not invalidate the greater point: those who can combine technical expertise with the ability to connect with an audience can be powerfully influential.

Consider Craig Jones' response posting to a Laurence A. Moran blog: *Sandwalk: Strolling with a Skeptical Biochemist*. The topic was *Lessons from Science Communication Training* and the original post was May 30, 2007.

The best thing any scientist can do is talk to people—at school, on the plane, in the bus. Recent PhDs often avoid this—they cannot explain, they think, without a basketful of jargon (I know of one who would say he was a firefighter to avoid explaining things). All too often scientists are told by funding agencies and such that they need to be more relevant to society. This is misinterpreted to say what your latest scientific endeavor will do to improve the lot of, say, shoe salesmen. This is wrong. In my work, I have to tell a lot of landowners about my research in order to place equipment on their land. It is generally the "gee, I didn't know you could do that" aspect that they enjoy hearing about—that I can record a magnitude 5 quake from halfway round the world, or determine just where the boundary between the crust and mantle is right under their house. And I can SHOW them this. Rekindling a bit of the awe of discovery in folks is what satisfies a lot of the public. Building on this will do science coverage more good than adopting the tricks of master hucksters; we don't need no stinking smoke and mirrors—we have science.

The goal of this book is to help those affected by the Brainiac Paradox mitigate the foibles that prevent their full contribution in the workplace.

This book proposes that there are certain foibles that serve as significant obstacles to some professionals' career success and enjoyment. By learning to recognize and address these foibles, they can more fully achieve their potential. Accomplishing this is not difficult, but nor is it something that can be achieved instantly or by robotically following a series of steps.

No Magic Pill

Consider that 68% of the adult American population is over-weight. Americans spend an astronomical $40 billion a year on weight-loss programs and products, yet the rate of obesity is increasing. Why are so many people still overweight, when they know the health and personal costs, and they have spent so much in an attempt to resolve it?

The reason is that certain behaviors are so stubborn and resistant to change that one-off development programs, like crash diets, rarely work for the long run. A point could even be made that they do more harm than good, because when they fail, they reinforce the participant's sense of hopelessness. In such cases, dieters will acquiesce to the problem, somehow rationalizing why they are not successful, or blame others. The same may be true for those affected by the Brainiac Paradox. Of course, there can be congenital factors (such as metabolism for weight and psychological/neurological for the Paradox) that can make change difficult or impossible. For most, though, all that stands in their way is not taking the right approach.

Despite the constant onslaught of revolutionary new pills, diets, or other gimmicks that promise easy, quick, and safe weight loss, experts have found time-after-time that the only proven approach is the basic formula of increased activity and decreased caloric intake. Furthermore, the only way to keep the weight off is a long-term change in attitudes, behaviors, and practices. The same is true with those affected by the Paradox. Just taking a class or participating in a workshop is not likely to correct deep-rooted behaviors. What is needed is an understanding of what contributes to effective communication and what detracts from it, combined with a methodical approach that supports real and lasting change. Moreover, just as the general solutions for weight loss are the same, whether one is 10 or 100 pounds overweight, solutions for the Paradox are usually the same, whether one's challenges are negligible or profound.

Summary – Chapter 4
The Best Revenge is Communicating Well

While technical professionals may disproportionally face communication challenges, they also disproportionally possess certain traits that are the raw material of effective communications.

- Passion
- Intelligence
- Depth of knowledge
- Verbal reasoning
- Topical relevancy
- Goodwill

When combined and used in the correct proportions, these are powerful ingredients for effective communication and can unleash their potential: others listen, heed, believe, and respond. However, when combined incorrectly they are ineffective and even counterproductive.

Over the years, I have observed a set of behaviors, attitudes, and practices that have repeatedly undermined the effectiveness of some technical professionals. In this book I refer to these as foibles and list the nine I believe are most consequential. I have found that even minor improvements in overcoming these foibles can pay large dividends. The goal of this book is to help those affected by the Brainiac Paradox mitigate the foibles that prevent their full contribution in the workplace. Towards that end, I have included insights, strategies, techniques, and tools for addressing each of these in the following chapters. More importantly, they are offered in conjunction with a methodology that facilitates the type of behavioral change necessary for lasting improvement.

– Chapter 5 –

Franklin's Gifts

Either write things worth reading, or do things worth the writing.
—Benjamin Franklin

It is hard to imagine the likes of a Benjamin Franklin living among us in the present day. Franklin was a polymath, the proverbial Jack of all trades, and master of *all*. He was a preeminent scientist, inventor, author, politician, philanthropist, and diplomat. His contributions in any one of these would warrant a prominent place in our history books; his achievement in all of them is extraordinary. It is as if some of the best aspects of Newton[5], Edison, Twain, Lincoln, Carnegie, and … Franklin (historian Gordon S. Wood called him the "greatest diplomat America has ever had") were spliced into one person.

Franklin was the consummate problem solver and throughout his life he tinkered, improved, and invented. His portfolio of inventions was remarkable both in its quantity as well as its diversity: the lightning rod, bifocals, flexible urinary catheter, Franklin stove, odometer, swim fins, and musical instrument (the Armonica).

As a social innovator, he was instrumental in establishing America's first subscription library, fire department, "paid city watch" (i.e., police), fire insurance company, and hospital. In addition, he founded the American Philosophical Society and the Academy and College of Philadelphia (later to become the University of Pennsylvania).

---

[5] In eulogizing Franklin, the British themselves called him America's Newton.

And as an economic innovator, he pioneered the concept of franchising (print shops) and championed the role of paper currency in the fledgling colonies. He created enough wealth by the age of 42 to be able to retire.

He spoke five languages and played violin, cello, harp, guitar, and of course, his own Armonica.

Franklin's Technical Gifts

As remarkable as all this is, it is his accomplishments as a scientist and communicator that are most relevant to the topic of addressing the Brianiac Paradox, and where, perhaps, he was most exceptional.

Unfortunately, an understanding of him as a scientist has been distorted by our youth-instilled caricature of him flying a kite to attract lightning. This belittles his scientific contributions and belies the esteem with which his scientific peers held him.

Franklin did not "discover electricity" as the general population often believes, but he contributed to its knowledge in profound ways – including the identification of positive and negative charge and the conservation of charge – due to his keen observation, careful experiments, and amazing insights. What's more, he put that knowledge to practical use through his invention of the lightning rod.

For most, his role as scientist ended with electricity, but there was significantly more. Franklin was the first to understand and map the Gulf Stream. He also proposed theories on a range of natural phenomenon, from the common cold to climate change (he theorized that the great eruption of Laki Volcano in Iceland accounted for the unusually severe winter in Europe that followed). He, along with scientist John Hadley, demonstrated the possibilities of cooling through evaporation, and he supported Christiaan Huygens' wave theory of light, which was predominantly ignored by the rest of the scientific community of the day.

Franklin's scientific accomplishments earned him numerous distinctions:

- Recipient of the Royal Society's Copley Medal (England, 1753), its highest honor and the equivalent to a Nobel Prize today (Franklin was the first recipient not born in England)
- Honorary degree from Harvard (1753)
- Honorary degree from Yale (1753)
- Elected as a Fellow of the Royal Society (England, 1756)
- Honorary Doctor of Law degree from the University of St. Andrews (Scotland, 1759)
- Honor of Freedom of the Borough of St. Andrews (Scotland, 1759)

- Honorary doctorate from Oxford University (England, 1762)
- Elected as member of the Académie des Sciences and the Society for the Encouragement of Arts, Manufactures & Commerce (France, 1772)
- Elected as member of the Société Royale de Médecine (France, 1776)

In short, Franklin was recognized as a great scientific mind (or philosophical thinker, as they were called in the day).

Incredibly, he was an equally gifted communicator, that is to say, he had an extraordinary ability to convey information in such a way so as *to constructively influence the perceptions and behaviors of others*. His surviving writings show a skilled tactical communicator, able to convey complex subjects simply, concisely, and persuasively, and his phenomenal accomplishments as politician and diplomat demonstrate his strategic effectiveness.

Franklin's proclivity in this area exhibited itself at an early age. He began writing for his brother's newspaper, *The New England Courant* when he was only 15 and ran the paper by the age of 17, while his brother was briefly jailed. By the age of 27, he had established himself with his own successful print shop and he started publishing the wildly popular *Poor Richard's Almanac*. In addition to such content as a calendar, weather predictions, and farming information, Franklin included axioms, witticisms, and proverbs that both reflected and influenced the values and ideals of the country. The success of the Almanac, and other shrewd business moves, allowed Franklin to retire young and to devote his time both to his scientific explorations and public service.

A proper summary of his political and diplomatic accomplishments would take far too much space, but suffice it to say that he faced a series of daunting diplomatic and political challenges and was remarkably successful in resolving them: repeal of the Stamp Act, The Declaration of Independence, treaty with France, peace treaty with England, and the U.S. Constitution, to name the most familiar, but far from all. Even some of his initial failures eventually turned to successes. His Albany Plan, which called for uniting the colonies "under one government as far as might be necessary for defense and other general important purposes," was the blueprint for the United States and proposed more than 20 years before the Declaration of Independence. In some cases, he was just too far ahead of his time. Few could match his sagacity.

It is a fitting testament to Franklin that he alone has the honor of signing all four of the seminal documents associated with the founding of the United States:

- Declaration of Independence (1776)
- Treaty of Alliance, Amity, and Commerce with France (1778)
- Treaty of Peace between England, France, and the United States (1782)
- U.S. Constitution (1787)

If George Washington was the steeple of the fledgling United States; Thomas Jefferson, John Adams, James Madison, and others were its major building blocks; and France was its buttresses; then Franklin was the mortar that held the entire structure together.

Franklin's Gift to Us

The chapter title, *Franklin's Gifts*, is a double entendre. It references the many exceptional personal gifts he possessed, but also the gifts he offers us via his advice and examples. Among his voluminous writings that have survived are numerous references that speak to aspects of the Brainiac Paradox as well as ideas that are helpful to overcoming it.

He offers us the example of his life: of ambition and compassion, of ego and humility, of industry and whimsy, of dogma and intellectual flexibility; in other words, the balanced man. He appears to have possessed an inordinate share of what is now commonly referred to as social intelligence.

Probably one of his greatest but less understood qualities is revealed in his axiom, "There are three things extremely hard: steel, a diamond, and to know one's self." Yes, he had his share of shortcomings, but what sets him apart was his awareness and acceptance of them. Rather than deny or paper-over his faults, as so many do, he acknowledged them and worked energetically and methodically to address them.

Furthermore, beyond the pieces of advice and wisdom he has left for us, is a methodology for self-improvement. He developed it for himself as a young man in an effort to overcome the "strong binds of [his] bad habits." He later planned to write a book devoted to the subject under the title, *The Art of Virtue*, but never completed it and his preliminary drafts were lost. However, he outlined the methodology in his autobiography.

In short, he wanted to live his life without committing any moral faults, and at the mere age of 20, set out to do so. Initially, he attempted this in whole; he felt he knew what was morally wrong and right, and he devoted himself to always doing the right thing. However, he soon found that whatever progress he made was soon lost. If he made progress in one area, he slipped in another.

Long-term success, he came to believe, depended upon a concerted effort to break specific habits and to replace them with new ones, and to do that required complete focus on only one at a time.

He identified a list of 13 *virtues* he wished to master, and organized them so that the mastery of each would facilitate easier mastery of the next. For example, first he tried to master the virtue of *temperance* because he assumed that temperance, especially as it related to spirits, would provide him more willpower when confronting the subsequent virtues. Next on his list was *silence,* followed by *order.* Silence would provide more mental clarity with which to master order, and mastering order would aid in achieving the next, and so on.

One at a time, he devoted his attention to avoiding behaviors contrary to that virtue. When he failed, he would tally his transgressions against that virtue in a worksheet located in a special book he created for the purpose. In addition, at the end of each day he would recall the day's events and tally his failings against all virtues. Tracking his lapses served to heighten his sensitivity to them, so that he might catch himself before making the same mistake the next day. The worksheet also served as a positive motivator, as he felt significant gratification whenever he could complete a day without having made any marks corresponding to the targeted virtue.

After a week, he figured his new habit strengthened and the old one weakened enough so that he could move on to the next. He would then put all his effort into mastering the new virtue.

When he got to the last of the 13, he started the process again, knowing that some backsliding would have occurred. He continued this way until he found that he could go extended periods of time without making marks on his worksheet.

And like him who, having a garden to weed, does not attempt to eradicate all the bad herbs at once, which would exceed his reach and his strength, but works on one of the beds at a time, and, having accomplished the first, proceeds to a second, so I should have, I hoped, the encouraging pleasure of seeing on my pages the progress I made in virtue, by clearing successively my lines of their spots, till in the end, by a number of courses, I should be happy in viewing a clean book.

Franklin's methodology speaks volumes about him: of his logic and practicality, his idealism, and his devotion to continuous improvement. The beauty of his methodology is that it is flexible enough to be adapted to just about any self-improvement goal. After all, a virtue is merely the opposite of an undesirable habit or inclination. For example, his first virtue, temperance, would not be a virtue if people were not inclined to do things in excess.

The remainder of this book borrows liberally from Franklin's methodology and his life's examples and writings. Franklin was the master scientist *and* communicator and why not draw from the well of his wisdom.

TEMPERANCE						
EAT NOT TO DULLNESS. DRINK NOT TO ELEVATION.						
	S.	M.	T.	W.	T.	F.	S
T.							
S.	*	*		*		**	
O.	**	*	*		***	*	*
R.			*			*	
F.		*			*		
I.		*					
S.							
J.							
M.							
C.							
T.							
C.							
H.							

This is a recreation of the worksheet Franklin used to track his progress towards moral perfection. The initials along the left side represent the 13 virtues he targeted, and those on the top, the days of the week. He would focus his efforts on one virtue at a time – in this case Temperance – "leaving the other virtues to their ordinary chance," and tracking his success with them only at the end of the day.

Summary – Chapter 5
Franklin's Gifts

Though the Brainiac Paradox suggests that the aptitudes that contribute to a great technical mind tend to run in an inverse proportion to those that contribute to effective communication, there are those who outright defy this, the polymaths mentioned in Chapter 1. There is probably no greater example of this than Benjamin Franklin. Franklin was referred to as Americas Newton and bestowed with his day's highest scientific honors (from America, Great Britain, and France). On top of that, he was (and still is) considered one of America's best writers and its greatest diplomat.

Going forward, Franklin will serve as a centerpiece for the book, not just because he is such an apt example of someone who could achieve the apex of scientific achievements while at the same time demonstrating an exceptional *ability to constructively influence others' perceptions and behaviors,* but because he was not necessarily born that way. While no doubt he was endowed with exceptional gifts, he also had some notable shortcomings, which he himself describes in his autobiography. In that same text, he tells of how, at the age of 20, he developed and implemented a methodology towards the goal of moral perfection. He identified 13 virtues that, if mastered, he believed would constitute moral perfection, and endeavored to master them all at once. When he failed, he tried again, but with a change: he would only try to master one virtue at a time. He devoted a week's effort on each virtue, and logged his progress in a special worksheet he created. After 13 weeks, he started the cycle over again. He continued doing so until he found that good habits had replaced his bad ones.

I can think of no contemporary person, and possibly none throughout history, who equals Franklin in combining technical achievement and communication effectiveness. What's more, among his voluminous surviving writings are numerous references to topics relevant to aspects of the Brainiac Paradox, as well as ideas that are helpful to mitigating it. We can learn a lot from listening to Franklin and following his examples.

— Chapter 6 —

The Brainiac Paradox Methodology

I judged it would be well not to distract my attention by attempting the whole at once, but to fix it on one of them at a time, and, when I should be master of that, then to proceed to another
—Benjamin Franklin

According to various studies, only approximately 10% of those making New Year's resolutions adhere to them. That is pretty abysmal when you consider that people were not making New Year's hopes or wishes, they were making resolutions!

The reality is that it can be very difficult to change ingrained behaviors. Basic willpower is not enough for most people. Scientists have found that habitual behavior is created by thinking patterns that create deeply furrowed neural pathways that bias future behavior, which in turn further reinforces those pathways, making modifications even more difficult. Change requires creating new neural pathways with deliberate thought and action, and reinforcing those with repetition.

It would seem that Benjamin Franklin intuitively understood this. The methodology he crafted when only 20 years old presaged the methods of modern behavioral scientists and conforms to ideas on neuroplasticity. "Contrary habits must be broken, and good ones acquired and established, before we can have any dependence on a steady, uniform rectitude of conduct," he wrote, as well as the need to guard against "the unremitting attraction of ancient habits and the force of perpetual temptations."

Some call Franklin the founding father of America's self-help movement. His autobiography has been credited as a major inspiration for all-time bestsellers such as Dale Carnegie's *How to Win Friends and Influence People*, Stephen Covey's *The 7 Habits of Highly Effective People*, and the foundation for various 12-step programs, like Alcoholics Anonymous.

In this book, I adopt his methodology to help those who could be said to be affected by the Brainiac Paradox. Franklin's goal was attainment of moral perfection. This book's is more modest: the avoidance of certain attitudes, behaviors, and practices that I have found to most hinder those in technical fields. I refer to these as foibles and identify the nine I believe are the most common and influential.

- **Denial**
- **Empathy** (deficient)
- **Jargon, acronyms, and complexity**
- **Verbosity, bloat, and excess**
- **Process bias**
- **Aesthetics** (inappropriate)
- **Collaboration** (deficient)
- **Credibility** (mismanaged)
- **Selling** (aversion to)

Also like Franklin, I prescribe working on one item at a time until the desired attitude or behavior replaces the old.

Franklin's methodology is a logical and straightforward approach, and anyone following it as designed will experience positive change. The challenge, however, may be in having the strength to *follow it as designed*. It requires time and discipline, and the will to stick with it. Not everyone can easily muster these.

Laying the Foundation

There are several factors that serve as pillars to successful change.

1. Strong motivation
2. Realistic goals
3. Progress metrics
4. Accountability instrument
5. Support mechanism

Read the following and make sure you are well positioned on all accounts. The more you comply with these, the greater your odds for succeeding.

Motivation

The methodology Franklin offered included all but the first and the last of the five above. Franklin's personal motivation appears to have been that of perfectionism, a powerful driving force for those with this compulsion. "I wished to live without committing any fault at any time; I would conquer all that either natural inclination, custom, or company might lead me into," were the opening words to his explanation of the methodology.

However, different people are motivated by different things and it behooves us to identify and tap into what works best for us. It can be positive motivation, maybe the success of a project or the next level of career success; or it can be negative motivation, seeking an end to unwarranted professional frustrations and setbacks. As you seek to identify what would best motivate you, do not worry about being *correct*: the specific motives are only for you and need not be shared. Health and wellness, for instance, may be the best *reason* to lose weight, but an upcoming school reunion (looking good) may be the best *motivation* – the thing that actually drives you down new neural patterns even as your brain coaxes you towards old ones. Thus, if there is a colleague who has taken advantage of you and the mere thought of him drives your blood pressure up, use him as a motivational device. Maybe you have a combination of things that will motivate you. Think through your options and indentify what is most likely to drive you once the fatigue of trying to alter old neural patterns sets in.

If at all possible, find a visual cue to keep the fires of that motivation burning. I had a friend in college who papered his dorm room walls with dozens of rejection letters from prospective employers. Rather than depress him, it fired him up. He said that every time he walked into his room they motivated him to work that much harder, not just to find a job but to ultimately succeed so he could prove all those organizations wrong. And it worked. He was a man possessed. Find something, positive or negative, that you can post in a place where you will often see it. It could be a word, a picture, an article, anything that will evoke a strong, even visceral response.

Realistic Goals

Franklin did not attempt to achieve moral perfection in one fell swoop. Instead, he methodically broke the overall goal down into a series of discrete goals. He then worked on them one at a time, not proceeding to the next until he felt his progress on the previous virtue well established.

In the case of the Brainiac Paradox, I have identified nine foibles that I have found to be the most common and influential in preventing some from making their full contribution in the workplace. Like Franklin's, I have arranged these so the taming of one facilitates the taming of the next. For example, the Denial foible is the first and must be overcome before anything can be accomplished. This is followed by Empathy, which is the keystone of effective communication; then a reduction in Jargon, which requires the development of a mental vigilance which, when acquired, helps address the next foible, and so on.

Also like Franklin, I have appended a short precept to each foible in order to help convey the desired intentions. For example, Temperance was Franklin's first virtue and he listed it as such: "Temperance – Eat not to dullness; drink not to elevation." The second virtue was "Silence – Speak not but what may benefit others or our self; avoid trifling conversation."

The foibles along with their precepts are as follows:

- **Denial**: *Take ownership of communication problems or failures.*

- **Empathy** (deficient): *Think in terms of the other person's interest. Listen.*

- **Jargon, acronyms, and complexity:** *Communicate in terms and concepts your audience will understand. Simplify.*

- **Verbosity, bloat, and excess:** *Accomplish more by communicating less.*

- **Process bias:** *Keep focused on the desired result.*

- **Aesthetics** (inappropriate): *Present an effective user interface.*

- **Collaboration** (deficient): *Be a valued team player.*

- **Credibility** (mismanaged): *Establish and maintain the credibility necessary to garner others' support.*

- **Selling** (aversion to): *Leverage your abilities and credibility.*

Metrics

A common management axiom is, "You get what you measure," which implies the converse: you don't get what you don't measure. If someone's New Year's resolution is to watch less TV, he is not likely to be as successful if he does not keep track of how much TV he watches.

At the end of each chapter there is an item entitled "Monitor, Assess, and Log." These are generic suggestions of what to measure. Use them to the extent they are relevant, but also consider creating others that are more specific to your situation.

Accountability Instrument

Coupled with the metrics you devise, you should have some additional mechanism to keep you in check and on track. Someone who wants to quit smoking, for example, may start out with a set amount of cigarettes each morning. Once she smokes those, she will not allow herself anymore. Then, at prescribed intervals, she decreases the number of cigarettes allotted for the day, until eventually there are none. For those with less willpower, consider that when author Victor Hugo encountered writer's block, he wrote in the nude and instructed his valet to keep his clothes hidden until he had completed a set portion of writing.

In Franklin's case, it was as simple as using a book to carefully track his progress on each virtue over time. Page 312 contains an example of a worksheet similar to Franklin's and that can be used for the various foibles. A blank worksheet for this purpose is downloadable from the *www.brainiacparadox.com* website.

Even as you focus on one foible at a time, you can monitor your success in maintaining your mastery of previous virtues to prevent backsliding (but keep your energy focused on the foible at hand). Once you have completed all nine, start over. Continue until you feel confident that the new neural patterns are well established and new attitudes, behaviors, and practices have supplanted the old ones.

Support Mechanism

Probably the greatest asset you can have in undertaking any long-term change effort is the help of colleagues, friends, and loved ones. They can provide the moral support to cheer you forward and they can serve as an added source of discipline when your other accountability mechanisms fail. When the going gets tough, it is just too easy to rationalize to ourselves about doing or not doing things, but those committed to assisting us will not be so easily deterred. In fact, just knowing others will hold us accountable may be enough of a motivation to keep us on track.

An even more important contribution they can make is by serving as a source of feedback and as a sounding board for your ideas and intended future efforts. Alternate perspectives are extremely valuable, if not crucial. It is especially helpful to have more than one, because hearing the same or similar feedback from multiple sources may be necessary to overcome the strongly-held beliefs or attitudes that are often the underpinnings of our current behaviors. In the process of writing this book, I shared drafts with various people. On some points, different people provided different, sometimes contradicting, suggestions. But on others, they generally agreed, and I felt more confident in implementing those changes.

Furthermore, beyond a source for general, objective input, you may know people who possess special talents or acuities you can recruit to assist you on relevant foibles. For example, the focus in Chapter 12 is aesthetics. If you are aesthetically challenged, it is far more useful to utilize someone who is strong in that area, as opposed to a colleague who may be equally disadvantaged.

Prep Work

With the preceding list of *success pillars* in place, there is a series of tasks that should be performed before commencing work on the first foible. These items not only support a better outcome but, in some cases, will also save time.

Assessments

There are three types of assessments you will be called on to perform, or have performed, for this book: self-assessments, historical assessments, and current second-party assessments. Some of these need to be performed at the onset. The combination of the three provides a rich cache of information from which to chart your course, gauge your progress, and to enrich the experience.

1. **Self-Assessments**

    At various times throughout the book, you will be asked to assess yourself on various topics. The first of these is a baseline assessment that should be performed before leaving this chapter. This will provide information useful to both organizing your efforts as well as measuring your eventual progress.

    A possibly more important benefit of this and other self-assessments are the insights they can provide when contrasted with the assessments of others. For example, you might think you are a great presenter, but when you ask others their opinions, they may point out shortcomings to which you were oblivious. Conversely, you may feel you have shortcomings in certain areas, but others may disagree and assure you not to overly concern yourself with those items.

In addition, when you compare all of your self-assessments with the input of others, you will have a better idea of the accuracy of your self-assessments. In other words, if you find that others' assessments are overall very similar to your own, you can feel more confident in trusting your self-assessments in the future. However, if you find that they are often in disagreement, then you know that you may have trouble with certain biases and blind spots, and that as a matter of course you should seek objective feedback before embarking on a communication or collaborative initiative, especially when the stakes are high.

Baseline Self-Assessment

Consider the following questions and write down your responses. Be as explicit and complete as possible. Note: some will not be relevant to students explicitly, but can be modified to address the spirit of the question.

- What is your ideal work environment?
- What external (things you do not control) barriers do you feel are hindering your ability to succeed?
- What do you consider your communication and interpersonal strengths?
- What do you consider your communication and interpersonal weaknesses?
- Which communication and interpersonal challenges have had the greatest negative effect on your career?
- Which audiences (individuals and groups) are important to your ability to perform (rank by declining importance)?
- What do you know about these individuals/groups? In particular, summarize what you currently believe is important to working effectively with them.
- What is your desired relationship with them?
- How effective is your current relationship with them?

2. **Second-Party Assessments**

    Next is the type of assessment referenced in Support Groups above. It calls for soliciting candid feedback from those who either know you well, and can provide candid and objective opinions, or those who have special expertise related to the foible you are trying to mitigate.

3. **Historical Assessments**

   These are past job performance appraisals, explicit or implicit
   feedback from post-project reviews, even comments you have
   received in emails. Maybe your organization has unique practices or
   tools that you can cull for relevant information regarding how
   others view you and/or your performance. The more of this
   information you can pull together the better, so be resourceful.
   You will be asked to refer to this material for various purposes in
   the following chapters, so it is suggested that you gather this
   information in advance and then keep it assembled for the
   remainder of the book.

360-Degree Reviews

A 360-degree review (also called a multi-rater feedback or multi-source
assessment) can be an extremely valuable tool for the purposes of self-
improvement. For those not familiar, it involves being assessed from a
variety of perspectives (superiors, peers, and subordinates) on a wide
variety of factors related to your performance and characteristics. While
there are variations on how they are performed, generally the responses
are anonymous and because of this may be more candid (more than
one source is recruited from the three categories, thus feedback cannot
necessarily be traced back to a specific person).

These can provide great insights into how others perceive our
communication and interpersonal characteristics. What's more, they are
valuable because of the different perspectives they incorporate.
Superiors, peers, and subordinates may see us in different ways, but
when they all recognize the same things, we should take special note.

If you have not had one performed on yourself, consider doing so
now. These are typically administered by the organization's human
resources department but others in your organization may have direct
access to this tool. If no internal sources are available, there are several
organizations that provide online tools for performing these, some for
free.

In any case, review the questions before having it performed. There
should be questions about communication, teamwork, leadership, etc.
As there might be an option for customization, consider adding
questions for areas not adequately covered by the default version,
preferably working with an HR representative or other knowledgeable
party. As queries are usually asked on a *strongly agree* to *strongly disagree*
scale, here are some that could be added, if not already present.

- Appears to be approachable and easy to talk with.

- Uses clear and uncomplicated language.
- Communicates concisely.
- Is a good collaborator and team player.
- Understands and values others' perspectives.
- Is an active and good listener.
- Is open-minded and flexible.
- Is willing to defer to others for the good of the group.
- Presents ideas or information in a well-organized manner.
- Presents ideas or information in a persuasive manner.

Hopefully, the tool you use will include the option for participants to elaborate on their responses via a comments field. If so, encourage them to use it.

Spend some time to get the right questions for the 360-degree review. It is a terrible to realize, "I should have asked that," after having numerous colleagues complete these surveys.

Recruiting Support

Following is a list of chapters in this book where it is suggested that you seek the input or feedback from outside sources. As you might want to distribute the load so as not to overtax any single individual, or to save some people for certain tasks, you may want determine an overall game plan at the onset. After reading each one, make a list of people who you think might best serve that role.

- Chapter 7 – "If They Haven't Heard It, I Haven't Said It"
  Two or more colleagues who will provide you candid feedback on your overall communication, collaboration, and interpersonal characteristics as well as the applicability of the specific foibles to you. Ideally these should be people who have seen a broad cross-section of your professional interactions and for an extended period of time, as well as those you trust to be candid and constructive in their views.

- Chapter 8 – "Audience-Oriented Communications"
  One or more people who are familiar with the audiences that are key to your success (the people who directly or indirectly affect the projects you are involved with, the funding available for your work, etc.) to help you understand how you need to communicate and interact with those groups. These need not be existing colleagues or

acquaintances. If a key audience is top executives in your organization, then maybe their executive assistants will share some insights. If it is a funding agency, then maybe someone who has a successful track record as a funds recipient from that agency will be willing to help.

- Chapter 9 – "So Your Grandparents Could Understand"
  One or more colleagues who are regularly present with you when you are involved in work conversations, making presentations, etc. Their task will be to help you catch yourself in the act of using unfamiliar words or concepts for a given audience. In addition, someone familiar with your key audiences and who can help you edit the key messages you will be creating.

- Chapter 10 – "Less Is More"
  One or more people who can read and assess whether your efforts to edit down excessive verbiage does not degrade the clarity of your messages. Ideally, these should be people with strong written communication abilities and who are also familiar with your field (though not so familiar so that they will have troubles recognizing when your writing is inappropriate for certain audiences).

- Chapter 12 – "Substance AND Style":
  Someone to provide feedback on the visual aesthetics of the communication pieces you create. Consider those who specialize in visual communication or who have a demonstrated knack in this area.

Miscellaneous Items
A couple more things to review before starting:

Write It Down
Just as in the above assignment, at several times you will be explicitly asked to write things down. Please do so. In some cases you may think you do not need to; you can just remember it. However, memory is not the point of the request, at least not entirely.

The intent is to guard against creeping determinism, a.k.a. hindsight. On any given topic we may have two or more conflicting opinions. We can agree with arguments for one point but simultaneously agree with arguments for the conflicting points. For example, I may think, "The stock market is going to go higher tomorrow because of …, so I should buy today," but at the same time think, "It might go down because of …, so I should sell today." Then, later, when I find out the stock market went down, I think, "I knew I should have sold all along."

It is not that we consciously try to play both sides. It is that the thought process associated with the correct choice (regardless of which one it was) is reinforced while the one associated with the incorrect choice is suppressed. Churchill said, "History is written by the victors," and I suppose so are neural patterns. While this is simply the brain trying to improve its odds of success next time, what we experience is the sensation that we always favored the succeeding notion, maybe even altogether forgetting that we had a conflicting view.

Obviously this phenomenon will cause problems if we are trying to assess the accuracy of our initial assessments. Writing things down forces us to commit. I can almost guarantee you that upon returning to your written statements after you have progressed in the book, there will be instances where you will be surprised by what you previously thought.

Optional Approaches to Using the Methodology

Each of the following nine chapters is devoted to one of the foibles. The methodology calls for you to address one foible, before moving on to the next. Franklin committed to one a week, but such a fixed timeline does not necessarily work for the Brainiac Paradox. The nature of the foibles are such that one may be mastered relatively quickly (e.g., denial) while others could take many months or longer (e.g., credibility). Furthermore, different people are affected by different foibles and to different degrees. For example, one person may have the most difficulty with empathy and collaboration; and another person with jargon, verbosity, process bias, and aesthetics; and another person just selling.

As such, each person's approach to overcoming his or her foibles is likely to be different. Because of the varying needs and approaches to problem solving, these chapters have been structured so that some foibles can be touched on lightly while others more thoroughly. Within each chapter are the following elements:

Part 1 –   *The Foible* – Introduces and explains the foible.

Part 2 –   *Remedies* – Discusses potential ideas, techniques, and tools that may assist the reader in overcoming the respective foible.

Part 3 –   *How To* – Provides step-by-step approaches for the remedies.

Part 4 – *Summary* – Brief chapter summary.

Part 5 – *Additional Information*
- Suggestions of things to monitor to help track progress overcoming that chapter's foible.
- A list of possible indications that the negative effects of that foible are waning.

Ideally, you will read chapters 7 through 15 in full and then return to Chapter 7 to start working on the foibles one by one. Doing so provides a broader understanding at the onset, which may help in addressing each foible. It will also provide familiarity with the various remedies, which may be of some immediate use, even if the respective foible is focused on later.

However, those who prefer to *solve the problem themselves* may prefer to just read The Foible part of each chapter and devise their own solutions. Or they may read it in combination with Remedies as a means of supplementing their own approaches.

Those who prefer a more prescriptive approach may start with the Remedies followed by the How To section. Some may even prefer to start with How To alone, only referring back to Remedies for instructions or elaborations on a given task.

You also have the flexibility of varying your approach based on the foible. For those that have been particularly troublesome for you, you may want to read the entire chapter as well as the additional resources listed on the *www.brainiacparadox.com* site, while for others only read the summary section of the foible.

That said, even if certain foibles do not appear to be an impediment, I believe there is value in working through them anyway. At the very least, this might prevent slipping into such behaviors in the future. After all, just as embedded attitudes and behaviors can be modified for the better, they can also be changed for the worse. This is especially true for those early in their careers or even still in school.

Caveat

One thing that should not be altered is the process of focusing on one foible at a time, determining its metrics and tracking performance against them. Taking shortcuts may still yield some short-term gains, but like those 90% of New Year's resolutions, they will not endure. It is only through devotion and repetition that most people can reroute their neural pathways.

Even if you are absolutely sure that a foible is inapplicable to you, it is wise to carry out those steps. If you are correct in your assumption, that will be apparent soon after you start monitoring your adherence. On the other hand, performing those steps may bring to your attention things you were overlooking.

Steps to Implementing the Methodology

Step 1: Conduct pre-work:
- Perform baseline assessment.
- Gather historical second-party assessment information.
- Create a list of individuals you will recruit for input, feedback, and assistance.

Step 2: Read through chapters 7 to 15 to develop an understanding of the nine foibles (optional).

Step 3: Undertake a focus on Chapter 7.

Step 4: Define both your individual goals, progress metrics, and tracking mechanism.

Step 5: Use the provided remedies, those of your own design, those from other sources, or any combination of these to whittle away at each foible.

Step 6: Keep a tally of your transgressions.

Step 7: Monitor your progress each day until either you note no marks on your tracking sheet, or you achieve the alternative goal you set for yourself.

> **Note:** If you find it impossible to attain satisfactory results on one or more foibles, continue to Chapter 16, which provides an alternative approach: collaborating with those of complimentary abilities or those who can provide specific support.

Step 8: Once you have satisfied the requirements of Step 7 for that particular foible, continue to the next foible and recommence at Step 4.

Step 9: When you have completed the ninth foible, read Chapter 16, and then return to the first and work through the series again. As you go through the second round of monitoring success with the nine foibles, you should be able to determine which foibles you will need to revisit on an ongoing basis in order to prevent recidivism, as well as those with which you may want additional external assistance.

Section III

The Foibles

This section introduces, explains, and offers remedies for each of the nine foibles that most frequently or materially impede the success of affected STEM professionals. **Note:** While some recommendations may seem quite elementary, keep in mind that the Brainiac Paradox affects people in different ways and to different degrees. What will be inappropriate for one person may be essential for another. Use or skip the offered remedies according to your circumstances.

– Chapter 7 –

If They Haven't Heard it,
I Haven't Said it

How few there are who have courage enough to own their faults,
or resolution enough to mend them.
—Benjamin Franklin

Foible: Denial

Precept: Take ownership of communication problems or failures

The similarities of the responses were uncanny. Over the years leading up to the publishing of *The Brainiac Paradox*, I have explained the book's premise to countless individuals and their reactions were almost always the same: first a smile of recognition as I described a paradox of talented STEM professionals who struggle with aspects of communicating or collaborating; followed by a nod of agreement as I noted that the more brilliant they were the more likely they were to struggle; and then a response something like, "Yes, I know someone just like that," once I had finished my explanation.

The consistency of their responses was reassuring, but at the same time there was something about this that troubled me: what I was not hearing. In not one of those occasions did respondents say they felt that this related to them personally. There may have been a few who acknowledged some general applicability, admitting to a type of communal culpability among those in technical fields, but not one who said, "That's me." Not one person, at least not initially.

More troubling still was how people reacted when they thought that I might by referring to them. While I did not make such a direct assertion, there were times when individuals read into something I said.

My friend Alice is a cancer researcher involved in some very promising studies. The first time I discussed the Brainiac Paradox with her, she smiled, nodded and responded just as the others I have described. She was sincerely intrigued by the topic and wanted to know more. Then one night, as we were making small talk at a party, she expressed her frustration with the rejection of her recent grant proposal. She could not understand why those reviewing it failed to see the blatant value of the research. I offered to review her next proposal before she submitted it – just to see if there were ideas I could offer to make it more compelling to her target audience. She paused and I saw a flash of realization came across her face. "He thinks the Brainiac Paradox applies to me!" She stared at me for a long moment, obviously astonished and affronted. Then she changed the subject.

Actually I meant no such thing. In fact, up to that point, she had given me no reason to believe this issue affected her. But then again, I had never worked with Alice. The detrimental aspects of the Paradox exist on a long continuum, from pronounced and continuous to slight and sporadic, and there are many who exhibit little sign of it in their private lives yet who may be hindered professionally. "The lady doth protest too much," I thought.

Alice was not alone in her apprehension. I encountered others who were prickly if they perceived any hint that I might be implicating them. It was obvious that this issue strikes a nerve.

I did not fully appreciate the implications until I had lunch with a former colleague, Chief Technology Officer Gary Robertson, at a local Indian restaurant. As we conversed over the spicy food and sizzling chicken, I worked through a series of boilerplate questions I was asking people with whom I formally discussed the book. Among them was, "What help is needed most?" It was intended to solicit his opinion on which foibles should be included, in which order, or receive the most attention. His response surprised me: "Getting them to understand that they need professional help with communication." I had not mentioned anything about the sensitivity I had already encountered. A light went on in my head: this was not just an uncomfortable issue – something I would have to tiptoe around – this may be an outright barrier. Denial was not just a consideration when dealing with the other foibles; it was an outright foible itself.

Non-Starter

Denial, of course, is amazingly powerful. It is the spell that possesses alcoholics, gamblers, and drug users, enabling them to career undeterred towards their destruction. Often, the spell is only broken – if it is broken at all – when the person hits rock bottom. European Statesman Jean Monnet said, "People only accept change when they are faced with necessity, and only recognize necessity when a crisis is upon them."

But the problems caused by the Brainiac Paradox usually do not trigger an, "I can't go on like this any longer" epiphany. It is a hindrance, a frustration, but it usually lacks the jolt necessary to break denial's hold. Hence, affected individuals may cruise along sub-optimized with no urgency for change.

Widespread denial would provide an additional reason why the communication development programs offered in universities and provided by employers have usually not delivered the desired results. How much effort is a participant likely to put into a program when they are thinking, "Why am I stuck here, when it is the guy sitting next to me who has the problem?"

Psychologist Tony Attwood says that denial is so pervasive among the technical professionals he counsels, that when doing an assessment, he has found it necessary to get the information from someone else, whether it be a colleague, a friend, a partner or family member. When he tries to have such clients honestly assess themselves they say, "'No, no, I am fine,'" adding, "It is almost as if they have built up a persona of perfection and arrogance – a denial of any fault – which is more to convince themselves than other people." And even when they admit there is a problem, they tend to try to minimize it.

"If you talk with first and second-level management, they will tell you, 'nah, it's going away. It used to be a problem but it is not that big a deal anymore,'" says Robert Scott, retired vice president of Innovation & Architecture, Global Business Services for P&G, and now with the University of Michigan's School of Engineering. "But if you talk to middle and upper management they all say it is a very real problem."

The Ninth and First

When I started this book, I had eight foibles in mind. After my lunch with Robertson, I had nine, and it was clear that Denial had to be the first one.

Denial presents a Catch-22 situation because the people who would most benefit from this book are those least likely to read it or to take action based upon it. They may only do so upon being urged to by a loved one, tired of professional frustrations spilling over into his or her personal life; if assigned to it by a boss, eager to unleash unfulfilled potential; or if suggested by a colleague, who recognizes the Paradox's career-limiting effects.

If denial is the foible, then acceptance is its corresponding virtue. It is the first step in any recovery program, like Alcoholics Anonymous' 12-step program, because without it all other effort is futile.

In order to break denial's stealthy spell, it may be necessary, or at least helpful, to better recognize and understand it.

Denial

Fundamentally, denial is a defense mechanism that engages when there is something undesirable that we wish not to face: something personally painful; the notion that we are not as perfect as we thought we were; that the problems we face are of our own making; the need for change; and so on. It comes in several forms:

- Absolute – "I do not have that problem."

- Blaming – "I wouldn't have this problem if it weren't for …."

- Minimizing – "It's not that bad."

- Deflecting – "The real problem lies with …."

- Rationalizing – "It's okay to be this way because …."

- Avoidance – "Nice weather we've been having."

Absolute Denial

Logical thinkers *tend* to be binary – either 1 or 0, true or false, yes or no, right or wrong. When faced with such extreme choices, it is understandable that some would exhibit absolute denial. This may explain the "persona of perfection" Attwood attributed to the group.

Blaming

It is the marketer's fault because they do not know how to provide requirements; the users' fault that they are not intelligent enough to know how to use the product; or management's fault because they cannot tell the difference between what is good and bad, and so on. One of the truest adages is, "Success has many parents, but failure is an orphan."

Minimizing

Some may say, "Communication may not be one of my strengths, but it is not a weakness." However, if it is not a relative strength (i.e., compared to one's peers), it is a weakness. Global outsourcing has diluted the value of strong technical skills in the fields of IT and engineering, and that is likely to extend to other high-paying technical fields. Despite potentially large savings offered by offshoring, one of the downsides has been communication issues. However, if employers have to deal with too many local employees who cannot communicate effectively, then they might as well deal with ineffective communicators overseas. On the other hand, strong technologists who are also effective communicators are much more difficult to find and/or replace; it makes them more marketable and increases their job security.

Deflecting

I once had a conversation with a pair of chemists who acknowledged this issue, but said it really only applied to engineers. Later that same week, an engineer said the problem was really only with physicists and the like. Not long after that I ran into an old friend who is an astrophysicist and he said it was mathematicians, and so on.

Rationalizing

"So convenient a thing it is to be a reasonable creature, since it enables one to find or make a reason for everything one has a mind to do," wrote Benjamin Franklin. Some may rationalize that the Paradox is unavoidable: there will always be some people who will understand certain things while others cannot, and this will lead to communication problems; it cannot be avoided. Maybe so, but the reality is those who are perceived as ineffective communicators will most often be the ones to pay the price for the ensuing problems. Those they fail to connect with are often their bosses, clients, customers, funding bodies, etc., and even though the fault may not be theirs alone, the repercussions primarily are. In such situations, *it is not enough to be right*. It is an unfortunate reality, but reality all the same.

Avoidance

Avoidance is the least of the denials, or the closest to acceptance. Essentially, the individual recognizes their personal applicability, but finds ways to avoid having to confront it directly. They keep themselves too busy or evade situations where this would arise.

Blind Spots and Norms

Besides denial, I believe there are other reasons some fail to overcome their challenges: perceptual blind spots (a.k.a., inattentional blindness). It is not a matter of the individual suppressing something that they know at some level to be applicable; it is that they honestly did not perceive it, just as a blind spot in a car can keep us from seeing other cars even when we are actively looking. We all have perceptual blind spots: certain realities that we just do not perceive. Sometimes they are obvious, such as when someone thinks they have a good singing voice, when they do not, or think they are funny, when they are not. Other times they are more subtle: things that are easily overlooked but can still significantly affect our ability to communicate or collaborate. Many simply cannot perceive their communication disconnects.

In the book *Vital Lies, Simple Truths*, Daniel Goleman writes, "The range of what we think and do is limited by what we fail to notice. And because we fail to notice that we fail to notice there is little we can do to change until we notice how failing to notice shapes our thoughts and deeds."

If You Do What You Have Always Done, You Will Get What You Have Always Got

Even those who "do notice" and "accept" the applicability of the Brainiac Paradox, are not automatically better off, if they do not also recognize the need to do things differently. Maybe they have long been told they need to develop their communication or teamwork skills and have tried to comply. They do what they think is best, or possibly what has been recommended by others, but even when those are shown to be ineffective they may cling to those approaches.

They would not make this mistake in their professional work. If faced with a dead-end, they would consider different approaches and try again, persisting until they were able to break the impasse. But when they face this in their personal affairs, they often fail to do so. It is a very human trait. An executive recruiter once remarked to me that the executives that have the hardest time marketing themselves are the marketing executives. And so may it be with problem solvers: they can solve almost any problem except for those relating to themselves personally.

This constitutes a different type of denial: denial of the need to do things differently. People suffering from this continue with flawed approaches, maybe even increasing their efforts, until they finally give up out of frustration and hopelessness.

Remedies:
Denial

Historical Assessments

At the end of Chapter 1 was a short series of questions intended to help determine the personal applicability of this issue. Ideally that tool would provide a more definitive assessment, but the Paradox's broad range of manifestations, both in terms of characteristics and magnitude, frustrates the creation of a single, concise and authoritative evaluation instrument. There are, however, a series of things you can do that may help validate, or invalidate, the initial assessment.

The first is to analyze any and all documents that assess you and your performance, or that provide clues as to how others perceive aspects of your communication, interpersonal and collaboration effectiveness. These may include job performance appraisals, 360-degree reviews, explicit or implicit feedback from post-project reviews, meeting notes, even comments about your performance from emails. Consider any possible situation where feedback related to personal or performance characteristics was recorded. For example, perhaps you presented at a symposium and the organizers captured audience feedback about your presentation.

Now pour through this information and look for common themes as well as assertive statements. Key words are communication, sharing, teamwork, collaboration.

Second-Party Assessments

Next, seek some input on communication, interpersonal and collaboration characteristics from those who currently work with you. Identify at least two, and ideally three or more people who know you well and frequently interact with you in the workplace. Find a time and place where you can discuss with each individually.

Ask them to assess you overall and then ask them questions about your performance related to each of the foibles. Request that they be candid with you and thank them when they are. Do not debate points on which you disagree. Just listen, ask for elaborations when you need them, and take notes.

When you are finished with the self- and second-party assessments, you should possess a better picture of the overall relevance of this issue for you as well as specific information regarding the applicability of individual foibles.

Type Assessments

In addition to work-related feedback, there are publicly-available *type* assessments that can serve as indicators. While they vary in terms of what they measure and how results are interpreted and used, they all share the advantage of being more objective, unlike the work assessments, which may be influenced by personal and organizational dynamics.

There are many of these available, but the three listed below are well established and can be taken online. The number of people assessed using these tools is in the hundreds of thousands, providing a wealth of information for researchers to draw upon. Thus, beyond just measuring you on certain scales, these offer a picture of how your characteristics compare to others in your field, other fields, men, women, etc. Furthermore, the providers of these assessments offer additional services that can help you make the most out of your results.

- **Myers Brigg Type Indicator**

- **Herrmann Brain Dominance Instrument**

- **Kolbe Conative Index**

Myers Brigg Type Indicator

An extremely useful tool for self examination is the Myers Brigg Type Indicator (MBTI). It is the most widely used and studied personality assessment tool and many people will already know their MBTI type. Because of its enormous database of tested users, it provides a rich source of information for those who want to better understand the implications of their psychological type, as well as, how to more effectively interact with people of other types. It classifies personalities according to four scales, each with opposing types:

Introvert/Extravert

- Introversion (I): interest flowing mainly to the inner world of concepts and ideas.

- Extraversion (E): interest flowing mainly to the outer world of actions, objects, and persons.

Sensing/Intuition

- Sensing (S): tending to perceive immediate, real, practical facts of experience and life.

- Intuition (N): tending to perceive possibilities, relationships, and meanings of experiences.

Thinking/Feeling

- Thinking (T): tending to make judgments or decisions objectively and impersonally.
- Feeling (F): tending to make judgments subjectively and personally.

Judging/Perceiving

- Judging (J): tending to live in a planned and decisive way.
- Perceiving (P): tending to live in a spontaneous and flexible way.

An MBTI type is denoted by the four letters representing the characteristic from each scale that most pertains to the subject.

Based on an analysis of quantitative and qualitative data from the CPP (Consulting Psychologists Press), the exclusive publisher of the Myers-Briggs instrument, those with Thinking and Judging (TJ) preferences are more likely to be associated with the Paradox.

Almost half of those in STEM professions are TJs. The breakdown for the component types are:

- **ISTJ** – 18%
- **ESTJ** – 13%
- **INTJ** – 8%
- **ENTJ** – 7%

The relevancy of these numbers is complicated by the fact that the distribution of the 16 different MBTI types varies across the general population, from 13% for ISFJs to just over 1% for INFJ. To factor this in, CPP assigns a Self Selection Ratio (SSR), which is a ratio of the percentage of a type within a field to the percentage of that type in the general population. The higher the SSR, the higher the correlation of the type to the field. The average SSRs among STEM professions for the previously listed four types are:

- **ISTJ** – 1.6
- **ESTJ** – 1.5
- **INTJ** – 3.5
- **ENTJ** – 4.3

Therefore, ISTJ and ESTJ are the most common types among STEM professionals (together representing almost one third), and ENTJ and INTJ have the strongest correlation to these fields. Still, this does not mean that these four types are direct indicators for the Brainiac Paradox. Keep in mind that the majority of STEM professionals (53%) are one of the 12 remaining types. Likewise, it does not mean that those who are one of those four types are likely to be technical. For example, construction managers are more commonly type ISTJ (24%), than are those in STEM professions (18%). Finally, representatives of all 16 types can be found in every field.

What makes **TJ**s most relevant to the Brainiac Paradox are some of their common characteristics:

- A tendency to think they are always right.
- Difficulties empathizing with others.
- A desire to control others and an aversion to being controlled by others.
- Inflexibility and resistance to change.
- Propensity for finding faults in others.
- Insensitivity to others.

These all could be said to impede communication and collaborative effectiveness, and individual references to these will appear in the coming foible discussions.

Now consider that the next tier of types associated with STEM professionals. INTPs and ENTPs each account for about 8% of those in STEM professions, or a total of 16% for NTPs (either INTP or ENTP). They both also have relatively high SSRs, at 2.5. However, the common characteristics for these types are far less associated with interpersonal challenges than the TJs above.

Thus, as a diagnostic tool, a technical professional with an MBTI type that contains TJ is more likely to be affected by aspects of the Brainiac Paradox, while those with a type that contains NTP, are less likely to be. In both cases, these should only be viewed as a single piece of data. They need to be considered in conjunction with historical, second party assessments, and possibly other *type* tools. As for the 27% who fall into the remaining 10 types, the correlations are too insignificant to say one way or the other.

Unfortunately, a shortcoming of MBTI as it relates to our quest is that it does not necessarily measure magnitude. While MBTI tests are scored on a scale of the four different factors, it mostly does not matter where on the scale the results fall beyond being on one side or the other, even if you are very close to the middle of the scale. Carl Jung, upon whose work the MBTI is based, believed that someone was either one or the other, and when combined into the complete four-letter type, degrees of one type did not affect the overall personality preferences.

Note: People who have taken the MBTI assessment more than once may receive different results on one or more values. This can happen when people are naturally towards the center of a given scale, but recent impactful events may have temporarily biased their responses.

To find out more information about MBTI go to *www.cpp.com*, or to take the test online, go to *www.mbticomplete.com*.

Herrmann Brain Dominance Instrument

The Herrmann Brain Dominance Instrument (HBDI) is another tool that can be used to help determine applicability as well as provide insights into improving performance. While MBTI determines psychological types and is based on Carl Jung's work, the HBDI seeks to measure thinking styles and builds on the brain hemisphericity work of Dr. Roger Sperry (discussed in Chapter 2). Ned Herrmann, while working at General Electric, developed the indicator to assist the organization with professional development. Herrmann added another dimension, the limbic system, to Sperry's left/right-brain dominance model.

No longer limited to left and right, Herrmann's model took into account people who were dominant thinkers in one of four quadrants.

Analyses of hundreds of thousands of profiles within the Herrmann Institute database indicate that technical professionals are typically dominant in the upper left quadrant but usually have secondary preferences in the lower left or the upper right quadrants. What's more, they tend to score uncommonly low – or are said to be resistant – in the lower right quadrant.

Unlike the MBTI tool, levels or degrees within the four segments are significant to how ones' HBDI type is classified and interpreted. Those who are very dominant in the upper left quadrant and very resistant in the lower right, would have a strong

Understanding the HBDI

While contemporary research corroborates the work of Sperry and Herrmann, it also demonstrates that characteristics are not always linked literally to the physical locations in the brain. The Herrmann Institute, which continues Ned Herrmann's work, states that the four quadrants should be seen as a metaphor for different thinking styles, acknowledging that the brain works as a whole system and is too complex to trace general characteristics to specific locations in all cases.

likelihood of exhibiting characteristics with the Brainiac Paradox. Those still in that quadrant, but closer to the center would be less likely to exhibit such characteristics.

For more information or to take the HBDI test online, go to *www.hbdi.com*.

Kolbe Conative Index

The Kolbe Conative Index seeks to measure one's conative preferences, conation said to be one of the three parts of the psychological mind, along with cognition and affection. Conation is associated with impulse, desire, volition, and striving. Therefore, while the MBTI and HBDI assessments seek to measure aspects of one's cognitive preferences or thinking styles, the Kolbe assessment seeks to measure how one actually does something or their "instinctive method of operation." Like MBTI, the Kolbe Index measures on a continuum of four scales, which are called Action Modes of Operation. They are labeled *Fact Finder, Follow Thru, Quick Start*, and *Implementor*. Rather than letters to determine type, assessments are comprised of four numbers, from 1 to 10, associated with each scale.

While the MBTI and HBDI can be useful general indicators for the Paradox, the Kolbe results can sometimes be used to help identify applicability within a specific field.

For example, engineers tend to score high in the *Fact Finder* mode, and very low in the *Implementer* mode. Those who score at the extremes (9-10) or (1-2) on each respectively, are more likely to exhibit characteristics associated with the Brainiac Paradox, and those with more moderate numbers, less so. For mathematicians, though, the marker is a very high score in the *Follow Through* mode. A very low *Quick Start* number is also an indicator, regardless of the individual's field.

To find out more about this tool and have the assessment performed, go to *www.kolbe.com*.

The Bottom Line on Type Assessments

None of these assessments is required, and there are some valid reasons one might prefer to skip them: none provides a definitive answer as to the personal applicability of the Paradox, the cost of these assessments can quickly add up, and they may cause one to focus on things that are not of prime importance. Recall that the best indication of applicability is the existence of communication problems, and the best way to determine those is through the personal, historical, and second-party assessments. For example, these *type* tools may strongly associate a characteristic to you, but if that characteristic does not cause you problems, and is not likely to in the future, then it need not be a matter of concern.

On the other hand, there are also good reasons you may want to use them. They offer a more objective perspective, they provide ways to compare yourself with other population segments, and the organizations providing these may offer important new insights or special recommendations based on your specific type. In addition, the more of the three you use, the more potentially rich those insights and recommendations. Just as astronomers may study celestial objects using different parts of the electromagnetic spectrum (e.g., visible light, radio, and infrared) and achieve a more complete picture by overlaying the resulting information, you can use these to obtain a richer understanding of yourself.

Changing the Paradigm
Of all the foibles, denial is simultaneously the easiest and most difficult to address. It is easiest because it requires no special skills, techniques, or prolonged practice; it merely takes a change of attitude. It is most difficult because it is often so entrenched.

The first step in mitigating the Brainiac Paradox's career limiting effects, is accepting personal responsibility for the success of communications and collaborations. Note, this does not necessarily mean accepting fault when things go wrong – only accepting the responsibility for making things right.

Years ago, I was given a book titled *If They Haven't Heard It, You Haven't Said It,* by Harvey Thomas, one of its co-authors. I was intrigued by the title. Brilliantly, I thought, in nine words it both alluded to so much of what is wrong with communications and provided the attitude necessary for overcoming the issue.

Most of us are rather thoughtless in our communications. We throw some message over the fence and just expect the recipient will catch it. When they do not, we consider it to be their fault – after all, we have communicated, right? A variation of this phrase, *If they haven't heard it, **I** haven't said it* turns that attitude on its head. Whether it is my audience's fault or not, I pay a price when my audience does not respond as desired. Implicit in this phrase is the forethought, the listening, the adjustment, and other elements that contribute to effective communication.

Mind you, it is not always easy. As much as I try to embrace this, I still may get frustrated or upset when painstakingly planned and executed communication activities fail due to audience apathy, or worse. After the adrenalin subsides, though, this philosophy forces me to recalibrate and persevere until my objective is achieved.

To a large extent, the remaining eight foibles identify some of the major reasons why our audience "hasn't heard it."

- Empathy – failing to factor in our audiences' perspective, interests, values, etc.

- Jargon, acronyms, and complexity – messages that are unfamiliar, too complex, or too difficult for our audiences to follow.

- Verbosity, bloat, and excess – message lengths that exceed our audience's capacity or desire to consume.

- Process bias – focusing on completing communication activities rather than on achieving communication objectives.

- Aesthetics (inappropriate) – communicating in ways that affront our audiences' various senses and negatively affect their opinions of us.

- Collaboration (deficient) – interacting in ways that our collaborators feel are unpleasant, unproductive, or unfair.

- Credibility (mismanaged) – underestimating the importance of what other people think about us.

- Selling (aversion to) – failing to adequately advocate and ask.

Overcoming these foibles, to the extent that they relate to you, is the key to more effective communication and interactions, and ultimately to professional success. The first step is acceptance, and achieving that is as simple as internalizing a variation of the above phrase: *If they haven't heard it, I haven't said it.*

However, internalizing the message takes more than good intentions. Recall from the earlier Franklin quote "… I concluded, at length, that the mere speculative conviction that it was in our interest to be completely virtuous was not sufficient to prevent our slipping, and that the contrary habits must be broken, and good ones acquired …." In other words, it is not enough to acquiesce; you must believe.

Make *If they haven't heard it, I haven't said it* your mantra. Say it to yourself repeatedly and over an extended period of time. Philosopher and psychologist William James said, "The greatest discovery of our generation is that human beings can alter their lives by altering their attitudes of mind. As you think, so shall you become." If you do nothing else but internalize, truly internalize, this mantra you will experience a significant change in your work experience and your overall professional satisfaction. If necessary, place this phrase, or a reminder of it, in several places you will see throughout the day. Most importantly, say it to yourself whenever you encounter a communication issue. This will help you avoid the traps of denial and other unproductive behaviors, and instead shift you into solution mode.

In the coming chapters a series of ideas, tools, and techniques are offered to assist you in overcoming each foible, but for Denial there is the only one: adopting the mantra *If they haven't heard it, I haven't said it.* It is that simple and that important. I personally have found this to be very powerful and trust you will also.

How To:
Own Your Communication Challenges

1. **Undertake an assessment of the communication, interpersonal and collaboration characteristics that may have thus far hindered your success.**

    ☐ Do any of the following ring true for you?

    - ✓ Absolute denial – "I do not have that problem."
    - ✓ Blaming – "I wouldn't have this problem if it weren't for …."
    - ✓ Minimizing – "It's not that bad."
    - ✓ Deflecting – "The real problem lies with …."
    - ✓ Rationalizing – "It's okay to be this way because …."
    - ✓ Avoidance – [switching the subject or other evasive techniques].

    ☐ Review existing documentation for feedback regarding communication and collaborative effectiveness.

    - ✓ Work performance reviews.
    - ✓ Post-project assessments.
    - ✓ Comments embedded in emails and other common communications.
    - ✓ Any other assessments performed in the organization as part of development, team building, etc.

    ☐ Seek new or additional feedback:

    - ✓ 360-degree review (if you have not already had one).
        - o These can be particularly useful because they are usually well suited to capture information relevant to this topic.
        - o They can be customized if the default questionnaire does not adequately cover all topics.
        - o They include multiple feedback from various levels (subordinates, peers, superiors), and are likely to solicit more objective feedback than most other assessment mechanisms.

☐ Engage a select few people requesting that they provide you feedback on your characteristics and performance as they relate to communication and collaborative effectiveness. Ask them to try to answer the way the average (general public) person would evaluate you on these, by answering with "average," "worse than average," or "better than average," for the first series of questions. You may ask them to elaborate on their responses when necessary but be careful not to come across as defensive or argumentative.

✓ Are my communications clear?

✓ Are my communications concise?

✓ Do I tailor my communications to the needs of different audiences?

✓ Am I conscientious, proactive, and timely about communicating information that others need or want?

✓ Are my communications aesthetically appropriate?

✓ Am I a good listener?

✓ Am I a good collaborator?

✓ Am I open and flexible?

✓ Am I pleasant to work with?

✓ Am I sociable?

✓ Do I adequately promote my opinions and ideas?

Also:

✓ What are my greatest strengths and weaknesses as they relate to communicating and interacting with others?

☐ Summarize the resulting feedback based on:

✓ What are the common themes or points?

✓ Rank each according to the extremity of the comments: low, medium and high.

✓ Rank each according to the consistency of the points. Did they appear: consistently, more than once, only once?

☐ Optional but recommended: participate in one or more type assessment tools. The following services provide online assessment, feedback, and advice. They may serve to corroborate and provide better understanding of the feedback collected above. These tools, especially the MBTI, are referenced several times in this book. While there are similarities between these tools, each provides specific focus and insights.

    ✓ Myers Brigg Type Indicator (MBTI). The most common of the "Type" assessment tools, the MBTI provides a rich collection of data, tools, and additional resources. Go to *www.mbticomplete.com* to determine your type online.

    ✓ Herrmann Brain Dominance Instrument (HBDI). Assesses thinking styles based on brain hemisphere dominance theory. Go to *www.HBDI.com* for more information or to take the online assessment.

    ✓ Kolbe Index. Assesses individuals' conative characteristics, how we instinctively do things. Go to *www.kolbe.com* for more information or to take the online assessment.

2. **Adopt the mantra "If they haven't heard it, I haven't said it." This is essential, even if you already believe you have mastered acceptance. Internalizing this will instill an attitude that will subconsciously and automatically facilitate a more constructive approach to communication and collaboration.**

☐ Repeat it to yourself regularly.

☐ Post it, or a reminder of it, in places that will keep it in the forefront of your thoughts throughout the day (pin a note to your board, add to your white board, make a screen saver, etc.).

☐ Do this until it is the first thing that comes to mind when you encounter ANY type of communication challenge.

Summary – Chapter 7
If They Haven't Heard it, I Haven't Said it

Though some may readily acknowledge that peers exhibit characteristics of the Brainiac Paradox, they are less likely to recognize or acknowledge it in themselves. What's more, they can be very sensitive to any suggestions that it might apply to them. This helps explain why such a prevalent and troubling problem persists, despite efforts by academia, industry, and others to address it. There is little hope of overcoming its destructive effects unless one can fully accept its relevance to themselves. Even if a reader goes through the remaining chapters and follows all the steps, their progress will be fleeting if denial remains.

While there is currently no specific and authoritative tool to determine whether the Brainiac Paradox is applicable to an individual, there are some tools that can provide additional clues. The Myers Brigg Type Indicator, the Herrmann Brain Dominance Instrument, and the Kolbe Conative Index are three different *type assessment* tools that can be conducted online and whose results may provide a more objective, albeit incomplete, indicator. They may also offer the advantage of additional insights and tools (offered by the type assessment providers), that could be helpful when addressing specific characteristics.

The key to addressing this foible is the mantra, *If They Haven't Heard It, I Haven't Said It*. It means that regardless of the reason for the problem, we need to communicate better, more, differently, until we succeed. Repeating this phrase to yourself regularly, and especially when communication issues arise, will help alter underlying attitudes, which in turn will affect our natural communication instincts and habits.

Monitor, Assess, and Log …

- When you find yourself in denial (any of its forms) when confronted with communication, interpersonal or collaboration challenges.

- When you encounter personal blind spots related to communication.

- When you fail to take personal ownership for the success of professional communications and interactions.

You Will Know You Are Overcoming This When …

- You react to communication and collaboration challenges with a problem-solving attitude, rather than that of denial, frustration, and combatancy.

- You are naturally more open to new methods and approaches for communicating.

- You find you are less aggravated by audience deficiencies.

– Chapter 8 –

Audience-Oriented Communication

He who falls in love with himself will have no rivals.
—Benjamin Franklin

Foible: Empathy (deficient)
Precept: Think in terms of the other person's interests. Listen.

It has been estimated that in any given conversation, we consume approximately 80% of our mental energy thinking about what we are going to say next, rather than listening to our partner. By instinct and conditioning, communication is egocentric. Our first communication is in the form of cries to signify our needs and ailments. Caregivers respond to these and in the process reinforce our perception that the world revolves around us. As we age, though, our universe expands to include others who are less interested in our needs and more so in their own. Faced with this reality, we develop a more complex awareness so that we can continue to achieve what we want from others.

This is the process of socialization, and early on we need help learning it: "Billy, if you want to play with Johnny's fire truck, you have to let him play with your dump truck." After a few years of social development, Billy, without prompting, will offer to let Johnny play with his video game so that he may play with Johnny's. In this case, Billy has learned that others have needs and desires similar to his own and that the key to getting what he wants sometimes requires meeting others' needs first. Years later, though, if Billy wants to fulfill his physical needs, he learns that it might not be enough to appeal to Amy's physical needs, but possibly her emotional needs as well. This exemplifies a new paradigm that is much more challenging, for it is no longer enough for Billy to project his own interests, desires, and motivations onto others; he needs to divine those of others, which may be much different from his own.

In the professional world, those prone to seeing their audience as *passive recipients* for the information they wish to share, rather than as *selective recipients* based on what their audience wishes to receive, are bound to be less effective communicators. Fortunately, humans are endowed with the sense of empathy (Merriam-Webster: "The action of understanding, being aware of, being sensitive to, and vicariously experiencing the feelings, thoughts, and experience of another ... without having [them] communicated in an objectively explicit manner"), which facilitates this social imperative. Unfortunately, not everyone is equally endowed. Some are born with an incredible ability to see things from others' perspectives – as if they had an intuitive crystal ball – some are quite oblivious, and the rest range somewhere in between.

To complicate the equation, some grow up in environments that foster empathic abilities and others not. Those without adequate natural gifts and the right developmental environment are likely to face a lifetime of difficulty in successfully navigating human interactions.

As discussed in Chapter 2, a lack of empathy is associated with Asperger syndrome (AS), which in turn is more common among those in technical professions.

Irrespective of AS, there are indications that empathy deficiencies may correlate with those who pursue STEM fields. In terms of the Myers Brigg Type Indicator (MBTI), empathy is associated with Feeling, or type F on the F-T scale, but the vast majority of those in various technical professions are at the opposite end: Thinking, or type T. And on the Herrmann Brain Dominance Instrument (HBDI) tool, people in those fields are more typically type A (analytical thinking) which is the opposite of type C, (interpersonal thinking), which is associated with empathy.

Sometimes it is not so much an actual deficiency of empathy as it is a relative deficiency. The cognitive landscape for some may be so different from those whom they need to interact with that the amount of empathy necessary may be just too great.

Other times it may be a kind of temporary deficiency. I say this because I have seen so many whose passions for certain topics can make them oblivious to others. Once they start in on that topic, they find it difficult to contain themselves. In conversation, they may overlook or simply disregard all verbal cues or body language indicating they have lost their audience. For those who have never been on the receiving end of this, imagine sitting through a friend's video from a recent trip. You may be sincerely interested, but only to a point. Before too long you are nodding off, and your spouse is snoring, and yet they continue undeterred, "… and here is Marge getting into our taxi cab in …."

Basic Communication Model

To better appreciate empathy's importance to communication, let us consider the Basic Communication Model.

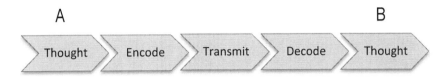

It starts with something in Person A's (whom we will call Adam) mind that he wants to convey to Person B (whom we will call Bernice). Adam encodes the information (e.g., words, body language, images) and transmits it to Bernice via some channel (e.g., verbally, email, presentation). Bernice receives the information and decodes it, analyzing it for meaning and resulting in thought. It is a sequential process, but in practice it is usually hierarchal and egocentric; the greatest effort is devoted to the first step, less on the second, even less on the third, and after that, it is up to the recipient.

Every step provides multiple failure points that can diminish the effectiveness of the communication. For example, say Adam wants to make Bernice laugh. As Adam combs his memory, he may recall a joke that is not very humorous to begin with. In telling it, he may not provide enough information to set up the joke properly. Adam's speech may not be clear and Bernice could misconstrue his words. Finally, Bernice may lack the experience or knowledge that gives context to the joke (e.g., golf jokes are usually only funny to those who golf).

Silence Dogood

Benjamin Franklin could not only peer into someone's mind, but climb right in and stretch out. He did it so thoroughly that he could write convincingly from a variety of personas. His first published pieces were under the name of Silence Dogood, purportedly a middle-aged widow from the countryside. The letters he wrote under her name, 14 in all, became extremely popular and it was some time before it was discovered that he was the author. This would have been a feat for anyone, but Franklin was only 15 years old at the time. He continued to utilize this practice of writing as different personas throughout his life.

While early composition classes instruct writers to be considerate of their audiences, that is not the same as being empathetic. Ann Herrmann-Nehdi, CEO of Herrmann International, tells the story of a doctor consultation to review some test results, "and he proceeded to talk in what I would perceive as a foreign language for about four minutes …. His language was obviously very accurate, but it was so laden with technical terminology that it was impossible for a layperson to understand what he meant. I almost burst out laughing," she said, as it reminded her of a *Peanuts* cartoon in which the adults' dialogue was indicated by just "wah, wah, wah …." When she expressed her bewilderment to the doctor, she learned that he was in fact trying to be considerate. "He felt like he would be insulting us if he spoke down to us, in other words, by not using accurate terminology. He would never want to be talked down to." In this case, following the Golden Rule of, "Do unto others as you would have them do unto you," was misguided. This example should not be taken to imply that the correct approach is to speak at an elementary level to non-technical audiences. While being spoken to at too high a level is exasperating, being spoken to at too low a level is insulting, and many make this mistake. Our goal should be to speak in terms that work for that specific audience.

The confusion between consideration and empathy may explain some of the friction that results from communication breakdowns: communicators frustrated because their efforts to be considerate are unappreciated, and audiences frustrated because they are not empathetic.

Remedies:
Empathy

Making a Connection

Effective communication calls for starting with the audience, then considering what they need/want to hear, how they need/want to hear it and how to transmit it – albeit in the context of what we want to share. This is audience-oriented communication. Lest the name mislead, it is not about deferring our communication agenda to our audience. If anything, it could be said to be more self-serving, because it is intended to ensure we get what we want from our audience ... by being responsive to our audience.

Think of the process the way a network systems analyst might approach connecting dissimilar systems of two companies. The high-level steps may be something like this:

1. Determine what information the recipient needs.
2. Determine the required data format.
3. Determine the best option of the available transmission modes/networks.
4. Determine what will need to be done on the sending end to have it properly encoded and transmitted.

The result is both parties are able to get what they need. Here is another way to look at it: egocentric communication can be compared to shooting blindfolded with a shotgun, i.e., shooting in the general direction of where we think the audience is and hoping that something finds the target, while audience-oriented communication is like taking careful aim using a rifle with a scope.

Our objective is to hit the bull's eye, but that requires knowing precisely where the target is and then having the tools to focus in on the bull's eye. Even then, just as distance, wind and other factors influence the path of the bullet, we need to take into account the factors that can influence our communications.

Of course, if someone is not highly empathetic (blindfolded), regardless of the reason, merely instructing him or her to be audience-oriented (taking careful aim) is not very constructive. The remainder of this chapter provides insights, techniques, and tools that can help one better see and target their audience.

When a Man Bites a Dog … The Elements of News

Benjamin Franklin's unique abilities and success as a communicator were largely serendipitous. If Franklin were born today, he would likely have matriculated directly through some technical field. However, the circumstances and timing of his birth placed him at the mercy of the apprentice system, which in many ways was like an arranged marriage of today; one's choice of profession was often dictated by convenience.

Franklin's father offered him a few apprentice opportunities from which to choose – what Ben really wanted was to go to sea – but in the end he was apprenticed to his brother James, a printer. Joyce Chaplin, author of *The First Scientific American: Benjamin Franklin and the Pursuit of Genius*, postulates that this had a profound effect on his intellectual development. "I think that you can explain a lot of things about Franklin by the fact that he had to get the newspaper out regularly, make sure he printed things that would sell; and so he had a very keen eye to what could be news, what would pay, and what would really let him get ahead …."

Whether or not Franklin was born with an innate ability to read people, his many years as a printer certainly would have been an important contributor. In a sense, each newspaper was an exploration of human nature. He could print what he thought would most interest his customers and then see what sold. Franklin could then make adjustments in the next edition and reassess – Philadelphia was a much smaller and more intimate city in his day and he likely would have personally known a great many of his subscribers, and how they reacted to certain stories. Through this process Franklin developed a strong sense of what interested others and how best to encode and convey it, a skill he perfected in writing and adapted to conversation.

In the journalism field this ability is referred to as news sense. While it is best learned on the job in a news organization, as Franklin did, news sense is a valuable skill that has long since been studied, codified, and taught in journalism programs. While intended for use by journalists and editors for the mass media, the various news elements have application for anyone who needs to anticipate what is of interest to a general audience. Editors do not dictate what news is, human nature does; they mostly just respond to it.

Following is a list of news elements that determine what should be included or excluded from a traditional news publication. Different news organizations or journalism schools might have variations of this list – reminding us how subjective this area is, even among experts – but this version is probably the one most commonly referenced.

There should not be any great revelations in these; most individual factors will appear to be basic common sense, yet parsing topics with this list helps overcome natural biases and reflexive thought patterns, providing new insights and perspectives valuable for targeting an audience.

Review the following and become familiar with them. Use the worksheet on page 314 as a tool when preparing material to present. A given topic need not rank high on all of these, but the more it does, the more likely a general audience will be receptive. Over time, with practice, these will become ingrained and you will be able to evaluate items newsworthiness without referencing this list.

- Timeliness
- Proximity
- Prominence
- Consequence
- Human Interest
- Conflicts, Crises, and Catastrophes

Timeliness
Timeliness has traditionally been very important in the news media. People tend to be most interested in things that are about to happen or that have just happened. Public interest is fleeting and the phrase, "that's yesterday's news" equates to "yesterday's bread." For example, if you have just been awarded a major research grant, that information will likely be of interest to others. But the impact dilutes as time passes.

Beyond mere assessment of topics, the timeliness factor can also be used as a way to package certain communications. For example, the anniversary of certain major events can provide an opportunity to communicate something. The first anniversary of the 9/11 attack, as well as subsequent anniversaries, provided the media the opportunity to revisit stories on terrorism, the victims, and so on. If there is something you wish to communicate that is not inherently timely, consider piggybacking on something that is. An IT security team, for example, might use the changes in daylight savings time – which have traditionally been used to remind people to replace batteries in smoke detectors – as a way to promote employees changing their system passwords. This simple connection will make the message more memorable and is likely to result in better compliance.

Another aspect of timing that affects the audience's receptiveness is the elapsed time since a similar communication has taken place. In newspapers, for instance, reporters may be less interested in a story if a similar one has been published recently. The audience is looking for *news*. The exception to this, though, is when the repetition represents a trend that in itself is newsworthy. For example, a major advancement in cancer treatment will be of significant interest. One that follows shortly after, though, will likely be of less interest, "We just did a story about cancer treatments." However, a third or fourth in close succession may represent extraordinary momentum in the battle on cancer and will again generate interest.

Proximity

It is human nature to be more interested in news that is close to us, whether physically or virtually. If something happens near where I live, even if there are seemingly no implications for me, I am more likely to be interested in it than if it happened at some distant location. Proximity, though, is not just geographical; it can be interpersonal. I will be more interested if it relates to people I know personally or professionally, even if they are on the other side of the world. It can also be topical; if World War II aircrafts are a particular interest of mine, I will pipe up every time they are mentioned or written about.

Proximity can be used to determine which audience to communicate with, or what information to share to a given audience. Colleges, for example, only send student honor announcements to the hometown papers of honored students because hometown papers are only really interested in the accomplishments of their local students. If the local paper received the full list of those receiving awards irrespective of where they were from, the recognition could get lost in the long list or it could seem to dilute the importance of the honor. By inverted logic, colleges that seek publicity in a certain market should make sure to publicize achievements from students from that area. The same logic can be used in the workplace, by taking into account the proximity of a given topic to our target audiences. For example, the engineering team may be interested in certain engineering developments, but if they need to reach an audience in marketing, they need to utilize topics that are close to marketers as a way to deliver their ultimate message.

Prominence

Size matters. So do numbers. Big-ticket projects generally will be of more interest than small ones. Projects that involve a large number of people will be of more interest than those that affect few. In particular, terms such as *largest, most, greatest,* and other superlatives tend to pique people's interest.

The prominence factor also relates to how important or well known the person, thing or topic is: a company vice president receiving some award is likely to draw more attention than a low-level employee receiving the same award. Prominence is not always a matter of rank; some individuals can be prominent merely because they are well known or well liked.

Just as proximity can be used for piggybacking on an otherwise minor topic, so can prominence. For example, in a university a topic that invokes the name of a well-known and respected retired physics professor will inherently draw more attention than it would otherwise.

Consequence

The extent to which a story has consequences for the audience has tremendous implications for its newsworthiness. A company going into bankruptcy is one thing; my company going into bankruptcy is another; a drug that treats some rare disease is one thing; a drug that treats my disease is another.

As with those listed above, consider how our topic affects our target audience. If there are no inherent direct consequences, we can look to piggyback on those that do. For example, in providing an update on a project to an executive team, rather than just listing the various challenges we have successfully overcome, we can discuss how the success should affect fiscal performance (which affects the executives performance bonuses – a major consequence for them). We still deliver our key messages, but by relating to consequences that affect our audience.

Human Interest

This is a very broad news factor, almost a catchall subcategory, which captures many of the elements that do not fit precisely with the others. Often it relates to topics that appeal to the readers' sense of curiosity, sympathy, empathy, irony, suspense, and other more emotionally-triggered responses. A researcher who has spent the last 20 years researching cures for breast cancer, who then gets it herself, creates human interest. An anthropologist who makes a significant discovery will be of interest to other anthropologists, not just because of virtual proximity, but because they may be able to relate to the experience.

Items that are odd and unique also trigger human interest. The classic example of this is often attributed to *New York Sun* editor John B. Bogart, who explained that, "When a dog bites a man, that is not news, but when a man bites a dog, that is news." We are drawn to the unexpected and unusual. Historically, carnival "freak shows" were a powerful example of this less-than-laudable aspect of human nature.

Conflicts, Crises, and Catastrophes

These have a significant effect upon readers' interests, and indeed are one of the key factors in the mainstream media; geographical, political, business, and social conflicts and crises dominate the top stories. This also helps explain why people slow down to gawk at car wrecks or why *The Real*

Housewives franchise is so popular. People are fascinated by other people's troubles, big and small. While we may prefer to avoid such topics, there are times when they are pertinent. For example, catastrophic weather events draw attention to the global warming debate.

Utilizing News Sense

There are two basic ways to use this list to support your communication efforts. The first starts with the topic we wish to communicate: we evaluate it based on timeliness, proximity, prominence …. This will help to determine who to communicate it to and how (and maybe if).

The second starts with the audience we wish to reach, and then we use news sense to determine the topic. The topic is merely a tool for reaching them. Once we have the right topic, we can either piggyback on it or transition to the topic we really want to cover.

One of the ways I have helped organizations raise their profile is by way of industry rankings, competitions, and awards. In most cases the problem with their previous unsuccessful attempts was that their entries focused on what they wanted to convey rather than on what the competition organizers wanted to hear. Generally, my approach to developing entries for these organizations was to sit down with key representatives and talk through the entry requirements. Entries usually come as a combination of specific questions related to quantitative information and essays that respond to open-ended questions. A typical essay question might be, "Describe the most significant accomplishment your organization has achieved in the last year." In my experience, the representatives typically consider the question literally, i.e., what was their biggest project. While this related to the prominence news factor, these projects often lacked other important attributes. However, when we brought the full consideration of news value to the discussion, we could usually find alternative topics that, while not as significant in pure magnitude, would be of more interest to the judges because it involved a bleeding-edge technology (timeliness), or because it was related to a major industrial trend (proximity), or just because there was such a compelling story to go with it (human interest). Even in cases where the biggest project was the chosen subject, taking into account various news factors allowed us to *spin* the topic in a more compelling way.

This approach was extremely successful, but it need not be limited to such venues. It can be used when dealing with an executive team, the board of directors, the media, and general public constituencies. For every communication we create, we should be able to answer the hypothetical questions, "so what?" and "what's in it for me?" from our audience's perspective; the more compelling the answer the more likely we will be to influence them.

Birds of a Feather

News sense helps us anticipate the interests of a general audience, but there are other tools that can help us replicate the abilities of those who are empathetically gifted.

Psychographics is a tool often used by marketers and political advisors. While demographics segment people by such things as age, gender, location, and income; psychographics segment people by such things as lifestyles, interests, values, etc. – in effect, how we think. For example, one psychographic segment most people have heard of is YUPPIE, which is derived from Young Urban Professionals (actually, its origin was in popular media and then adopted by marketers). Another is DINK: Dual Income No Kids. Each of these are associated with a small set of characteristics that can be extremely effective in determining which market segments will be interested in a product, what future products should be developed, and more importantly, which messages will influence consumers and how they can be most advantageously delivered.

A similar approach can be used to segment audiences in an organization. Certain psychographic segments naturally occur or are created by the nature of people's work. For example, job levels often correspond with many shared values, motivations, communication preferences, etc. The top executive team of an organization may share many of these, even though they represent different areas of the organization and have different backgrounds. Middle managers may share more in common with others of the same level across an organization than they do with the top executives of their discipline. The same goes for base or entry level employees.

Almost anybody would communicate differently with a CEO than an entry-level employee, but that difference is likely more about the time and effort they put into the communication, and less about the message. Understanding the psychographics of these various groups allows not only for the creation of more effective communications for each audience, but for developing communications that will be effective across all audiences (by understanding the factors that are common to all audiences).

This does not mean that everyone in a particular group shares the identical defining characteristics. Nor does it mean any given individual falls into only one segment; they can qualify for several depending on how the segments are defined. See page 316 for a representative sample of a tool created for one type of organization; it provided a reference tool when designing a communication program as well as a way of teaching others to target their audiences effectively.

Follow the Grain

While developing your own segments, do not just assume that they will be organized according to job level or function.

Technical professionals, as defined by this book, are a loose psychographic. If you were to analyze all who fall under this umbrella term, irrespective of their specific field or level, you would find certain characteristics more prevalent with this group than others, or the general population as a whole. We expect this group to be more intelligent, logical, and rational; to value such things as objectivity, facts, and precision; and to be motivated by innovations, solutions and being fairly recognized for their contributions. Again, not all will align with these characteristics, but enough do – whether a rocket scientist or a basic lab technician – to guide interactions with this group.

Individual Psychological Types

News Sense helps us with large general audiences and psychographics with subsets of those. Next, individual psychological types provide us another way to target audiences, even individuals, more effectively. For example, CPP, the exclusive global publisher of the MBTI, offers the book *Introduction to Type and Communication,* which draws upon hundreds of thousands of MBTI profiles and years of analysis. For each of the 16 MBTI types, it presents various findings and insights, both from the perspective of the communicator and the audience. It categorizes these into areas such as Communication Highlights, What They Want to Hear, When Expressing Themselves, Giving/Receiving Feedback, and others. It also provides general Communication Tips for each type, as well as a list of Do's and Don'ts. Following are examples of some of the information provided for ISTJs (Introverted, Sensing, Thinking, and Judging), the most prevalent type among STEM professionals:

Communication Highlights
- Straightforward, practical, logical, and efficient.
- Independent, self-sufficient, and self-reliant.
- Focused on facts, details, and results.

What They Want To Hear
- Exactly what is expected of them.
- Clear feedback and step-by-step procedures.
- Detailed facts and information relevant to their situation.

Communication Tips for the ISTJ

- Balance your practical, task-focused approach with consideration of the needs and situations of the people involved. Make a conscious effort to develop rapport and connect with others.

- Remain open-minded and listen without judgment to others' perspectives.

- Develop patience for interruptions and changes in plans.

- Attend to and acknowledge personal responses, and avoid coming across as blunt, detached, or impersonal.

For *Introduction to Type and Communication* to be most useful, we need to know our audience's MBTI type. Unfortunately, in most cases we will not have access to that information. If you can ascertain your audience's type, great. If not, page 2 of *Introduction to Type and Communication* provides descriptions of the various Preference Pairs, which may help you estimate your audience's type. While you cannot depend upon this approach to provide you with an accurate assessment, it may work in some cases and get you close in others.

Following are insights that can help us when communicating specifically to type ENFP (Extravert, iNtuitive, Feeling, and Perceiving), which represents ISTJ's opposing preference pairs.

Communication Highlights

- Outgoing, optimistic, caring, genuine, and compassionate.

- Energetically and enthusiastically encourage and persuade others.

- Champion changes that provide possibilities and improve processes for people.

What They Want To Hear

- People's experiences, feelings, thoughts, viewpoints, and ideas.

- General guidelines and information, not specific directions or commands.

- Theories and models that will enhance growth, learning, and development.

Communicating Effectively with ENFPs
Do

- Be supportive, build rapport, and focus on collaboration and cooperation.

- Discuss ideas and possibilities to enhance people's processes.
- Focus on people's needs and feelings in situations.

Don't
- Be overly judgmental, logical, or analytical.
- Focus mainly on structures and routines or on facts and details.
- Debate, argue, or critique points without first finding common ground.

The combination of insights of your own type as well as your audience's, provides extremely useful guidance. As you research audiences you have worked with in the past, you are likely to experience epiphanies as to why previous efforts have failed.

Two Ears and One Mouth

The preceding represents proven techniques that we can use to become more audience oriented in your communications, but the fundamental secret, like Dorothy's in *The Wizard of Oz* (the ruby slippers and the chant, "There's no place like home"), has been in front of us all along … listening.

Listening is the Holy Grail of audience-oriented communication. It has been preached by our parents and demanded by our mates; it has been a central theme of such best-selling books as *Men Are from Mars, Women Are from Venus*; *Crucial Conversations*, and *How to Win Friends and Influence People*; and yet, we rarely practice it as we should. If we really want to narrow our focus on the audience's needs, we must listen.

Listening, though, is about more than paying attention. As Daniel Goleman says in *Social Intelligence*, "Full listening maximizes physiological synchrony, so that emotions align …. Listening carefully, with undivided attention, orients our neural circuits for connectivity, putting us on the same wavelength. That maximizes the likelihood that the other essential ingredients for rapport – synchrony and positive feelings – might bloom."

While Franklin did not focus on Listening as a specific virtue, his virtue of Silence: "Speak not but what may benefit others or our self; avoid trifling conversation," is really just a variation of it. In his autobiography, Franklin confesses mixed results in his effort to master certain virtues – "On the whole, tho' I never arrived at the perfection I had been so ambitious of obtaining, but fell far short of it, yet I was, by the endeavor, a better and happier man than I otherwise should have been if I had not attempted it…." Though he may have fallen short on some virtues, there is no question that he succeeded with Silence. Both those who knew him well and his brief acquaintances frequently commented on his unique practice of silence and intense listening.

He also reveals his thoughts on the subject in an article he wrote, *Remarks Concerning the Savages of North America,* (excerpt available at *www.brainiacparadox.com*) in which he lambasted the practices of "civilized society" – in this case the British House of Commons – by comparing them to the "savages" of North America.

The beauty of listening as a self-improvement goal is that it can provide immediate results. Not only does careful listening help us tune into our audience, it also builds the goodwill that makes them more likely to listen to us. On many occasions I have heard people say – when describing why they liked a person so much – something akin to, "They listened to me as if I were the most interesting and important person in the world."

Through careful listening, we can ascertain the needs of our audience … so that they can meet ours. Taking time to listen saves us time.

Mix It Up

For listening to be most effective in helping us become more audience-oriented in our communications, it is necessary for us to be exposed to diverse groups of people. Over time, human nature, cognitive dissonance, career specialties, and societal norms tend to heard us into groups that share similar experiences, values and views. In such situations, listening well is relatively easy, but likely yields less of what will truly be helpful to us. It is like joining a gym and working on only our arms, because that is what is already strong, leaving other muscle groups to atrophy. We have to mix it up to get the best payoff.

If we deliberately expose ourselves with diverse groups, especially those similar to our key audiences, we are likely to find it easier to connect with our key audiences when it really counts. But more than that, doing so exposes us to potentially valuable ideas, perspectives, and information, which we would not have otherwise.

When Pixar Studios built a new headquarters building, it very deliberately designed it to force its employees to intermingle. The design not just encouraged, but forced people from different areas to mix. The original plan even went as far as specifying that there only be one set of bathrooms for the 600 plus employees located there (it eventually compromised on two, when employees argued that was going too far). Employees concede that many of their best ideas, or important sharing of information, happens in chance encounters with individuals whom they otherwise would not have had contact.

Keep in mind, that it is not just about seeing, but being seen. At one organization where I was employed, there was an engineer who was a very talented caricaturist. Every year, at Bring Your Children to Work Day, he volunteered in the lobby to draw pictures of the visiting kids. During that brief stint he was able to meet a diverse cross-section of the organization (parents accompanied their children), demonstrate that he was more than "just a technologist," and generate a tremendous amount of goodwill from all he encountered.

Reading

Reading may be another way to supplement your exposure to different perspectives and approaches. Novels usually contain extensive content related to characters' inner voices that, while fictional, can still provide a rich panorama of someone's mind's eye.

The value of this has been demonstrated by researchers Emanuele Castano and David Comer Kidd at the New School for Social Research in New York City. They had participants read a selection of literary types – literary fiction, popular fiction, serious non-fiction, and a control group reading nothing at all – and then had them take a series of tests. The research found that after reading literary fiction, people performed better on tests measuring empathy, social perception and emotional intelligence. This was true whether the participants liked to read literary fiction or not. However, those who read popular fiction, serious non-fiction and those in the control group did not improve. The researchers attributed the difference to the less explicit nature of literary fiction. It leaves more to the imagination, thus forcing the reader to make inferences and to sensitize themselves to the emotional nuances of the characters.

While autobiographies and memoires would not share these characteristics, I believe they also would be helpful. They can provide an intimate peek into how others think, what they value, how they have reacted to various events in their lives, and generally, why they have done what they have done.

The key, of course, is in the selection: seeking out voices that are similar to those we are trying to better understand and attune ourselves to, rather than just reading what we have always enjoyed.

While reading is a helpful supplement to actual interactions with others, it is not a substitute. Just as Franklin could use the regular publication of his newspaper to test and assess the reactions of others, it takes actual interactions to test and assess our ability to read others.

How to:
Become More Audience Oriented

1. **Adopt practices that will help you tune into your audiences, see things from their perspectives, and that ultimately facilitates the synchronization of minds.**

   ☐ Listen well.

   ✓ Eliminate distractions (turn off computer displays, put away phones, etc.) when you are having a conversation with someone so you can provide full attention.

   ✓ Follow the guideline of speaking only half as much as you listen.

   ✓ Maintain good eye contact (this may take some practice for some).

   ✓ Present body language that communicates that you are open and interested.

   o Keep your body facing your audience.

   o Lean forward, not backward.

   o Do not cross your arms.

   ✓ Do not interrupt or signal that you are about to interrupt.

   ✓ Practice active listening.

   o Strive to read your audience's body language and other non-verbal communications.

   o Carefully consider what they are saying both literally and implicitly.

   o React (smile, frown, etc.) accordingly.

   o When their message is complex or unclear, summarize what you believe they have said to confirm your understanding.

   o When you do not understand, patiently ask clarifying questions.

☐ Read others' communications carefully.

- ✓ Dedicate your full attention to what you are reading.
- ✓ Pay careful attention to the implicit, as well as its explicit messages (can be difficult as there is no body language and inflection to help guide us).
- ✓ If the message is ambiguous (or possibly offensive), confirm the intention before reaching conclusions or undertaking actions.

2. **Increase your exposure to diverse groups (especially those important to you and/or those whose perspectives you find hardest to understand).**

☐ Determine where to focus your efforts.

- ✓ Draw up a list of the various distinct audiences whom you work with or depend upon.
- ✓ Rank according to those with whom you have the greatest empathy (can see things from their perspective; even anticipate how they would react to certain situations).
- ✓ Review those groups towards the bottom of the list (those you understand the least) and evaluate them in terms of their importance to your success.
- ✓ Select the top three among these as your initial targets (work on the next three once you complete these).

☐ Develop a plan for activities that will provide you exposure to your target audiences.

- ✓ Consider places or activities members of your target audiences are likely to be engaged.
- ✓ Internally, you could volunteer for cross-function activities:
  - o United Way campaign
  - o Intramural teams
  - o Lunch-time enrichment programs
  - o Health and wellness initiatives
  - o Community relations initiatives

✓ Externally, you could:

  o Take a class with a local college or community center (e.g., if you do not understand artsy types, take an art class).

  o Join an organization that includes a mixture of people (e.g., Toastmasters, Rotary).

  o Get involved at your place of worship.

  o Get involved with community improvement projects.

✓ If you read your organization's internal communication material or your local paper with this in mind, you will find numerous opportunities to expose yourself to diverse groups.

☐ Read books that may provide you insights to your key audiences.

  ✓ Books written by those similar to your target audience.

  ✓ Literary novels with characters similar to your target audience.

3. **Seek a basic understanding of what interests other people.**

☐ Start by studying the elements of news (see the list and a description of the elements starting on page 131). This will develop your news sense.

☐ Whenever you have something specific to communicate, analyze it against the series of news elements to determine how best to present it. The News Elements Tool on page 314 can help you do this more objectively and easily.

  ✓ Doing so will help guide what aspects of your communication can serve as a "hook," something that will grab their attention and facilitate their reception of the rest of the message.

  ✓ With continued practice, you will eventually be able to evaluate a given topic's potential interest to a general audience without referencing the tool.

☐ Note how the audiences you most commonly or crucially deal with respond to the communications you share. This will refine your news sense.

  ✓ Pay attention when others indicate feedback in some form.

  ✓ Query people as to what they may have found most interesting or useful as well as what they did not.

4. **Develop and Use Audience Analysis Tools**

☐ Create an Audience Analysis Worksheet.

✓ Download a blank Audience Analysis worksheet from *www.brainiacparadox.com*.

✓ Evaluate your key audiences to determine common perspectives, attitudes, values, etc., which can be important to how they receive you and your communications. Reference the example of the Audience Analysis Worksheet on page 316 as a guide and follow the instructions provided there.

☐ Reference when creating communications for, or preparing to meet with, key audiences.

5. **(optional) Use MBTI to help you communicate more effectively with individuals.**

☐ Determine your Myers-Brigg type (MBTI) and that of your target audience.

✓ Have an official assessment performed on yourself, if you do not already know your type.

✓ Attempt to ascertain your audience's type (many people have already been assessed for the MBTI).

✓ Study the profiles and key characteristics of your type, as well as those of your audience.

☐ Use these tools to facilitate more effective communication with your key audiences.

✓ Acquire a copy of *Introduction to Type and Communication*, published by CPP.

✓ If you do not know and cannot ascertain your audience's MBTI type, review the type descriptors in the book to see if you can estimate their type.

✓ Calibrate your communications based on the insights this tool provides about you as the sender, and your audience as the receiver.

Summary – Chapter 8
Audience-Oriented Communication

Through the process of socialization we learn that for us to get what we want and need from others, it is necessary to meet the wants and needs of others. The problem is that it may not always be clear what others want and need. Often we need to do a bit of mindreading, and that takes empathy.

Empathy is the most important success factor for effective communication. Some are gifted in this regards, but others struggle to divine the thoughts, attitudes, and motivations of others. An empathy deficiency, sometimes referred to as mind blindness, is one of the key characteristics of autism and Asperger syndrome. It also alluded to in the descriptions of the most common cognitive types associated with technical professions. To complicate matters, even those who could be said to be empathetically typical may have troubles reading other audiences if their education, background, and professions place them on very different cognitive, environmental, and experiential planes than those whose minds they need to tune in to.

Whatever the reason, those who do not possess adequate empathy must either develop it … or fake it.

Developing empathy comes from improving listening skills, exposing oneself to diverse audiences and even reading works by or based on those with unfamiliar perspectives.

Faking it is done by using processes and tools to do analytically what those with strong empathetic skills do intuitively. Learning the *elements of news* helps us anticipate what would be of interest to a broad general audience. Audience psychographics can help us to communicate to specific groups.

Finally, personality-typing tools (e.g., Myers Briggs) can be used to help us communicate more effectively by allowing us to factor in both our and our audience's preferences, biases, and perspectives.

Monitor, Assess, and Log …

- When you are talking more than listening.

- When you catch yourself communicating based on what you want to say rather than what your audience wants/needs to hear.

- When it appears you have not properly understood, anticipated, or accommodated your audience.

You Will Know You Are Overcoming This When …

- You are able to successfully anticipate your audience's informational desires and needs on a regular basis.

- You notice that others seem to listen more carefully to you.

- You observe a significant decrease in confusion or communication disconnects.

- You find you are able to build rapport with groups that were previously distant.

– Chapter 9 –

So Your Grandparents Could Understand

Clearly spoken, Mr. Fogg;
you explain English by Greek.
— Benjamin Franklin

Foible: Jargon, acronyms, and complexity

Precept: Communicate in terms and concepts your audience will understand. Simplify

In the forward to *A Brief History of Time*, Stephen Hawking wrote, "Someone told me that each equation I included in the book would halve the sales. I therefore resolved not to have any equations at all. In the end, however, I did put in one equation, Einstein's famous equation, $E = mc^2$. I hope that this will not scare off half of my potential readers." Hawking's book went on to become one of the top sellers of all time, with more than 10 million copies sold.

It should be no surprise that technical complexities, terminology, formulas, jargon, and acronyms are barriers to effective communication with non-technical audiences (and some technical audiences). In fact, though denial may be common foible, as explained in Chapter 7, on this topic there is little dispute; most people in technical fields recognize and own up to this foible.

There are legitimate reasons for the existence of this foible. Terminology that is common, even essential, in certain fields might never be uttered by those in other fields. Besides, acronyms and abbreviations can be a valuable shorthand, reducing the burden of the repeated use of compound words and long names. But it is more than just jargon that impedes effective communication between technical and lay groups. The underlying concepts and frames-of-reference that may be fundamental to one group may be foreign to another.

Language and thought patterns are deeply engrained and are difficult to alter even when we strive to. Consider the monolingual traveler visiting a country where his language is not spoken. On a conscious level, he knows people will not understand him and yet he reflexively asks questions or makes requests without hesitation, and then will do it again with someone else just moments later. Similarly, it is understandable if certain specialists find it difficult to effectively calibrate their communications for those outside their fields. In fact, it is often the incomprehensibility of such language that by itself designates one as a Brainiac to lay people.

While no Brainiac, I experienced a little of this myself when I tried to teach my father to browse the Web. It was in the late 1990's and at the time he was about 80 years old. Probably the most complicated piece of modern technology he had experience with was a TV remote. He was intrigued by the information I could instantly access on the Internet and was interested in learning how to use it himself. I thought it would be wonderful for him, but I also anticipated it would be difficult. To minimize the learning curve I got him WebTV. For those unfamiliar with it, WebTV was an early Web appliance that had no operating system you needed to understand; you just plugged it in to your telephone line and TV, turned it on, and then you could browse the web. "It can't be much easier than this," I remember thinking.

As you can guess, it did not go well. I showed him how to plug everything in, turn it on and then said, "Okay, click on the box that says 'Start Session.'" He looked up at me with a puzzled look. I realized he did not know how to use a mouse. "Oh, you see, this is a mouse and you move it to move the pointer," I explained. Again he looked at me. "Oh," I continued, "the pointer is this little arrow-like device on the screen," Not long after I taught him what the pointer was, I had to explain the difference between the pointer and the cursor. And on it went. It did not take very long for me to realize that to effectively teach him, I had to un-know so much of what I knew reflexively. Every question he asked or mistake he made highlighted how much knowledge I took for granted and how much time it would take to teach him.

It was not that he was unintelligent – he participated in the development of radar during World War II – and even at his age, he was still mentally sharp, but I was having problems teaching him technology that was less complicated than what I had already taught my 4-year-old son. The problem was that his framework for understanding machines and how they worked were firmly established after a lifetime, but that framework had largely been supplanted by new – digital – paradigms.

It is challenging for those who have devoted years to studying and practicing in a narrow area of science, math, engineering, or technology to put aside all the knowledge and terminology that is the mainstay of their world in order to communicate with non-technical people. Furthermore, just about all professionals use jargon, buzzwords, and acronyms: marketers, musicians, accountants, etc.

However, there are some cases where its use may not be so innocent. "It appears as if some feel a need to show how smart they are by conveying how complex their work is," says IT executive Mark Cybulski, a sentiment echoed by others in my many discussions on this topic.

For those who legitimately struggle with properly calibrating their language for various audiences, I offer the following techniques.

Remedies:
Jargon, Acronyms, and Complexity

Sensitizing

Many years ago, I was a member of Toastmasters (a club that focuses on the development of public speaking). Most of the meetings were dominated by members taking turns presenting in front of other club members. Part of the developmental process called for one person to be assigned *the bell* with the instruction to ring it anytime the speaker used a verbal crutch (*ums*, *uhs*, etc.). Many of us use these extensively without even realizing it. The idea behind the bell ringing was to raise such usage into the presenter's consciousness.

The first time I made a presentation in front of the group, the bell rang almost constantly. It was embarrassing at first, then annoying, and finally aggravating. "How the heck can I deliver this speech with that damn bell ringing!" I thought to myself. However, the anxiety created by the bell raised my awareness of the use of verbal crutches, and like a lab rat that gets a shock whenever it performs a certain function, I increasingly learned to catch myself before vocalizing each verbal crutch. As I progressed, my presentations were choppy – I hesitated just as I was about to use a crutch – but before too long I edited myself more fluidly and the bell was rarely rung.

In another situation, a meeting facilitator gave everyone in a brainstorming session Nerf balls, with instructions that if the speaker used inappropriate language, got off target, went too long, etc., we were to throw our Nerf Balls at them. As strange as this may sound, it worked extremely well. The ludicrous nature of the action created laughter, which disarmed any defensiveness that otherwise might have ensued.

Even though the bell or Nerf ball approach will not likely be appropriate for you, there are other, more subtle techniques that can be used that serve the same purpose. The trick is finding a way that provides immediate feedback.

For example, you might recruit one or more people who are regularly in attendance at your presentations, discussions, or other verbal interactions, and explain what you are trying to achieve. Ideally, they would not be someone with too similar a background – lest they be deaf to any transgressions – but sometimes that is the only option. Work out a signal they can use whenever you use jargon or difficult to understand concepts with your audience. For example, an accomplice could scratch his nose each time, or make a series of checks on a piece of paper within your eyesight.

Such actions might go unnoticed by others, but if done correctly and practiced, it will soon be as obvious to you as a ringing bell.

Sensitizing can work particularly well with acronyms or jargon, where the inappropriate use is relatively clear-cut, but possibly less effective when trying to avoid complex concepts or explanations.

Key Messages

It would seem that one of the reasons Hawking has been able to keep inherently complex concepts easily understood is the nature of his communication process. He has advanced ALS (amyotrophic lateral sclerosis, commonly referred to as Lou Gehrig's disease), so that his only means of communicating is in writing, and laborious writing at that. It takes him a great deal of time to write each sentence, time that allows him to be very deliberate about what he says.

Given enough time, most could carefully craft messages that would be more understandable and compelling, but that is unrealistic considering the demands and pace of our lives. So, while we may be able to develop a filter that will limit our jargon and acronyms, that does not help us much when trying to convey unfamiliar or complex concepts to lay audiences on the fly.

Among the most useful advancements in software programming have been those related reusable code. As logic and functionality often repeat within or across programs, software language developers have increasingly incorporated ways for code to be reused, from simple subroutines in early languages to feature-rich program objects today. This approach saves coding time and reduces program size as well as improves reliability (redundant code increases fault points).

Now consider how much of what we communicate is actually novel. Most will find that there are certain messages that they convey, concepts they explain, or questions they answer multiple times, some repeatedly over time. Despite this, they may struggle each time they try to communicate these. Dealing with these ad hoc is both wasteful (we likely say it a little differently each time in hopes of saying it better than the last) and risky because there is an increased chance of miscommunicating or being construed as inconsistent.

This is not just a problem for those in science, technology engineering, and math. In particular, this is important for politicians, corporate leaders, and others in high-profile positions. Their words can have great power and others may scrutinize them carefully; so anything that can help them communicate effectively, accurately and consistently is very valuable. Those who provide communication support for such people usually create some form of prepared and practiced messages. Though they may come in different forms and be referred to by different names (key messages, talking points, position statements, etc.), I will use the term key message generically here, except when a specific subtype is referenced.

Key messages are to communicators what reusable code is to programmers. They save time, improve consistency and, in particular, allow those using them to be very deliberate about what they communicate ... and what they do not. Often they are part of a larger communication strategy, orchestrated so that all the key messages contribute to a larger message. Once created, they can be used, reused, or repurposed in a variety of ways. With them, the communicator is more likely to remember important points and to deliver them in the most effective manner. Without them, even the most practiced presenter may take off on a meaningless tangent or stray into dangerous topical territories. When political analysts say that a candidate is "on message" or "off message," what they are referring to is how closely they are adhering to their key messages.

Key messages are especially helpful in navigating sensitive topics when dealing with the media, where a couple misplaced words can greatly change how a given message is received by the audience.

As they relate to us, the deliberative nature of their creation allows us the time and perspective necessary to create an effective and understandable message. We can edit out jargon, acronyms, and concepts unfamiliar to our audience while at the same time, adding information and explanations that clarify our meaning. We can also enlist others to review them and confirm their effectiveness in advance of their usage. In addition – for those who are not naturally gifted presenters – they provide us an opportunity to practice and memorize messages, so that they can be delivered more fluidly.

Basic Key Message

We start with the basic key message that, once created, can be repurposed for other specific uses (elevator speeches, sound bites, etc.). There is no universal format for them, but most professional communicators use a construction that calls for an initial statement, followed by secondary statements, and supporting points, as follows.

- Key Message
  - Supporting message one
    - Proof point
    - Proof point
  - Supporting message two
    - Proof point
    - Proof point

Example:

- *ACME Inc. is dedicated to being a good corporate citizen.*
  - o *We are a leader in environmental stewardship.*
    - ▪ *The first organization in our segment to build all Energy Star compliant products.*
    - ▪ *We have eliminated the use of all Volatile Organic Compounds in our production processes.*
  - o *We contribute to the economic and social wellbeing of the communities in which we operate.*
    - ▪ *We have developed special training programs that have lead to the employment of 500 people who have traditionally been considered "unemployable."*
    - ▪ *We are the largest contributor to free medical clinics near our various facilities.*

The key message should be able to stand alone, as does, "ACME Inc. is dedicated to being a good corporate citizen," but they are strengthened, and made more versatile by the inclusion of secondary messages and proof points. Two of each is provided here, but three or more may be desired based on the topic and usage. Also, while the proof points used in this example are primarily facts, there are other types that may be used:

- Examples
- Statistics
- Analogies
- Metaphors
- Anecdotes
- Comparisons
- Third party endorsements
- Others (e.g., graphics, URL links, etc.), which while not necessarily deliverable verbally, can be used for documents, presentations, etc.

Analogies can be particularly effective when you need to convey a complicated or abstract concept in terms your audience will understand. For example, Carl Sagan's use of the Cosmic Calendar – in which time since the big bang was mapped to a one year period and by this scale, the first modern humans would not have appeared until 11:54 p.m. on the last day of the year – brilliantly and simply conveyed a perspective of time that would have been unfathomable had he stuck to pure numbers.

Thought experiments, like Einstein's Elevator or Schrödinger's Cat, are other examples of how complex concepts can be conveyed in ways accessible to most.

Once you have a relatively full stable of key messages, they can be repurposed for specific communication needs.

Elevator Speech

An elevator speech, for example, is a variation, or combination, of key messages and is one of its most useful tools. The elevator speech is defined as what one would say if they had their target audience alone in an elevator – figuring about 30 seconds for the elevator ride. Creating one provides a ready, concise and theoretically compelling response to the question: "So, tell me a little about yourself? your project? your team? your organization?" and so on. It can be used for any situation where you want to be sure to make certain points quickly and effectively, whether it is small talk at a party or during a job interview.

To demonstrate the value of these, try this exercise. Ask yourself how you would respond to, "Tell me a little about your current work?" coming from a member of an audience that is key to your success.

Look for a place that you could actually try it – for example in your automobile while you commute to work – and provide your response aloud. Most will find this difficult to do well. We may be confident that we know what we would say and how we would say it, but when forced to actually verbalize it, we likely will not express things well, take far longer than 30 seconds to answer, or forget to include key points.

To create your elevator speech, start by reviewing the list of key messages you have already created. Likely you will have already addressed the points you would like to make in your elevator speech and all that is necessary is editing them into one cohesive statement. Based on an average rate of 150 spoken words per minute, you have 75 words with which to work. Of course, the 30-second timeframe is somewhat arbitrary – I would wager that few elevator speeches are actually delivered in elevators – so you can go a little longer if necessary, but if you make it too long, you will probably not be able to deliver it in its entirety when you get the opportunity to use it. As such, you might even want to create a few variations, based on different audiences or scenarios.

More than basic key messages, elevator speeches should be committed to memory as their opportunity for use is, by definition, unpredictable.

Q&A's

Questions and Answers are another essential communication tool. They can be helpful in preparing us to deal with the questions we frequently receive or, more importantly, to deal with potentially difficult topics. While reactive and sometimes defensive in nature, a properly considered and composed Q&A can turn a negative inquiry into a positive assertion of one of our key messages.

Q&A's are tricky, though, not just because they require creating responses to difficult questions, but because we are likely to avoid preparing for difficult questions in the first place. Few people are willing to ask themselves the right question. If they are preparing for a potentially controversial or contentious subject – one for which they find that they have no good answers – most people have an uncanny knack for avoiding them or reengineering the question until it matches an answer they are willing to provide. It is like developing a product to meet a load specification and finding that the materials or processes necessary to meet those specifications are too costly; some may be tempted to alter the requirements or tolerances until a cheaper solution will work.

Can't Handle the Truth

In my experience, the higher level a person is in an organization, the more likely they are to disregard preparation for tough questions.

Their authority may allow them to control the discourse within the team, avoiding the topics they do not wish to discuss, but this can leave them dangerously ill-prepared when questions come from above or outside.

Others just disregard tough questions altogether. In either case, this can be dangerous.

Depending on the stakes involved, this is an area where it can be very valuable to enlist the help of an expert communicator. A professional can help keep the "real questions" at the top of the list. They can also help deal with questions that have greater potential consequences, i.e., major public relations or legal implications.

Those circumstances aside, creating Q&A's is just an extension of the key message process. The basic formula is:

- Create questions that are likely to be asked and/or that would be difficult to answer spontaneously.
- Respond with a brief, honest answer followed by mitigating statements and proof points if possible.
- Transition to one of your key messages.

Example:

Question: Can we achieve significant savings by out-sourcing or off-shoring your services?

Answer: *On some superficial levels that may seem to be the case, but when evaluated as a whole, out-sourcing and off-shoring can end up being more expensive. ACME Inc. analysts researched this and found the true cost is on average a multiplier of X compared to in-house operations. Corporations ABC and DEF found this out the hard way and had to bring operations back in-house after costly experiments with off-shoring. Besides, our team has an in-depth knowledge of our organizational processes and culture, which would be impossible for an outside service provider to match.*

The Best Policy

When dealing with difficult issues, honesty truly is the best policy. Many try, and a few succeed, crafting answers that avoid the truth or to outright deceive. In doing so they risk damaging their credibility and alienating their audience to a far greater degree than an admission.

If you are dealing with a challenging question, give an honest answer and then use the redirecting technique to change the subject to a key message that can cast the issue in a more positive light.

Sound Bites

Sound bites are a variation of key messages, usually intended for the media. As many will do at least one media interview in their career, it is useful to understand these. Besides, the characteristics of a good sound bite (short, powerful, and memorable) make them a valuable communication tool for many purposes.

Sound bites are a response to the declining space for quotes the news media – especially broadcast – provides for any topic. According to research conducted by Daniel C. Hallin, based on samples of network evening news broadcasts from presidential elections from 1968 through 1988, the average sound bite declined from 43 to 9 seconds.

With so little quoted material used, it is important to ensure your key point is included. To achieve that, your message should be short, powerful, and include one or more elements that may make it memorable. For example, they may be:

- Provocative: "It's the economy stupid," used by James Carville, lead strategist to Bill Clinton, to focus the election discussion on a key weakness of the incumbent, President George H. W. Bush.

- Unexpected: "Senator, you are no Jack Kennedy," used by Lloyd Bentsen in a vice presidential debate to deflate the perception that Dan Quayle was the "new JFK."
- A pun: "If the glove doesn't fit, you must acquit," used by Johnnie Cochran to emphasize a seemingly contradictory piece of evidence in the OJ Simpson trial.
- Humorous: "God doesn't play dice with the universe," attributed to Albert Einstein.
- Rhetorical: "The only thing we have to fear is fear itself." Franklin D. Roosevelt's words at his first inaugural address resulted in one of history's most famous quotes.
- Ironic: "Today I consider myself the luckiest man on the face of the earth," said by Lou Gehrig to fans at a special farewell ceremony, as the fatal disease that would take his name forced him to quit baseball.

How to:
Communicate without Jargon

1. **Sensitize yourself to the use of jargon and acronyms, etc., as well as concepts unfamiliar to your audience, so you can catch yourself before using them.**

☐ Recruit others to provide you with immediate feedback upon use of inappropriate words or concepts.

    ✓ Depending on your circumstances, you may be able to do this openly, with one or more constituencies.

        o Explain you are trying to eliminate the use of unfamiliar terminology and concepts (most will be impressed by your intentions and more than willing to assist you).

        o Have them signal you when you violate some prearranged rules.

    ✓ For circumstances where you are not able do this openly, indentify one or more individuals to assist you.

        o Develop a covert system for them to provide real-time feedback, for example:

            ▪ An audible system, such as cough, throat clearing or tap of a pencil (may be conspicuous at the beginning of this process when violations are likely to be many).

            ▪ A visual system, such as scratching the nose, adding a stroke to a tally list, or other silent signal.

☐ If the previous approach will not work in your situation, develop your own system to note when you transgress. For example, you could record your presentations or other verbal sessions, and then play them back afterwards, listening carefully for slips.

    ✓ Tally your use of inappropriate words or concepts.

    ✓ Keep a master tally, which can be used to track your progress.

☐ Continue doing this until you find that you can consistently catch yourself before using unfamiliar terminology.

2. **Develop a library of carefully-crafted key messages that you can use to explain even the most complicated concepts to any audience without difficulty.**

☐ As a start, create a dozen or so key messages, using the format of primary message, supporting messages and then proof points. These are for topics you commonly need to describe, explain or share in some way.

✓ Review your ongoing projects, responsibilities, and relationships to flesh out a full list of topics you should be prepared to address. Special emphasis should be placed on topics that are typically difficult to explain to those outside your group. Think in terms of a couple of categories.

o Core messages: these relate to core elements of your purpose, beneficial characteristics, direction, etc. While the wording of these may change over time, the ideas they are addressing should be relatively fixed.

o Strategic messages: relates to messages that will help further your work, projects, career, etc.

o Frequent messages: relates to information you regularly relay in your work.

o General Messages: any message outside of the above categories that you believe you need to be prepared to deliver.

✓ Craft a primary message of 25 words or less that makes a definitive and discrete statement.

✓ Create 1-3 supporting messages (25 words or less), which elaborate on the primary message.

✓ For each supporting message create 1-3 proof points. As some of these proof points, such as anecdotes, do not lend themselves to 25 words or less, no limit is assigned, but an effort should be made to make them as concise as possible.

o Examples

o Statistics

o Analogies

o Metaphors

o Anecdotes

o Comparisons

- o Third Party Endorsements
- o Others (do not overlook graphics, URL links, or other supporting visual information that can be helpful for documents, presentations, etc.)

   Note: A single proof point can be used for more than one key message if needed.

- ✓ Review all your key messages.
  - o Replace or eliminate jargon, acronyms, and other terminology that would not be familiar to a broad audience.
  - o Consider using the news elements evaluation and audience analysis tools to evaluate your messages for maximum relevancy to general and key audiences.
- ✓ Put them aside for a couple days and then read them anew.
- ✓ If possible, share them with someone who well understands your audience's perspective. Ask them to point out where you still need to simplify or if they see better ways to say it.

- ☐ Create the additional key messages you will need to be adequately prepared for your traditional needs.

- ☐ Reassess your needs and messages on a regular basis.

- ☐ Create topical key messages as needed. These are messages used to deal with acute topics or issues.
  - ✓ The format is the same.
  - ✓ The difference is that these are usually intended to be used for a fixed period – hence disposable – such as a product launch. They can however, be added to your stable of key, or even core messages.

- ☐ Create an elevator speech(s).
  - ✓ Identify one or more topics you need to be able to address succinctly and articulately at any time and without notice.
  - ✓ Draft an approximately 75-word pitch for each.

- o The target length is based on a 30-second speech at an average 150 spoken words per minute. Hence, it can be longer or shorter based on how you are likely to use it.
- o If possible, draw on content from the key messages you have already created.
- o Practice delivering these aloud to yourself until you can do so fluidly without referencing notes and within the target time you have set. **Don't Skip This Step**, otherwise your elevator speeches likely will not be effective.
- o Next, practice delivering to someone (spouse, friend etc.). Adjust as necessary based on their feedback.

☐ Create sound bites from some of your key messages.

- ✓ Determine which topics' may require sound bites (media interviews, presentations, speeches, etc.).
- ✓ Craft messages that are short (a dozen words or less) and memorable (something provocative, funny, surprising, etc.).
- ✓ Get feedback and update or replace as necessary.

☐ Create Questions and Answers (Q&A's).

- ✓ Create a list of questions for which you should have prepared answers.
  - o Questions you are most frequently asked.
  - o Questions you are likely to receive based on upcoming events.
  - o Questions that you would most hate to be asked.
- ✓ For questions regarding potentially negative topics, create short answers for each that provide an honest response, but then transition to positive points (the positive points can be pulled from the key messages already created).
  - o The length of the answer is not restricted, but the shorter the better in most cases.

☐ On a regular basis, review and practice the various messages created above, until you can deliver them accurately with ease. This is especially important for elevator speeches which, by design, are intended to be delivered without notice.

Summary – Chapter 9
So Your Grandparents Could Understand

Everyone knows that simpler is better, but too few practice this. Thought and language patterns are deeply ingrained and it can be hard to recognize when we are using inappropriate language or concepts, let alone avoiding such mistakes before they are made.

The first step to addressing this is to sensitize ourselves so that we can catch unfamiliar words or concepts before uttering them to a lay audience. This entails working with someone who can provide us real-time feedback when we error. With repeated implementation, this feedback will help us anticipate – and thus avoid – inappropriate communications.

Of additional help are key messages, Q&A's, elevator speeches, sound bites, and other messages that can be crafted long before their intended use. Advance preparation allows us to edit these for audience appropriateness – avoiding jargon and unnecessary complexities – and optimize these for overall effectiveness. With practice, you will be able to fluidly deliver compelling, coherent, and consistent messages as needed.

Monitor, Assess, and Log ...

- When you use words or concepts that are inappropriate for a particular audience.

- When after an exchange you find yourself regretting what you said or what you failed to say.

- When problems ensue because people did not fully understand you.

You Will Know You Are Overcoming This When ...

- The actions of others indicate they accurately understand your requests or guidance (i.e., less problems because they did not understand).

- You are able to capitalize on fleeting opportunities by delivering a compelling message to key audiences.

- You are able to address tough issues adeptly.

- Communicating with non-technical audiences is not much more difficult than communicating with your technical peers.

– Chapter 10 –

Less Is More

He that speaks much, is much mistaken.
—Benjamin Franklin

Foible: Verbosity, Bloat, and Excess
Precept: Accomplish more by communicating less

On a cold, wet fall afternoon of 1863, Edward Everett, the most noted American orator of the day, gave probably the most important address of his life. It was a beautiful and moving speech of 13,607 words and took almost two hours to deliver. Shortly after Everett finished, another speaker took the podium and made some short remarks of a mere 269 words. The next day Everett wrote to that second speaker: "I should be glad if I could flatter myself that I came as near to the central idea of the occasion, in two hours, as you did in two minutes."

The later orator was Abraham Lincoln and the event was the dedication of the Soldiers' National Cemetery at Gettysburg. Everett's was a masterful presentation, but it is Lincoln's we remember (ironic considering it contained the line, "The world will little note, nor long remember what we say here …"). Lincoln's address demonstrates that a few words can be more powerful than many. Less is more.

After Jargon, the most common foible is Verbosity, even though it is sometimes the result of good intentions. On more than one occasion when consulting with someone for the first time, they would say to me something akin to, "I just want you to know, I believe you can never communicate too much." They could hardly be more wrong.

Noise

In just the last 25 years, we have gone from a paper-based workplace – which by its very nature could only move so fast – to a digital and wireless environment that bombards us with text, sound, and video at all hours of the day and in all places. I can now share more information faster with someone across the globe than I could with someone across the hall 25 years ago. I can reach them whether they are at work or home, or anywhere in between. While in theory this enables a very fluid workplace, with information being shared at near the speed of light, the reality is that it has opened the floodgates for a bloated informational environment. Just as gas expands to fill a void, content expands to the limits of our digital and cognitive bandwidth.

I recently participated in an organization's annual leadership conference, which included an activity intended to teach some Lean Manufacturing concepts. In it, the group of about 150 corporate leaders was divided into groups of 10. The exercise called for each group to be given a set of the same business processes along with instructions to complete as many as they could in 10 minutes. After the first run, they were asked to meet as a group and come up with changes in the processes so that they could deliver more of the end product (a stamped piece of paper) in the same 10-minute period. The activity was run again using the new processes, and afterwards additional changes were made and tried. This continued for several cycles. Eventually each group realized that by simplifying the process and supporting it through informal communication in which a verbal *pull system* replaced the traditional written system, huge productivity improvements could be achieved.

Teaching Lean may have been the objective of this exercise, but the most striking takeaway for me was the apt illustration of the part "noise" plays in our day-to-day operations.

All 15 groups were located in the same immense hotel ballroom. As informal communication – in this case verbal communication – became more important to the process, the room got louder, and as it got louder it became more difficult to hear teammates, and this resulted in mistakes during the process. To compensate, everyone began to speak even louder, which led to a spiral of escalating noise and mistakes. Eventually everyone was shouting. By the end of the exercise, the room sounded like a crowded athletic arena. This was a metaphor for the modern workplace.

The average person is bombarded with so much communication that they have long reached the saturation point. It is difficult for them to process what they receive and recall what they process: problems ensue. The reflexive solution – the issuance of even more communications – only makes the problem worse. Unfortunately, some in technical fields have a tendency to be particularly "noisy" in this sense. Their papers, presentations, even emails are frequently longer and more numerous than most audiences can afford and are willing to accept. Then, when they sense that their communications are being misunderstood or ignored, they create even more, hoping to break through.

At one organization, after the IT department sent out emails updating the entire organization on its response to the increasing problem of spam, more than one employee replied by complaining that the IT Department's emails themselves were spam. They had been increasing the amount of communications they issued to keep people informed about ongoing developments, to address questions they frequently received, and to combat mistakes they saw users making. They thought that was what a good IT department should do. Unwittingly, the one thing the IT team had succeeded in communicating was that these messages were not of immediate importance and could be put off or ignored. And, because important messages were mixed with, and diluted by, nice-to-know messages, system problems actually increased.

Yes, you can communicate too much.

Pressure to Be Verbose
As with most of the foibles, there are some reasonable justifications for this one. By default, the topics these professionals deal with are often quite complex and do not lend themselves to abridgment, even when communicating with technical peers. The problem increases exponentially when trying to communicate to non-technical people. Many struggle with this and, as one IT executive said to me, "think that if they just keep talking, eventually the other person will understand." Furthermore, precision is a relatively common value among technical professions, which results in even longer and more tedious (to non-technical people) communications.

Training and education also play a part. "We were trained to write a certain way," said one scientist. "We spent all of graduate school having any artistic expression beaten out of us, and instead were instructed to write in a very formal, precise, and lengthy manner." An engineer added, "We are so taken in by all the data and the figures. That's what we do. We think 'This is great stuff. Why wouldn't you want to see this? I want to show you what I did so that you can see I am doing a really good job for you. I want the A!'"

Still others suffer from the notion that the value or importance of a document is directly related to its size. Once, after creating a briefing book for the company's CEO – carefully crafted to contain the same content in one quarter the length of previous briefing books – a colleague said to me, "You can't give him this! It's not thick enough!"

Finally, when communication failures lead to problems, technical professionals are often held responsible, justifiably or not. Hence, they may feel an understandable compulsion to communicate more, if for no other reason than to provide defensive cover.

The complexity of technical subjects does present a challenge, but it should not be an excuse. As Albert Einstein is quoted as saying, "Any intelligent fool can make things bigger, more complex, and more violent. It takes a touch of genius – and a lot of courage – to move in the opposite direction." Rarely are there things so complex that they cannot be simplified – and strengthened in the process.

Time Is Money and Communication Is Time

Think about how much time could be saved, and how much more productive we could be, if we could be relieved from consuming just half the communications we currently receive. The vast majority of people are very inefficient communicators, generating many more words than they have to in order to support their business activities. As a result, their communications are less effective.

The next time you compose something, keep in mind that after a certain point, every sentence you add increases the chances that your audience will not finish reading your message or will read it less carefully. The same goes for the number of types of communications you send to achieve a certain communication goal. For example, if you send a status update on a key project too frequently, eventually the recipients will not read all of them or not read them completely.

Endless Meeting Loop

For some fortunate few, meetings are short and infrequent, but for many they consume a significant portion of their workweek, and still others, the majority of it. In concept, meetings are an ideal way of communicating: they are a personal, multi-directional, and immediate means of sharing information and thus facilitating quick decision-making. In practice, though, many are often no more than glorified water-cooler discussions. Groups will meet for great lengths of time with little focus or discipline, fostering discussions that are three parts filler for every one part relevant content. Rather than results-oriented activities, they become performances, with participants taking turns trying to score points by making the most noteworthy comments, by asking questions intended to undermine others, or simply to command the most time on the stage. What's more, though consensuses may be reached and decisions made, they are often done in such a haphazard fashion – with later points superseding ones made earlier in the meeting – that a day after the meeting, it may be difficult for participants to recall exactly what was decided or achieved.

To the extent we organize, or can influence the running of meetings, it is in our best interest to ensure meetings are purposeful and well run. It is actually a way to score some extra points, as everyone appreciates it when meetings do not waste time and when they achieve what they were supposed to.

If we can learn to communicate the same information with less, we can greatly increase the overall effectiveness of our communication. To achieve this, though, takes forethought, strategy, creativity, and practice. The forethought and strategy most often come into play when planning communication for large projects and programs, which will be covered in the next chapter. First, though, we must learn to be more concise in all our communications.

Remedies:
Verbosity, Bloat, and Excess

Scope

One of the factors driving excessive communications is scope. People try to achieve too much in the space of a single communication. Common wisdom is that the most an audience is likely to take away from any communication – whether a document, presentation or speech – are three things. The more that is attempted beyond that, the more the communication is diluted. And the more it is diluted, the less control there is of what is retained; your audience may remember certain things, but they may not be the things you most want them to recall.

Hence, when you create a communication, you should try to limit yourself to three key things (can be less) you want them to take away. You can then focus on delivering those messages clearly, bolstering them with compelling supporting information and using repetition to ensure they sink in.

Trimming and Boiling

An opening scene in the movie *A River Runs Through It*, portrays the main character's experience in his youth of being home-schooled by his Presbyterian minister father. "Being a Scot," he narrates, his father "believed that the art of writing lay in thrift." Accompanying the narration is a visual of the boy looking on as his father sits, savagely editing his paper. He then returns it to the boy saying, "Half as long." The boy runs off and later returns with a new version. The father edits it as before and returns it to the boy: "Again, half as long."

Just as good computer programmers seek to write applications that can achieve the same desired outcome in the fewest lines of code (or at least they used to), or electrical engineers seek elegant solutions that achieve the desired functions with the least components, good business communicators should seek to achieve their communication goals with the least communication elements.

In journalism, the process of editing to make a bloated story more concise is called *trimming* and *boiling*. Trimming refers to editing out unnecessary information and boiling refers to rephrasing so that the same information can be conveyed with less words. As an example, following is an actual email (minor changes have been made to eliminate personally identifiable information) sent to all employees from the Information Technology department of a major corporation.

IMPORTANT MESSAGE - PLEASE READ IN ITS ENTIRETY
We have had many requests for online phone number lookup capability over the last couple of years. To meet this request, we have continually improved the online phone book on the corporate intranet site. With up-to-date information, it has become an increasingly valuable tool for people and is one of the most popular features on the corporate site.

Previously, we elected to give you, the user, the ability to keep your own information up to date. Unfortunately, this self-administered approach has not been as successful as anticipated. Currently approximately 30 percent of employee information in the phone directory is missing, inaccurate, or incomplete. It is critical that all employees update their information to provide a reliable, quick source of directory information. As a gentle reminder, you will receive an e-mail periodically like this to show you what the directory says about you and give you an easy way to update the phone book if something has changed. Please take the time to review the information below and click "YES, THIS INFORMATION IS CORRECT" or "NO, THIS INFORMATION IS NOT CORRECT".

If the information is correct, thank you for keeping it current, and taking the time to verify it. If the information is incorrect, you will be directed to the directory update utility, where you may make the required changes.

Once you have clicked yes or no you may delete this email.

On behalf of all those in the organization who depend on accurate information, we thank you for your participation in keeping the phone book accurate.

Not such a long message (264 words), right? Based on average reading speed of about 225 words per minute, it should take only about 1 minute and 10 seconds for each employee to read. However, consider that this particular message was sent to all employees at a large organization. There were roughly 10,000 employees with corporate email accounts, so approximately 194 man-hours (almost five weeks) may have been consumed if every employee read that message in full. Following is an alternative version that has been trimmed and boiled.

PLEASE READ AND RESPOND AS REQUESTED
The online phone number lookup capability is one of the most valued functions of the corporate web site. This system relies on employees to keep this information up to date, but approximately 30% of employee information in the phone directory is missing, inaccurate, or incomplete.

As a reminder to keep this information accurate, we will be sending an e-mail to you periodically with your directory information. Please take the time to review the information below and click, "YES, THIS INFORMATION IS

CORRECT," or "NO, THIS INFORMATION IS NOT CORRECT." If
clicked on "NO" a web page will open where you can edit your information.

Thank You

As can be seen, some superfluous material has been deleted and other items
have been rewritten to use fewer words. It is now 113 words, less than half
the original. Now, let's see if we can trim and boil it to "half again as long."

PLEASE RESPOND AS REQUESTED
The online phone information system relies on employee data maintenance, but
approximately 30% of information is inaccurate. IT is going to send periodic e-mails
with your directory information, asking you to either confirm the information or click
on a link that will open a web page for editing.
Thanks

This version is 54 words, which is half the last version and almost one fifth
of the original. The resulting text may or may not be too austere, but it
serves to demonstrate that we can boil and trim extensively and still achieve
the objective. Consider a hypothetical situation where the first message was
sent to half of the employees in an organization and the last message was
sent to the other half; which do you think would have resulted in better
compliance among its respective recipients? If you believe it is the first,
recall that this was an actual email used in a corporation and it started with
the plea, IMPORTANT MESSAGE – PLEASE READ IN ITS
ENTIRETY. Obviously previous messages were not.

Inverted Pyramid

For those times when it is absolutely necessary to create a very long email
or other document, consider another journalistic technique: the inverted
pyramid structure.

This approach calls for prioritizing information and starting with the
most important and essential information first, followed by the next most
important, and so on down. In journalism parlance, the first sentence is
called the lead (sometimes called the hook because it is designed to capture
the readers interest), and should give the reader a sense of what the entire
piece is about. If properly done, each paragraph should be self-contained
message, in that the communication still makes sense, no matter at which
point one stops reading it. The last half to one third of the story is usually
background information: of interest to some, but not essential.

This approach has two very practical advantages for newspapers. The
first deals with how people usually read newspapers: reading the first
paragraph or two of the stories attached to the headlines that look

interesting and reading even more if the first couple of paragraphs hook them. The second has to do with limitations of pre-digital newspaper production. Stories had to fit in "news holes" but the size of the hole was approximate. Using the inverted pyramid style, typesetters could eliminate one or more of the final paragraphs without severely affecting the integrity of the story.

In workplace communications, this approach limits the damage when audiences start skimming after reading the opening lines, or do not finish at all.

The first iteration of the previous email example starts with, "We have had many requests for online phone number lookup capability …." It is not until the third paragraph that the main point of the communication is mentioned. This is called "burying the lede *[sic]*" and it is a natural tendency among those accustomed to reading and creating scientific papers, which may start with background information, methodology, etc. Laypeople, however, usually want the "so what" answered towards the beginning and if they do not find it there, they are not likely to continue very long, whether it is reading a document or paying attention in a presentation. That is one reason why key messages are such good building blocks for communications. They present our key points concisely and up front, followed by the proof points and other information necessary to support them.

The final iteration of the trim and boil example above did not follow a strict inverted pyramid style either. Following is a revised version that does. While still not the best way to craft this message, as much as possible of the original wording has been retained to better illustrate the transition of the first iteration to the last.

In an effort to ensure employee directory information remains accurate, Information Technology will begin sending periodical emails to all employees requesting they check their own information and make corrections if necessary.

After checking their information, the email will ask the recipients to click on, "YES, THIS INFORMATION IS CORRECT," or "NO, THIS INFORMATION IS NOT CORRECT." Selecting the second will open a web page where recipients can edit their information.

This online phone number lookup system relies on employees to keep this information up to date, but approximately 30% of employee information in the phone directory is missing, inaccurate, or incomplete.

It is one of the most valued functions of the corporate web site and the Information Technology team wishes to ensure it remains so.

Thank You

The first paragraph contains the main message, albeit at a very high level. The second provides additional information that clarifies the first. The last two provide background information, which is nice to have and may provide additional information as to why, but is not essential to all readers. The recipient could stop reading after any of these paragraphs.

The inverted pyramid structure is not always the preferred approach, but at the very least we should make sure not to bury the lede. Keep the most important information towards the top.

Use pictures, graphs, bulleted lists, headers, etc.

If one picture is worth a thousand words, than it stands that pictures may be a key to achieving more concise communications. You should look for ways to replace long narratives with visual elements. Graphics will be discussed in more detail in Chapter 12.

Practice Makes Concision

The process of trimming and boiling and using the inverted pyramid is easy, but practice is necessary for this to become habitual. However, for those who like problem solving, this may be an enjoyable challenge.

Take a short document, email, or other item you have written and edit it, trying to reduce its length by half. Once you have achieved that, see if you can make it "half again as long." While you do this, make sure you order information from most important to least. Then share your attempts with a trusted source, preferably a non-technical person, and ask them to summarize what they read, to ensure the desired points are still getting across.

When you feel you have the knack for this, edit all your key messages to make them as concise as possible. This not only improves your key messages, but gives you additional and relevant practice. In addition, concise key messages are even more preferable when you need to deliver them verbally.

Use the same process with most of your writing going forward. I say most, because one can get a little carried away. Yes, there are times when we need to be ruthless in our quest to be more

Redundancy, Redundancy, Redundancy

Saying the same thing repeatedly, or with minor variations, is one of the key contributors to verbosity, but it too has its place. Often audiences need to hear a message several times before they will retain it. The key is to do it purposefully and sparingly. The adage, tell them what you are going to tell them, tell them, and then tell them what you told them, is often sound advice.

concise, but in most cases we just need to be careful … moderate … considerate. Editing text is like preparing a steak for grilling: excess fat should be removed, but if we go too far, we will lose much of the flavor.

This process also takes more time than you might have in certain situations. As French mathematician Blaise Pascal once wrote, "I have made this letter longer than usual, only because I have not had the time to make it shorter." With practice, you can communicate more concisely with relative ease and speed. Continue this process until you feel – and your sources concur – that you could not edit the documents any more without jeopardizing the integrity of the content. From then on, continually take stock of your communications to assure they are no longer than necessary.

Another practice that may help is the use of Twitter – or something like it – that absolutely restricts the user to short communications (140 characters in Twitter's case).

Force similar restrictions on yourself. Set limits for the number of words in an email, the number of pages in a report, the number of slides in a presentation (and number of words on a slide), etc. As everyone's situation is different, it is impossible to provide a single set of recommendations for these. Instead, you will need to determine what limits makes sense for you, or better yet, have someone help you set these. Note, these should be thought of as outside limits and not a license to use the full amount; we should always strive for as concise a message as is practical.

Meetings

The solution to most meeting problems is simple: some structure and discipline. As a regular practice, meetings should include certain basic elements:

- Meeting objective(s).
- Agenda that is distributed to all invitees before the meeting.
- Established leader or facilitator who will keep discussions on track.
- Note taker (including attendance and late arrivals).
- Review of decisions made at the end of the meeting.
- List of action items, who is responsible and by when, and any other relevant specifications.
- Distribution of notes and assignments after the meeting.

Those organizing a meeting of any significant length, should include all of these at a minimum. And those invited to such a meeting, should request – and if possible, demand – that these be part of it. Likely there will be resistance, but if so, ask those objecting to consider the costs of the meeting. Just as the widely distributed wordy emails translate into significant dollars wasted, so do meetings. Imagine the sum of the average hourly compensation of the members in a meeting. The cumulative hourly cost of a meeting can be sobering and can help focus attention on the obligation to use that time wisely. It can also help resolve a common problem: late arrivals. Time consumed waiting for the arrival of key individuals serves no productive purposes, other than possibly allowing a little time to build rapport among those members who have arrived. Honor other people's time and require they honor yours.

Short meetings do not require such formality, but caution must be exercised or they will evolve into long meetings. One trick to prevent this is to require any meeting lacking the listed requirements above, to be standing only. Standing is a great way to keep people concise and on track. Even these short meetings should include a review of decisions and assignments at the end of the meeting.

How to:
Communicate More with Less

1. **Narrow the scope of any communications to no more than three key points.**

   - ☐ Write a very brief statement for each (writing, as opposed to just thinking them, forces us to commit to specific points, which in turn, fosters clarity).

   - ☐ Prepare supporting points for each.
     - ✓ Either draw from the key messages created in the previous chapter or develop new ones.

   - ☐ Stick to these points when delivering.
     - ✓ Your audience may steer you in a different direction, and as a good listener you should be responsive, but always steer the discussion back to your remaining points.

2. **Use the Inverted Pyramid structure for most messaging.**

   - ☐ Organize your material in descending order of importance.
     - ✓ In the first few sentences, the basics of who, what, when, how, and possibly why should be answered.
     - ✓ The following content can be used to elaborate on the opening sentences, with content listed in order of decreasing importance.
     - ✓ The end of the message can be reserved for the background information, which may be of interest but is nonessential.

3. **Trim and boil your writings.**

   - ☐ Read through your draft and remove text that is nonessential. Consider:
     - ✓ Do you **really** need to say this? For example, review the opening remarks in the example used earlier: *"We have had many requests for online phone number lookup capability over the last couple of years. To meet this request, we have continually improved the online phone*

book on the corporate Intranet site. With up-to-date information, it has become an increasingly valuable tool for people and is one of the most popular features on the corporate site."

- ✓ Have you said it already somewhere else in your text and if not, could you?

☐ Read through the remaining text to see if rewording would allow you to communicate the same thing with fewer words.

- ✓ Use active rather than passive voice.
  - o *What is needed is* becomes *We need.*
- ✓ Avoid unnecessarily dramatic wording.
  - o *Now is the time for all good men to come to the aid of their country* becomes *the country needs good men to act now* or even *help the country now.*
- ✓ Avoid cliché and wordy phrases.
  - o *At this point in time* should be just *at this time.*
  - o *That being said,* could be *however.*
- ✓ Look for opportunities to replace two or three small sentences with one compound sentence.

☐ Do not go too far.

- ✓ Do not cut out so much that you omit essential information.

- ✓ If you boil too much, your writing may become drab and sterile.

- ✓ Combining too many sentences into one compound sentence may lead to confusion.

☐ Aim for clear, concise yet still palatable communications.

☐ Practice.

- ✓ Trim and boil recent writings to get the hang of it.
- ✓ Challenge yourself to see how far you can go and still retain a strong, effective message.
- ✓ Use this technique in future writings.

4. **When creating or editing documents, consider replacing long narratives with visuals, tables, etc.**

   ☐ A picture or graphic, possibly accompanied by a brief caption or explanation, may communicate your message better.

   ☐ Tables, bulleted lists, or other formatting alternatives can also present information more concisely than a straight narrative.

   ☐ Keep in mind that beyond just making messaging more concise, these tools can make communications more clear and memorable.

5. **Do not let meetings waste time.**

   ☐ For any meeting you run (or can be an influence in running), require:
   - ✓ Meeting objective(s).
   - ✓ Agenda that is distributed to all invitees before the meeting.
   - ✓ Established leader or facilitator who will keep discussions on track.
   - ✓ Note taker (including attendance and late arrivals).
   - ✓ Review of decisions made at the end of the meeting.
   - ✓ List of action items, who is responsible and when, and any other relevant specifications.
   - ✓ Distribution of notes and assignments after the meeting.

   ☐ For short or impromptu meetings:
   - ✓ Require all attendees to stand.
   - ✓ You can skip most of the items required for the sit-down meeting, but still review decisions and assignments at the end.

Summary – Chapter 10
Less is More

There is an outdated sentiment that the more information we share, the better. However, the digital age has delivered technology that reduces traditional communication hurdles, unleashing a flood of information far beyond our ability to consume. The result is less effective communication.

Whether a result of the challenge of concisely and accurately conveying complex concepts, or simply because of professional norms, those in STEM fields have a reputation for being verbose. As a result, some technical professionals find that they are ignored, tuned out, or avoided.

We can become much more concise by keeping the scope of our communications narrow (three or less key points), prioritizing information (using inverted pyramid format), utilizing editing techniques to convey the key points as efficiently as possible (trimming and boiling), and leveraging key messages when communicating verbally. Likewise, good meeting practices will save time and produce better results. Less is more.

Monitor, Assess, and Log ...

- When the scope of communication was too large.

- When written communications could have been briefer.

- When written communications were poorly organized, i.e., burying the lede.

- When you said more than you needed to in conversations or presentations.

- When you violated good meeting practices.

You Will Know You Are Overcoming This When ...

- You get a sense that others are consuming your communications in full.

- When participants do not seem bored, preoccupied or do not interrupt you in your presentations.

- Others' eyes do not glass over in conversations.

- Others compliment you on how well you run your meetings.

- It is apparent that meetings are more productive.

– Chapter 11 –

It's Not the Journey, It's the Destination

Never confuse motion with action.
—Benjamin Franklin

Foible: Process Bias

Precept: Keep focused on the desired result

"You eat too much junk!" says Janice Pasetti to her overweight teenage daughter, Edda.

"So, you smoke!" Edda retorts.

Janice grinds her cigarette into an ashtray, "There, I quit!"

Edda responds by throwing her Twinkie into the trash, "There, I'm skinny!"

On more than one occasion, this scene from the 1990's television sitcom *Grand* flashed into my head while listening to clients express their exasperation over failed communication efforts. They show me their detailed and beautifully formatted communication plans, pointing to the checked-off tasks saying, "See, I've communicated!"

Those affected by this foible are typically at their best when working with things rather than people. They are more likely to focus on completing communication "deliverables," rather than on achieving objectives. They mistake *communication, the process* with *communication, the objective* and unfortunately all too often set themselves and their audiences on confrontational paths.

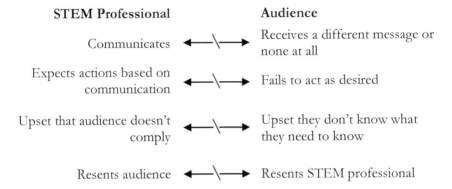

STEM Professional		Audience
Communicates		Receives a different message or none at all
Expects actions based on communication		Fails to act as desired
Upset that audience doesn't comply		Upset they don't know what they need to know
Resents audience		Resents STEM professional

Process's Place

Of course, good processes and disciplined execution are valuable, even essential in many technical fields, so I am not arguing against them. I am merely suggesting that they be put into the proper context.

Processes are created to assist us to achieve an end, and it is that end that must reign supreme in our thoughts and actions. As obvious as that appears, it is easy for us to lose sight of that among the demands of our everyday struggles. What starts as legitimate good intentions and a means for delivering predictable and reliable results can evolve into rigidity.

This issue seems to be in the comedic crosshairs of the movie *Office Space*, in the form of the much-derided *TPS reports*. While the purpose of these reports is never explained, they are portrayed as useless timewasters, yet something upon which management is endlessly fixated. As a plot element, they symbolize all the processes that, while possibly useful at some time in the past, become the ends in themselves.

Processes must remain subordinate to the objectives. If for some reason a given process does not contribute towards an effective achievement of a goal, it must be changed. Likewise, if the goal changes, so might the process need to be.

To facilitate a better understanding of this foible, it may help if I share what I have found to be its three most relevant contributing characteristics as it relates to communication and collaboration.

1. Flawed communication instincts
2. Stubborn adherence to flawed instincts
3. Perfunctory implementation

1. Flawed Communication Instincts

Despite its many manifestations and nuances, much of the Brainiac Paradox can be generalized as a tendency for flawed communication instincts, at least as they relate to diverse audiences. Thus baring some type of external guidance, no matter how much time and effort affected individuals devote to communication activities, the results are likely flawed: junk in, junk out.

2. Stubborn Adherence to Flawed Instincts

Considering the inordinate evidence for the existence of this issue, it is surprising how stubbornly some cling to those erroneous instincts. I cannot tell you how many times someone has asked for my assistance after suffering ongoing communication problems – even prefacing the request with a statement like, "communication is not one of my strengths"– only to find out later that they were already set on what they wanted to do. At first, they would cooperate as I assessed the situation. But when I gave them my recommendations they would resist, saying that they still wanted to do the [communication tool du jour]." If their desired solution was inappropriate, I would explain why, to which they would respond, "We still want to do the …."

I call this the *newsletter syndrome* because historically the kneejerk solution to any organizational communication problem has been to create a newsletter. It is not that newsletters are inherently bad or inappropriate; it is just that they are not the answer to everything.

This phenomenon is the counterpart to the business executive who specifies a certain technology, vendor, etc. (of which they know little) because, "I read this article," "saw this advertisement," or "talked to this guy on the plane."

It is important to note that the newsletter syndrome not only leads to ineffectiveness but can also be outright harmful. It is like the person who calls his doctor to say he is sick and asks the doctor to send a prescription for antibiotics to the local pharmacy. The doctor explains that antibiotics are only effective for certain ailments, and insists the person come in to be examined first. Some patients, however, persist until the doctor relents and provides them the antibiotics anyway.

This is less likely to happen nowadays, though, as the health industry has come to realize that such casual practices with antibiotics are not benign. The overuse of antibiotics has resulted in resistant strains of certain bacteria, which in turn is costing many lives and threatens ever-more dangerous health problems in the future.

The same type of *resistance* may develop among audiences when they face excessive and inappropriate communication. Eventually the audiences are conditioned to disregard the offending source, filtering out the important as well as the trivial. And once that happens, the perception can be difficult to reverse.

A secondary problem with both is that while the subject is using the antibiotics, or distributing the newsletter, they are forestalling the actions that would actually help them, potentially putting themselves at the risk of immediate harm.

Naturally, there will be times when the patient may just be right. They will come in for an examination as requested and it will be determined that antibiotics were indeed the proper course of treatment. The same is true for those who insist on certain communication approaches … or business executives who want to prescribe certain technologies. Maybe a newsletter is the most appropriate approach, but it is careless and risky to proceed without proper evaluation.

3. Perfunctory Implementation

Whatever problems are created by the previous issues are exacerbated by perfunctory implementation. It is similar to making an apple pie, but accidentally using a mock apple pie recipe and then failing to notice there are no apples among the ingredients. Erroneous communication plans are to be expected; but it is the unchecked follow-through that cements the problem.

What's more, the very traits that are beneficial in many technical fields (e.g., precision, discipline, and rigor) may predispose some to this error. They are conditioned to operate on the assumption that if they follow certain steps faithfully, they will consistently achieve certain results (predictable results are the building blocks of science, technology, and math). The process of communication, on the other hand, is notoriously imprecise. One cannot count on a given communication being received a certain way. Recall the Basic Communication Model from page 127:

A ▸ Thought ▸ Encode ▸ Transmit ▸ Decode ▸ Thought ◂ B

Imbedded in each of those few steps are countless potential failure points. What goes in is rarely exactly what comes out. This eventuality is the basis of a children's game, *Telephone*. For those who are unfamiliar with the game, it starts with a brief story, joke, or description that is whispered into the ear of a child. That child, in turn, whispers it into the ear of the next child, and so on through a series of children assembled in a line or circle. Along the way, some children will tell the story incorrectly, others will hear it incorrectly, and still others will interpret it incorrectly. When the last child hears it, they repeat it aloud for everyone's enjoyment for invariably the communication has morphed in amusing ways.

The problems illustrated by this game only increase in adulthood as matters of context, biases, and motives further muddy the communication process. The only precise predictable result in human communications is that results cannot be predicted precisely.

I am not suggesting that communication planning is pointless. Just the opposite. "By failing to prepare, you are preparing to fail," said Benjamin Franklin. Though the uncertainties of communication cannot be eliminated, they can be reduced significantly through the process of careful communication planning.

Unfortunately, very few people plan their communications and even fewer plan them effectively. Sure, they may do so to the extent they answer the following questions:

1. What do I need to communicate?
2. Whom do I need to communicate it to?
3. How should I communicate it?
4. When should I communicate it?

Recall, though, the definition of effective communication used within this book: *the ability to influence others' perceptions and behaviors constructively.* Answering the above questions does little to ensure a desired result (as discussed in Chapter 8, these are communicator-oriented rather than audience-oriented) nor does it help minimize communication failure points along the way.

Note that when I said, "Very few people truly plan their communications," I was referring to everyone, not just those in technical professions. The sad truth is very few people know how to conduct effective communication planning. Not even all *professional communicators* know how to do effective communication planning and among those who do, not all practice it. This is the result of an additional paradox: those who most need effective communication planning processes and tools do not know them, and those who know them are in the least need of them. The latter is based on the assumption that the majority of those who pursue communications as a career have natural associated talents. They inherently know the right communication approach, just as others might know the right approach to solving a difficult equation. They also understand the inherent limitations of communication planning and thus are likely to be more flexible and responsive during the implementation.

Remedies:
Process Bias

An essential step to becoming an effective communicator – one who consistently achieves desired outcomes – is embracing the perspective of communication as a result, not a task; a destination, not a journey. It takes *results-oriented communication*. This entails conducting the planning necessary to identify the tools, strategies, and tactics that are most likely to deliver desired results and then monitoring, adjusting, and persisting until the results are achieved. A good communication planning process helps you:

- Ensure you are targeting the right perceptions and behaviors.
- Better understand your audiences.
- Avoid wasteful and possibly even detrimental activities.
- Identify opportunities for communication synergies.
- Organize your communication activities.
- Execute effectively.
- Follow-through until your goal is achieved.

I have developed a tool that can help you develop good results-oriented communication plans. It is concise and easy to use and can be scaled to support any communication need, from a single email to a large-scale project implementation.

The bad news is that in order to make full use of this tool, it is probably necessary for you to first understand and practice a more formal communication process. Many may be tempted to skip this, as only a few are likely to be involved in the type of work that requires formal communication plan creation (i.e., large projects dealing with complex topics, multiple audiences and over an extended period of time). But even if this is true for you, there are still valuable reasons for learning and practicing it. Doing so fosters the development of certain attitudes, processes, and sensitivities that are important to small scale communication planning or even on-the-fly interactions.

Formal Communication Planning
Following is an outline of a formal communication process. Some communication professionals may use a different processes (and, as

mentioned, some none at all), but this one provides a good framework for learning to create effective communication plans.

Formal Communication Plan Creation Process

1. Define problem
2. Define goal
3. Identify target and auxiliary audiences
4. Determine a strategy for each audience
5. Determine the objectives necessary to successfully fulfill the audience strategy
6. Determine which tasks are necessary to achieve those objectives
7. Execute
8. Assess and recalibrate throughout execution
9. Persist until goal is achieved

1. Define Problem

Yogi Berra said, "If you don't know where you are going, you might wind up someplace else." While the goal (audience perception or behavior) drives the process in results-oriented communication, it is important to make sure you have the right goal, especially if this is an effort you expect will require significant time and resources. As such, it is worth investing a little effort into analyzing the problem you are trying to resolve, or the opportunity you are trying to seize. You cannot always assume that the obvious item is the correct one. In manufacturing, for example, a quality problem might be attributed to a piece of machinery. But by using the 5 WHYS technique, engineers may trace it back to a relatively

Communication Planning Terms

As the terms goals, objectives, strategies and tactics are often used differently by different people, following is their intended meaning as used in this book.

Goal: end-result desired.

Objective: one or more specific achievements that contributes to attainment of the overall goal. Objectives are usually quantifiable while goals need not be.

Strategy: a plan of action that results in an outcome greater than the sum of the individual tactics.

Tactic: a discrete action that contributes to attainment of objectives.

obscure cause (e.g., the machine problem was caused by a part failure; why the part failure? because of a lubricant problem; why the lubrication problem? because of a change in vendor who supplied the lubricant? and so on). In *Defining the Problem*, on page 191, there is an example of how this may work within a communication plan.

---

5 WHYS
Technique used to determine a root cause. Starts with asking why in regards to a problem, then asking why to the answer. This is repeated up to five times, or until the root cause of the problem is determined.

After you create your problem statement, verify; ask yourself if this is THE item you are trying to tackle. The act of asking yourself questions is a quick and relatively effective way to test validity. While we may unconsciously play a game of denial with ourselves – ignoring what is difficult or unpleasant – it is difficult to consciously lie to ourselves. If necessary, use the 5 Why technique. Likewise, writing it down forces us to commit to something specific.

2. Define Goal
With the problem statement in hand, the goal is usually fairly self-evident. Nevertheless, care should be taken that the goal be stated and understood with great clarity: what behavior or perception are you seeking. By the very nature of results-oriented communication, this will be the constant reference point for all subsequent activities. Any ambiguity here is likely to be magnified down the road.

3. Determine Which Audiences Need to Be Influenced
Inherent in your goal is one or more audiences. However, depending on the circumstances there may be many audiences that must be influenced by your communication. In fact, sometimes the only way to influence your key audience is by influencing another audience, who in turn, influences your key audience.

For example, the goal of the communication plan in one case was the approval of a new corporate software system. The decision was to be made by a committee of corporate division heads. Obviously they were a key audience, but upon further investigation, we found that these division heads looked to certain "power users" within their organizations for opinions about system changes. As a result, it was upon these power users that we focused much of our communications activities.

Importantly, in addition to the primary and secondary audiences you specifically target for action, also carefully consider those you need to include for information. Failing to do this can create significant problems, either real (such as resource or timing conflicts) or perceived (people upset they were not kept in the loop).

4. Determine a Strategy for Each Audience

A good audience strategy comes from working through all the factors at hand to find the most efficient and effective approach for achieving what is desired from that audience.

Many years ago, I worked for an American Red Cross Blood Services region. Because of declining work-place donations, my team and I were given a goal of increasing the number of donors scheduling appointments at regional donor centers. To reach these donors we had traditionally used public service advertisements and special promotions, and the first thought was just to do more of these.

However, after considering some evolving factors, we came up with a new, inexpensive and effective strategy. The evolving factor was the explosion of cell-phone ownership (early 1990s). There were dozens of Red Cross vehicles on the road each day in the metropolitan area. With the large red crosses on white vehicles, they were very noticeable. Our strategy was to add stickers – in particular at windshield level – on the back of the truck, which said, "To donate blood, call 1-800-GIVE-LIFE." Our public service announcements and promotions had already created the awareness of the need to donate. Now, commuters stuck behind those trucks in rush-hour traffic were susceptible to impulse, and would use their cell phones to make appointments. We experienced an almost immediate 15% increase in donations even as similar Red Cross Blood Services regions were experiencing declines at their donor centers.

As you determine strategies for specific audiences, also keep in mind your other key audiences. You may indeed need a specific strategy for each audience, but sometimes one less-than-perfect strategy might serve more than one audience. The ability to consolidate activities is desirable – they require less effort for both you and your audiences – but must be balanced against any potential loss in effectiveness suffered from skipping the optimized strategies for individual audiences.

5. Determine the Necessary Objectives to Successfully Fulfill That Strategy

As you work through the various steps, determine which objectives are necessary for you to achieve your overall goal. In the system software implementation example provided above, the objective for the division heads was to get support from five of the six (we figured a single opponent would probably not hold out against the other five members). The power users audience varied by division, but our overall objective for them was to get enough support to influence the five division heads.

6. Determine Which Tasks Are Necessary

In this step you define which specific tasks must be completed to support the preceding goals, strategies and objectives, when they need to be completed, and – if more than one person is involved with its execution – who is responsible for what tasks as well as other details necessary to support a collaborative effort (e.g., who approves communication pieces).

7. Execute

You've planned your work, now work your plan.

8. Assess and Recalibrate Throughout Execution

Retired Four-Star General and former U.S. Secretary of State, Colin Powell said, "No battle plan survives contact with the enemy," and the same is true of communication plans.

In any extended communication activity, you can expect to face challenges and changes along the way and if you do not adjust, your odds of success are greatly diminished. This lack of assessment and adjustment is the primary reason so many of those clients (mentioned at the beginning of the chapter) were frustrated that their beautifully designed and formatted plans did not work.

Imagine navigating in a small sailboat on a rough sea at night and your goal is a harbor marked by a lighthouse in the distance. To help guide you, you have a compass and a chart, which shows the location of various hazards. You can use these tools to plan your approach, but you cannot solely rely on the resulting plans. The winds can shift, the tides or currents can pull you off course in unpredictable ways, or uncharted hazards may come into view as you proceed. The same is true for communication. The environment is dynamic and you need to regularly assess your progress and course-correct as necessary. The assessment activity does not have to be elaborate. It may just be a matter of paying attention to your audience's reactions or asking a couple questions of representative audience members.

9. Persist until Goal is Achieved

Another Yogi Berra'ism is, "It ain't over till it's over," which is, in fact, quite profound. When involved in long-term communication initiatives, it is easy to become fatigued and lose focus or energy. In such cases it can be tempting to declare "good enough" and move on.

While it is okay to change your measure of achievement, it must be a conscious decision based on an honest assessment, and not one driven by weariness, boredom or neglect.

However, when a goal should not be compromised, stick with it. Persevere.

Non-Linear Communication Planning

The formal process offered is based on a logical series of steps, but sometimes when conducting communication planning, the shortest distance between two points is not a straight line, and it may be better to change the order of various steps. For example, this process calls for identifying the audience before developing the strategy, which makes logical sense. However, there can be situations when it makes sense to create a strategy before a specific audience is identified.

As an illustration, consider a candidate running for office. Her goal is to win election to the office. In this hypothetical case, let's make the playing field equal for her and her opponent: they are similar in experience, funds raised, and overall likeability, and the constituent voters are evenly split among conservatives, liberals, and independents. Based on this scenario, we would expect the candidates' stands on various issues to be a key determinant of the election outcome. Her stand on any given issue will gain her votes among some and lose some among others. Likewise, some issues will greatly energize supporters (and opponents), while others less so.

For her to achieve the desired perception (a majority of voters prefer her) and behavior (supporters turn out to vote), she needs to correctly calculate which issues will maximize her votes. Only after she has done that can she identify what audiences she must target.

As a different example, the communication channel/medium may be the determinant variable. In the early days of social media, savvy communicators recognized the growing influence and potential of these sites. They started with the communication channel and then figured out how they could exploit it.

Brainiac Paradox Communication Planning Method

With study and practice, the formal communication process should significantly improve your track record for achieving desired perceptions and behaviors. The reality, though, is that only the most disciplined individuals will use it for anything less than high-stakes or large-scale initiatives. It just seems like too much trouble for day-to-day communication planning needs.

Communication Planning Tool

Communication Goal:

Audiences/ Stakeholders	As Is Perceptions/ Behaviors	Desired Perceptions/ Behaviors	Issues/Potential Barriers	Communication Strategy	Key Messages	Communication Channels	Timing
-	-	-	-	-	-	-	-
-	-	-	-	-	-	-	-
-	-	-	-	-	-	-	-
-	-	-	-	-	-	-	-
-	-	-	-	-	-	-	-
-	-	-	-	-	-	-	-
-	-	-	-	-	-	-	-

That, in part, is why I developed a communication-planning tool, which is powerful, yet quick and easy to use. While the formal process uses a linear, narrative approach to drive communication planning, this one uses a grid (worksheet) format and short abbreviated entries. Detailed instructions for how to use it are provided on page 318, but in short, it works by organizing different audience information into horizontal rows, and collecting communication factors for each audience according to column headings. The advantages of this approach will become clear when you begin to use it. As information is added to the various cells, it is possible to see how they affect previously-entered information, and adjustments can be made accordingly. It is almost like a Sudoku puzzle, where some items are provided, and then others must be determined, and possibly changed, until everything fits. Not only does it drive optimized communication for each audience, but also it allows the analysis of similarities and overlaps along vertical columns, which can drive optimization of the overall communication plans.

For example, one column captures the communication channel preferences/plans for each audience (face-to-face, email, pull system, etc.). If there are several audiences that are to receive the same messages, and there is a common channel from among their top three preferences, then you may want to consolidate communication: it can be better to have one *very good* approach than to have many *perfect* approaches. The magic will come when you arrange the various communication fixed elements and variables in a manner that leads to the best outcome with the least amount of effort or tradeoffs.

In addition, it is extremely scalable. You can use it to sketch out the thought process for the creation of a single presentation or drive the communication planning process for a massive project. I use it all the time and I am constantly amazed how it helps. Even when I believe I know what to do off the top of my head, I find that when I go through the process and consider each element requested in the tool, I discover overlooked elements, important relationships between elements, or more effective ways to execute the communications.

It is hard to appreciate the many virtues of this tool until it has been used. Try it out. Practice it. Even modify it according to your specific circumstances if need be.

Putting It to Work
The results-oriented communication approach is malleable to many needs. Following is an example of how this approach was scaled for a small, but crucial, initiative.

> **Situation:** The email system at a large organization was scheduled to be down for maintenance for a few hours over the weekend. From experience the email team anticipated complaints from one or more angry executives who would be travelling overseas at the time and whose, "one chance to catch up on email" would be prevented by the action. Even though the email team always sent out notices about upcoming service outages, that did not matter to these executives: "IT screwed up" was what they perceived and remembered. I was asked what I could do to help them avoid this problem in the future.

Defining the Problem
Problem Statement: Initially it may have been, "System outages may affect and anger business executive." But was that *the* problem? No, the problem was that executives were ignoring warnings and holding the IT team responsible. New problem statement: "Executives are ignoring system outage warnings." But again, was that *the* problem. We were getting there, but not quite. Remember, *If they haven't heard it, I haven't said it.* The real problem was that something about the executives or the way the team communicated with them resulted in them ignoring or disregarding the communications. Thus, "The current system outage reporting approach is ineffective with executives."

Defining Goals and Objectives
The goal, of course, was to perform such maintenance at the allotted time without raising the ire of any of the executives. And, if we had stuck with the *Executives are ignoring system outage warnings* problem statement, the objectives would have been to *get executives to pay attention to system outage notices.* That would have driven solutions like, send more messages, or send them sooner, or even – God forbid – embed some

flashing red text that says, "Warning – system outage this weekend." But the ultimate problem statement led to a different objective: *Devise a system-outage notice approach that will ensure executives are aware of and plan around system outages.* That, in turn, drove a different approach to finding the solution.

Defining and Assessing Key Audiences

With our audience and objective identified, we needed to determine the scope of the communication by doing the as-is and to-be analysis. As-is: executives were unaware of the upcoming outage. To-be: not only awareness (perception), but we wanted them to plan around the outage (behavior).

Next we considered what issues or barriers would impair the ability to achieve the objective. The main issue was that emails were used to alert the organization about planned system downtimes, but they were not effective with these executives: first, they already received too many emails each day to handle adequately; and second, they had been conditioned to ignore emails from IT because they were too numerous and usually unimportant (at least to them). Finally, even if they did read the email, the message required the executives to plan ahead in order to avoid the outage, but many relegated management of their calendars to their executive assistants.

Solution

The idea for the solution arose from the last barrier in the previous item. The executive assistants were a group these executives did not ignore. And not only did they manage the calendars of the executives, but they were well versed on how their respective executive preferred to receive information. If we could work through the assistants, we could likely achieve our goal.

Strategy Development

All we needed to do was send the communication to the executive assistants, and ask that they make sure their boss would get it. However, remember the objective (the beacon of light that guides us): *Devise a system outage notice approach that will **ensure** executives are aware of and plan around system outages.* Therefore, we called several and explained the situation and our objective. They were more than willing to help – a frustrated executive was an unhappy boss to them. They gave us additional ideas on how this approach could be implemented.

Messages and Channels

In this case, the channel (executive assistants) was the strategy and the message was a short, to-the-point version of what had been sent before earlier system outages.

Assessing and Adjusting

This is one of those cases where no news was good news. If the weekend passed and there were no frenzied calls or complaints, we would be tempted to declare victory. All the same, we followed up with the executive assistances and asked how it went, and if there were any additional insights. Some had suggestions and we incorporated them and then institutionalized the process for future similar communications.

This example demonstrates that if you follow the general process and ask yourself the right questions, eventually a solution will come into focus. In this case the right question was, "If they are ignoring IT, to whom do they listen?" It was a simple and very effective solution, and the whole thing – working through the communication-planning tool, contacting a few executive assistants, executing the plan and following up probably took less than a total of 30 minutes.

How to:
Be a Results-Oriented Communicator

1. **Practice using the formal communication planning process.**

   ☐ Indentify some perceptual or behavioral goals you could use to practice this process.

   ✓ Ideally this would be a more elaborate communication project entailing multiple audiences, communication vehicles, and an extended time-period.

   ✓ If nothing currently fits the bill, think about something you may want to achieve in the future, or possibly something you attempted to achieve in the past. You will not be able to practice the actual execution, but this will allow you do most of the other steps.

   ☐ Create a written plan based on the steps starting on page 185.

   ☐ Execute your plan (for those who can).

2. **Practice using the Brainiac Paradox communication planning process.**

   ☐ Identify some small-scale perceptual or behavioral goals. Goals that relate to a:

   ✓ Limited audience, possibly only one person.

   ✓ Limited time-frame (immediate or near term).

   ☐ Goal examples include:

   ✓ Achieving a particular team decision after a presentation.

   ✓ Receiving a positive evaluation after a one-on-one meeting.

   ✓ Receiving a particular response to an email.

   ☐ Use communication-planning steps 1-7 on page 318 for each goal.

   ☐ Stay focused on your goal and adjust your activities as necessary.

   ☐ Remember to use whenever success is essential and/or the stakes are high.

Summary – Chapter 11
It's Not the Journey, It's the Destination

Logical and linear thinkers are inclined to be process-oriented communicators. Communications are seen as a series of steps that, when completed, will deliver the desired results. But actual communication programs often do not transpire as expected and any communication activity that does not account for that will be in doubt.

To compound the issue, rather than conduct analysis to determine which communication tool and channel would likely work best based on a given set of circumstances, there is a tendency to use the same old cliché set of communications tools (e.g., newsletters) or to hop on the bandwagon of more trendy tools (e.g., the latest social media app).

To become effective communicators, we need to become results-oriented communicators, which requires three basic elements:

- A planning methodology that drives the highest likelihood of success in attaining the desired perception or behavior.

- A willingness to monitor audiences and adjust plans along the way.

- A commitment to persist until the desired outcomes are achieved.

The communication tools provided in this book support all of these.

Monitor, Assess, and Log …

- When you undertake important communications, whether large or small, without proper planning.

- When you catch yourself focusing only on the execution instead of the desired result.

- Whether you are unable to achieve the desired perception or behavior among your audiences.

You Will Know You Are Overcoming This When …

- You observe a noticeable improvement in your ability to achieve what you want from others.

- You find that your communication efforts require less time.

- You sense that the goal of this book – mitigating the foibles that stand in the way of you making your full contribution – is coming into sight.

– Chapter 12 –

Substance AND Style

Well done is better than well said.
– Benjamin Franklin

Foible: Aesthetics (inappropriate)

Precept: Present an effective user interface

By the early 1990s, the race for dominance in the personal computer market had narrowed to two primary platforms: IBM compatibles using Microsoft's operating system (a.k.a. PCs) and Apple Computer and its proprietary operating system. Before too long, it appeared, there would be only one.

History has repeatedly demonstrated that when there is media to be shared and there are incompatible systems, the market prunes competitors until there is a single standard. Years earlier, the Beta Video Tape format lost out to VHS, and years later, HD-DVD would lose out to Blu-Ray. In the personal computer showdown, IBM and Microsoft had huge advantages. PCs were the standard of the business world and had a much larger share of the personal computer market. PCs were also less expensive and had more software and hardware options.

Yet Apple did not succumb. In fact, after teetering at the edge for a time, it came back to gain significant market share, and in 2011 it overtook HP to be the single largest individual producer of personal computing devices (if tablet and smart phones are included in the count). That same year it was designated the top global brand by Millward Brown, who conducts the annual BrandZ rankings. Finally, since 2012, it has been alternating places with Exxon for the designation of world's most valuable company.

So what explains this remarkable turnaround? Was it the discovery of some game-changing technology? Not really. While Apple has established itself as an innovation leader, most of the products introduced during this whirlwind of growth were variations of existing products and technologies – others' MP3 players predated the iPod, others' smartphones predated the iPhone, and still others' tablets predated the iPad. Was it enormous spending on marketing? No, in 2009, Apple only spent half of what Microsoft alone did on advertising, and far more was spent by the competing hardware manufactures that used Microsoft's operating system. Was it a robust distribution channel that outflanked the competition? No, if anything Apple products are less convenient to purchase than most of its competitors.

A clear distinguishing factor, and the thing I believe explains the success, is aesthetics. By this, I do not just mean the physical aesthetics of the products themselves – for which they are the undisputed leader – but the aesthetics of the overall user experience offered by Apple compared to its competitors. Apple computers have a reputation for being easier to use, more intuitive, and even more stable (the operating system is less susceptible to system crashes and malicious software attacks). Even their customer support is rated superior to the various PC hardware and software vendors. As a whole, Apple products provide a far more aesthetically pleasing user experience and, as a result, the company has developed an almost cult-like following. One hears of PC users switching to Apple computers, but rarely of Apple users switching to PCs, unless required to do so for business reasons, and even then, they do so grudgingly.

Recognizing this disparity and the implications, Microsoft has invested enormous sums to replicate Apple's aesthetics (the operating system is the most important factor affecting the user experience). Despite their resources, though, they have yet to catch up.

I believe a primary reason for this is the contrasting personalities of the two organizations. It could be said that Apple is more a right-brain organization (spatial, holistic, artistic, symbolic, intuitive, creative, and gestalt), while Microsoft is more a left-brain organization (logical, mathematical, linear, detailed, sequential, controlled, and analytical). Indeed, Apples have long been far more popular among right-brain types, such as artists and musicians, while PCs have been far more popular among most technical fields as well as accountants and other left-brain types. Microsoft's inability to close that gap is a result of its design instincts (what makes logical sense to its developers) as opposed to Apple's (what makes intuitive sense to its customers).

Personal User Interface

Each of us presents a user interface – the sum of the experiences we create among those who interact with us – which has an enormous affect on how others respond to us. This user interface is based on not just our direct personal interactions with others, but also indirect interactions in the things we create (e.g., documents, presentations, etc.). Several of the virtues previously covered relate to important aspects of our personal user interface (simplicity, empathy, and concision). Any improvements we can claim in these areas will have already improved our overall user interface, but there are still other attributes that can help or hurt us. How we look and sound, how our communications look, and how difficult it is to find and use the information we share, are also influential factors. Whether we are easy on our audience's eyes, ears, and minds can easily overshadow the content of our messages or the assessment of our work.

Some are naturally lucky in these regards. They are personable, attractive, and they have a knack for creating and presenting material that is appealing to others. They are like nectar to bees. They inherently draw others to themselves. Even if they lack other attributes – maybe they are not the most intelligent, accomplished, and even, dare I say, ethical – they can parlay their relationships for personal and career success. On the other hand, there are others who may be intelligent, accomplished and principled, yet who struggle because their overall "user interface" is not as appealing. It is a victory of style over substance, and those who have worked for any length of time will be familiar with this.

As the concept of aesthetics is somewhat nebulous and ubiquitous (everything has aesthetic characteristics), we will categorize and focus our attention on three elements:

- Visual communication aesthetics – how our communications look.

- Usability aesthetics – how easy it for others to use the information we share.

- Personal aesthetics – how we look and sound.

Visual Aesthetics

Thanks to computers and a proliferation of graphic-related applications, there are many ways to "dress up" basic text and graphics but, like the five-year-old that gets into her mother's makeup, the results can be rather garish in the unskilled hand.

When I think of this foible, I think of Doug, an IT operations manager I worked with several years ago. He was frequently required to distribute organization-wide emails about system upgrades. These required employees to perform certain tasks, or to avoid others. Despite his numerous communications and best efforts, he was frustrated to find that many employees did not comply with his instructions. As a result, he used increasingly-dramatic formatting to draw attention to important points in his emails. Of course, everything seemed important to him so he used the full arsenal of formatting tricks. Emails would contain a multitude of fonts, type sizes, colors, bolding, underlining, and italicizing. He would even format some text to blink. Not only were the results visually overwhelming (likely to invoke a seizure among susceptible viewers), but they did not work; since the reader's eyes were drawn to everything at the same time, they were drawn to nothing in particular. And, beyond just being ineffective, they reflected poorly on him, and indeed his entire department.

For those with whom the Paradox is believed to be related to left-brain dominance, we would expect a struggle in terms of the attributes related to the right-brain, which is generally associated with special aptitudes of space and creativity. Certainly not all will be challenged in this area – recall the engineer who was a gifted caricaturist from page 140 – but some are.

Communication Logistics Aesthetics

Communication channels can be divided into two basic types, push and pull. Push communications are those that you actively distribute (push) to your audience (emails, reports, phone calls), while pull communications are those that you provide access to, but that depend upon others to access them (web sites, libraries, shared folders). While the two share some aesthetic sensibilities, they also present different paradigms. By their very nature, pull communications are potentially more powerful (only those who desire the information will go to the trouble of pulling it). If done well, pull communications can be very effective; if done poorly, they can frustrate and alienate an audience.

I painfully recall a communal network drive, referred to as the T: Drive (I assumed for Team though I never confirmed), at one place I worked. It was established to support a large Enterprise Resource Planning (ERP) development team. At the time, this network drive represented a great advancement in the ease of sharing a massive volume of documents among the 200 plus member team.

However, there was no established organizational structure or usage guidelines and the drive became chaotic. Everyone with access could use it in any way they wished. The drive was a black hole of information. I estimate there were more than 50 primary folders. And most of those had several levels of subfolders.

The confusion and difficulty created by the lack of organizational logic was compounded by poor labeling. While some of the folder names were explanative and intuitive, most were enigmatic, redundant, or outright misleading. The same was true for the file names. Names often only made sense to the person who created them. Moreover, people were not even consistent, so a person creating two similar documents might use very different naming approaches from one day to the next. Hence, even if you did decipher what was meant by one file name, it did not necessarily help you when looking for the next.

Eventually, we cringed whenever we heard, "It's on the T: Drive," in response to a request for information.

Personal Aesthetics

An unfortunate but obvious truth is that our appearance has a great affect on how others perceive us, and more importantly, how others behave with us. Even before we say a word upon meeting someone, they have likely made significant assumptions about us … and we them. For example, Yale University Professor of Psychology Marianne Lafrance conducted research in which participants were shown an above-the-shoulders picture of a stranger and asked how they would describe them. All participants saw the same exact picture, with the exception that five different hair styles where digitally edited in. The participants had radically different views about the person's intelligence, wealth, personality, etc., all based on the version of hairstyle they saw. Now extend that to the clothes we wear, our eyeglasses, our hygiene, etc. How many of our relations are handicapped at the outset?

Philosophically, this is a challenging topic. We know it is a moral failing to judge someone by his or her appearance, but it is almost impossible to avoid completely. It is instinctive: a hardwired survival skill. Ages ago, when faced with new circumstances, it was sometimes necessary to react first, and think second. Thinking first could consume the crucial milliseconds that would make the difference between life and death. This is where the spindle cells mentioned in Chapter 2 are believed to be important, providing a shortcut between parts of the brain that facilitate this type of reactive head start. Today this functionality appears to have been adopted for social expediency, giving us a head start on who we like, respect, are attracted to, and who we should feel the opposite towards. Consciously we may think one way, but we remain influenced by unconscious impulses.

Virtually all are burdened by this trait. If you do not believe so, consider Hedy Lamarr. For those unfamiliar with her, she was one of the most glamorous stars of the *Golden Age* of motion pictures. In fact, it was she, not Betty Grable, who was voted by GIs as the most popular pinup girl during World War II.

She is also credited with U.S. Patent 2292387, "Secret Communication System," which she devised at the onset of World War II. Its purpose was to prevent enemies from jamming Allied radio-guided torpedoes. It is the basis for today's Frequency-Hopping Spread-Spectrum Radio

Hedy Lamarr

Transmission technology – crucial to cell phone operations. That feat seems incongruous with her appearance, does is not? Obviously the military technicians assigned to consider the submission did not take her seriously. They rejected it and told her she could do more for the war effort by helping to sell war bonds. Now consider the accompanying picture of Golda Meir. Would Lamarr have faced the same fate if she looked like

Meir? It is impossible to know, but she likely would have had a better chance.

A different example of this was when my son attended an economics class of a small liberal arts college he was considering attending. About 10 minutes into the class, a very large student, who my son correctly guessed was a

Golda Meir

"Not being beautiful was the true blessing …. Not being beautiful forced me to develop my inner resources. The pretty girl has a handicap to overcome."

football player, lumbered into the lecture room. "Great," my son thought, "it was just this type of dumb jock I was hoping to get away from at a school like this." Before he could even settle into his seat, the professor asked the latecomer a question about the material on the board, to which, "this guy gave the most intelligent and articulate answer I could imagine."

Finally, I recall when, as a college resident assistant, a young female chemistry major on my floor poured her heart out to me about a guy she liked, but who did not return her sentiments. "He was too superficial to see beyond someone's looks and see her true worth," she pined. Ironically, it was clear that the only reason she was attracted to him was his looks, not because of intellectual or other potentially noble characteristics.

The reason I belabor this point is because I have witnessed this issue become a major obstacle for so many people. The idea that ability, exertion, and contributions could be trumped by matters of style affronted their sense of logic and fairness. Over time, the resentment would build until it undermined their ability to perform; they did not respect or like the people for whom they worked and no longer cared about their job. By showing the ubiquitous nature of this, I am hoping those affected can work past it. We are all victims and perpetrators of this in some ways, and as such, it is fruitless to bemoan this human shortcoming and instead factor it in to our interactions with others.

Voice Aesthetics

Jerry Lewis' *The Nutty Professor* may be film's first depiction of the archetype geek, the over-the-top stereotype featuring buckteeth, unkept hair, and thick glasses positioned halfway down the nose, all clad in a lab coat with a loaded pocket protector. Upon his appearance in the movie, we immediately understood who this character is intended to be. Consider, however, that a blind person listening to him speak in the movie would probably have known the character just as quickly. It is not the content of what he said that would tip them off, but the way Lewis' character said it.

Characteristics of our voice – tone, clarity, tempo, intonation, and accent – convey perceptions of us, just as how we look and dress. Have you ever become well accustomed to the voice of a radio personality, only to be shocked when you see what they actually look like? Absent a visual, we create images to accompany the voices we hear. And when those voices do not match the actual faces, we are taken aback. The point is that not only do our voices convey an image of us, but an indelible one. Furthermore, the more the voice and visual seem to concur, the more powerful the impression, either good or bad.

For the vast majority, voice is a relatively unimportant characteristic. Our voices may convey an image of us, but it is a benign one. There is, however, a small minority whose voices convey a very vivid perception, which may hamper their professional efforts. Consider Paul, whom I referenced at the beginning of Chapter 1. He had a soft, nasally voice that lacked intonation or an appropriate cadence. Someone performing a screening interview over the phone might dismiss him as a candidate shortly into the call based on his voice.

The Tale of Two Professionals

Imagine two new employees. Each has identical intelligence, experience, education, drive, and work ethic, but they present two different user interfaces. Each starts in the same position in the same type of company.

The first looks like the Dwight Schrute character from the TV sitcom *The Office* and speaks in a drab overly precise voice. His written communications are accurate but are long, confusing, and visually unattractive. His presentations cram too much text into too small a font size on a single slide. When he does include graphics in his presentation, they actually distract because they are of poor quality, the wrong size, distorted or inappropriate in some other way. He prefers to work alone and when he must collaborate, he does so grudgingly, minimizing the interactions and keeping it "all-business." He rarely laughs, smiles, or makes any effort to connect with others on a personal level. He does not proactively share information, he is slow to respond to others' requests, and the material he does make available is difficult to access and use.

The second looks like Rainn Wilson, the actor who plays the Dwight Schrute character. His clothing, glasses, and hairstyle are professional but not particularly stylish. The tone, tempo, and modulation of his voice are unremarkable. The communications he creates are for the most part focused, concise, and well organized. He incorporates quality graphics that facilitate better communication and that serve to break up the accompanying text. He is not necessarily outgoing, but he is pleasant enough and easy with which to build a rapport. He is conscientious about proactively sharing information when it would be of assistance and does so in a way that makes it easy to use.

Now, consider these two just five years into their careers. Despite matters of *substance*, which are identical, the second one will almost certainly be on a much better career track. Fast forward 20 years, and we should expect that the outcome would be very different. Obviously the first person is an extreme, but the description associated with the second is not on the other end of the spectrum; it is *average* and well within reach of most people.

Remedies:
Aesthetics

Fortunately, aesthetics is one of those things where modest improvements deliver the greatest relative returns. It is similar to someone preparing a house for sale. They can spend tremendous sums to make upgrades in order to attract buyers – redo the kitchen or create a new master suite – but they are not likely to recoup those investments. On the other hand, some cleaning, painting, and basic landscaping can make a house much more marketable with only a small investment. What these modest improvements do is allow the potential buyer to imagine what they can do with the house, without being distracted by minor things that may exaggerate any shortcomings.

And so it is with our personal aesthetics. Minor improvements can remove the distractions that prevent others from seeing the benefits they may experience from working with us.

- Visual aesthetics – how our communications look.

- Usability aesthetics – how easy it for others to use the information we share.

- Personal aesthetics – how we look and sound.

Visual Aesthetics

Primum Non Nocere (first do no harm), is one of the seminal principles of the Hippocratic Oath. It stems from the all-too-common reality that in our sincere efforts to do well, we often make things worse. Those not skilled in graphics should take heed. Graphic design and other aspects of visual communication are difficult crafts to master and there are literally thousands of books that have been written to help individuals do them better. In the end though, people's potential in this area is usually limited by their innate aesthetic aptitudes, just as their singing ability is limited by their vocal chords and sense of pitch. Some will have hidden abilities that can be developed and polished, but most will not. Even the latter, though, can benefit greatly by simply avoiding the common mistakes that most draw negative attention. This is equivalent to doing the basic "cleaning, painting, and landscaping" for real estate, versus doing major upgrades.

Go with the Flow

Probably the best advice on this topic is to follow organizational norms. Use whatever formatting seems to be preferred in the organization. If your organization has a graphics style manual, follow it. If document templates are provided, use them. If you feel urges to "do something special" to call attention to your work, ignore them. Even if your organization's practices are lacking, at least your communications will look no worse than the rest.

Having made that point, there are a couple specific things to consider.

Limit Formatting Variations

Good design usually incorporates some variety in text formatting, but not excessively. As Franklin said on a similar topic, "It's like salt, a little of which in some cases gives a relish, but if thrown on by handfuls, or sprinkled on things at random, it spoils all." It is okay to have some variation in text size, color, and other formatting options, but do so sparingly and consistently. Likewise, you can use bolding, underlining, etc., but use them sparingly unless called for by traditional writing conventions, such as italicizing the titles of creative works.

Different fonts have different personalities and as such can be used to add another layer to communications, but nonstandard fonts should only be used when they make a specific contribution. For example, you may use a cursive type when creating an electronic invitation. In general, serif fonts (the ones with the added flourishes at the end of each stroke), are easier to read in body text, while san-serif (text without such flourishes) are preferred for headlines and presentation slides.

Specifying an ideal type size is impractical. Different uses require different sizes, and different typefaces have different apparent sizes. This is Garamond in the 12 pt. font. **This is MoolBoran in the 12 pt. font.**

An additional undesirable aspect of some emails created by Doug – referenced earlier in this chapter – was that he centered all the text, which is not appropriate for the body text. Almost as bad is full justification, which is text that aligns to both the left and right margin, as in the case of this paragraph. Centered text may seem to give the text more flair, and full justification may give documents an overall polished look, but anything other than left justification, makes text more difficult to read. Our eyes and brains are conditioned to starting the next line at the same place and processing letters and words at fixed distances from each other. To achieve full justification, word processors insert extra spaces between words (professional systems may also add spaces between letters). These create what amounts to reading friction. It takes longer and is more tiring to read such documents. Compare this paragraph to the last; you might notice it harder for your eyes to glide across the page than when the formatting is left justified and the spacing between words is uniform. In this one, your eyes will likely move in a slightly more choppy manner. Even if our audience does not realize it consciously, full justification can be grating. For almost all of your documents, use left justification for the body of your text, though centered text for certain purposes, such as titles and headers, is fine.

Pictures, Graphs, etc.

The importance of visuals has become even more important in the digital age. Consider the importance of images to news reporting. Newspaper publishers and TV news producers have long understood the appeal of images. Even before photography, newspaper publishers included sketches of major events (even if the person doing the sketch had not witnessed the event) to accompany their stories. Traditionally, though, the graphics were subordinate to the stories; the text content of a story determined how prominently the story would be displayed and how much space or time would be devoted to it. Nowadays, though, the tail seems to wag the dog. Images are often the determinant of what makes it into the news and how prominently it is displayed.

The inclusion of a photograph or illustration not only satisfies certain visual expectations, but can also be extremely helpful in conveying a message. Considering all this, it is surprising that visuals are not included in more communications. It is not as if they are hard to come by. Most software tools (e.g., for word processors, spreadsheets, presentations) include libraries of pictures, clip art, and shapes, and if those are not acceptable, they offer ways to create or import additional options.

Other Visual Elements

If photographs or illustrations are not an option or are inappropriate, consider other design elements that will break up long documents.

- Graphs and charts can be an excellent way to both dress up a document visually as well as enhance its communicative power.

- Bullets and/or numbered lists not only break up text, but often make the content more concise (by eliminating redundancies) and clear (it is easier to recognize and delineate what is and is not within the scope of a given idea).

- Sidebars (self-contained text elements enclosed in a box, or set off in some other way) not only add visual variety but can also enhance the communicative function of a piece.

- Headers (in a text format that sets it off from the body text) both interrupt long spans of text and organize the text into logical segments.

Let Form Follow Function

Unfortunately, like the gaudy use of text formatting, visuals can be used incorrectly or excessively, actually detracting from a communication. It may help those without a graphical flair to think of graphic elements in relation to a document, as they would punctuation in relation to a paragraph. Each guides the tempo, ensures clarity, emphasizes certain points, breaks ideas into digestible chunks and provides an overall personality to the item.

That last item is an important one because it underscores the point of consistency. Whatever approach is taken, it should seem to flow through the piece, lest it appear disjointed.

The key is to let the form follow, and indeed enhance, function. If, for example, you are making a pitch to a committee, and they will have your proposal in hand as you speak, you will want to replace or accompany as much text as possible with charts and graphs. Recall visuals rely on the right hemisphere of the brain while language on the left. Charts and graphs will allow them to more easily process the visual material and your words simultaneously. Few will be able to read and listen well at the same time.

Exception to "Going with the Flow"

One case where following the organizational practices may not be advisable is in the formatting of presentation slides, signs, and other communications where the apparent size of the text is not fixed. While text on a computer screen or in a printed document will normally appear the same size to all readers, those that are projected will have different apparent sizes based on the size of the image, the audience distance, and ambient lighting.

This exception is necessary because so often organizational norms in this area are deficient. Presenters try to squeeze too much text into a single slide, at least for the conditions in which the material will be displayed. For example, you might be able to get away with small text if you are displaying the slide on a huge screen in a small dark room, but even then it should only be done when absolutely necessary. If creating slides for a location that can be accessed in advance, it may be wise to test it (viewing from the worst seat in the room), especially if it is an important presentation.

Generally, if there is doubt about something being too small (or too large), it probably is.

In terms of the graphical elements in a slide, the key things to consider are relevance (are they graphics for graphics sake), size (must be readable from whatever condition your audience will see it), audience appropriateness (cute clip art might not be appropriate for a serious leadership group), and quality (grainy, out-of-focus photographs, distorted, or pixilated graphics). It has been said the best movie musical scores are the ones the audience does not notice. The same may be true for the use of visuals in various communication pieces.

If you still struggle with elements of design, enlisting the assistance of someone with strength in this area should be considered. It does not have to be a professional; it can just be someone who has a demonstrated aptitude for creating attractive and appropriate communications. If someone like this is not available, you should at least share drafts of important pieces with others to get their feedback. Despite your best efforts, it may be hard to tell whether your finished product is spot on, wildly off target, or just has a flaw or two that screams out. Ideally, those who assist you will be familiar with your target audience and their preferences.

Software Templates

One suggestion given was to follow organizational templates, but many organizations do not provide them. If that is the case, another option is the templates and style devices that are provided with most document creation software (word processors, spreadsheets, or slide presentations).

These cannot only improve the overall look of your documents, but also accelerate the creation process because they primarily involve filling in the blanks. At the risk of beating a dead horse, you must be careful to select those that are most appropriate. Just because they are created by professionals does not mean that they are right for every situation.

Create Your Own Templates

Sometimes, when dealing with a recurring need that is not satisfied by off-the-shelf solutions, creating a custom template is useful. Custom templates not only save time in the long run, but also establish a pattern that can improve the readability of shared information. Once an audience becomes accustomed to the template's design and organization, it will be easier for them to process the information contained within.

Consider the typical daily newspaper. We can pick up any example from across the country (at least those that are still in print) and in most cases quickly find the information we need, even if we have never read that particular paper before. This is because most newspapers follow certain design conventions that we have become accustomed to over the years. The first section of the paper is for general news, followed by sections for features, sports, etc. Content within each of these sections also follows patterns: a table of contents will be in the lower left or right hand column of the first page. The masthead, a small boxed section with information about the paper, is included in one of the first few pages of the first section, and so on. Yet, despite these common conventions, *USA Today* looks different from the *New York Times*, which looks different from *The Chicago Tribune*. The conventions reduce the number of variables the reader has to deal with – thus making it easier to process the information – even if other design elements distinguish one publication from another. A more contemporary example of this is software menu design. Apple was early to realize (Microsoft later followed) that reusing the same basic menu design and layout across various applications made it easier for users. Even if a particular application would benefit greatly from a proprietary menu structure, the overall usability would be impaired; this would require the user to learn a new interface each time, or adjust to a different one when switching between programs.

If you distribute the same type of information on a recurring basis, consider creating a template or set of conventions that reduce the time the recipient needs to process the information. Recall Doug, the operations manager mentioned earlier in this chapter. I created some templates for him that he could use for almost all the organizational communications he typically distributed. I assessed the scope of what he was trying to do and analyzed why what he was doing – beyond the gaudy formatting – was not working. I found that just about everything he did made it more difficult for his audience. In addition to the loud formatting, his messages were issued too frequently, were too long, and not well organized.

To help, I created three very basic templates for him: *Urgent Bulletin*, *Action Required Bulletin*, and *Information Bulletin*. Each had a relatively similar layout: a text box with various subcomponents that would fit entirely within a screen page.

Within the main text box of the template was a series of headings. For example, the Urgent template had the following elements, always listed in this order:

Audience

This described in a single short sentence, to whom this was applicable: those using certain software, with certain computer models, etc. This way, most of those to whom the message was not applicable could determine this at the very top, before they had to read through other irrelevant information (recall that Doug had no way of segmenting email distributions and instead had to distribute these to the entire organization).

Summary

A short, one sentence summary of the subject of the notice, e.g., a system down for maintenance over the weekend. This provided another potential way for readers to determine the applicability of the message without reading other unnecessary information.

Action Required

This included one or more bulleted actions the user was instructed to do. These were very short and prescriptive. Do this first, then this, etc.

Details

Here is where any additional information necessary to explain the bulletin was included. There could be several bulleted lines in this section, but never so many that it prevented all the information from fitting on one screen. If this space was insufficient, links to intranet pages with more information were provided.

Assistance

Instructions or links for those who had questions or needed additional assistance.

The *Action Required* template included these same items, but was distinguished by the orange background color for the header (the rest of the template was black type on white background), as opposed to red for the Urgent template. It also included a Do By field after the Action Required field.

The *Informational Template* was largely the same except for the blue background text for the header, and the elimination of the Action Required element. Each template was dated in case a new bulletin on the same subject superseded a previous one.

While there was nothing fancy about the design of these templates, they were extremely effective. Information was ordered with the intention of providing the most important information first. Think of it in terms of a decision chart: the template was designed so that various audiences could quit reading the template at the earliest opportunity.

Not only were these communication tools more concise than the emails Doug had been sending, but over time the consistent formatting trained the users so they could process these more quickly.

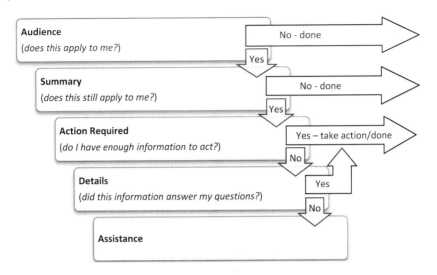

We even developed a system for creating consistent and communicative subject lines for the emails, which improved their usability. For example: "IT INFORMATION Bulletin: Email System Down for Maintenance Saturday," or "IT URGENT Bulletin: Computer Virus Widespread Throughout Organization," and so on.

I should note that I also ended up creating User Guidelines for the templates, prescribing how they were to be used – and not used – after Doug started reformatting the template to more closely resemble his previous communications: longer descriptions after each informational item, reordering so that the explanation was on the top, and altering text colors and sizes. Old habits die hard.

Beyond solving Doug's problems, other groups within IT adopted the approach. Then the Building and Grounds department asked permission to create a version of the template that they could use for facilities announcements (e.g., "the south parking lot will be closed for repaving"). Finally, even the corporate Internal Communications function adopted this approach. We were thrilled; after all, the more consistency there was across various departments, the more effective the format would become. We just worked with the other groups to ensure uniformity, while also delineating the various templates. For example, we assigned different colors to different groups. This was important, because beyond just email distribution, administrators would often print out the bulletins and post them on corkboards in break rooms. The colors immediately let audiences know who provided the postings.

Almost everyone has some information they share on a regular or frequent basis: maybe project updates, incident reports, etc. By utilizing a consistent approach that is most useful and less demanding on your audience, you will improve the perception of your personal user interface.

Information Accessibility Aesthetics

The ease or difficulty with which someone can *pull* our communications has a significant influence on our perceived personal user interface. Good usability casts us in a positive light, and poor usability aggravates our audiences. It does not matter if we have repeatedly told them where certain information is, or sent them a link – *If they can't find it, it doesn't exist.*

Collaborative software has come a long way in facilitating the sharing of information across groups, but the problem of difficult-to-locate information persists. Whether using SharePoint, a shared drive, a web page, or any other repository, if information is shared it should be organized in a manner that is intuitive to our audience. I emphasize that last bit: to our audience. Even repositories that attempt to organize things logically and carefully often miss the mark because they are only logical to the team maintaining the information.

For example, I was once charged with redesigning a corporate IT intranet site. The site was intended to both provide a collaborative tool for the IT team as well as a self-help tool and information source for non-IT system users throughout the organization. The existing site demonstrated some attempts at a logical and easy to use interface, but only for the IT team. Navigation options were presented according to the internal team structure and many of the team names were only understandable to those within IT; there was no intuitive connection between some of the function names and what that function did.

Even if the user found the correct section, the technical information intended for the IT team was comingled with the information intended for users. And, because individual items were not always labeled intuitively, users might have to open many pages before they could find the information they were seeking, if they could find it at all.

Without going into too much detail, the redesign included navigation that both segmented the key audiences as well as categorized the information into sections on the front page. Content primarily aimed at general employees was on the left, under the header of *Products and Services.* The navigation buttons were *Desktop Systems, Business Systems, Telecommunications,* and so on, each with a couple elaborative words underneath to help the user better understand the content. Clicking on those navigation buttons lead the user to all information that related to that topic – no matter which IT team supported it. Another set of navigation buttons was provided on the right side of the main page, under the header *IT Team Information* with navigation buttons labeled *IT Strategic Direction and*

Goals; Current Projects; Organizational Charts and Contact Information; and *IT Research, Best Practices, and Industry News*. By segmenting the two audiences at a high level, it made it easier for both groups to find relevant information while also providing more intuitive access to all information (a general employee, for example, might want to locate a certain IT employee from the contact information under the IT team information).

While this specific example may have little relevance for some, the underlying principle is universal: organize information in a manner that it is the easiest for your audience(s) to find and use.

Labeling

Of course, well-organized information may be of little use if the user does not recognize what they are looking for when they navigate to the correct location. We need to label things so that users can easily identify them. The most straightforward way to accomplish this is to name things so they are intuitively descriptive. A broad range of audiences should have a good idea of what is contained in a given file from the name alone. Beyond that, the file name has to work within the context of other files that may be around it. Intuitive naming does not do much good if the files and content are quite similar. For example, if I arrange to meet someone for the first time at a location and say I will be the one with the blue shirt and the red baseball cap, the assumption is that I should be easy to identify. But what if several people at the location also fit that description. By using a little extra effort when labeling folders and documents, you will likely save your colleagues, and maybe even yourself, frustration when trying to locate them later.

A way to simplify this task, while simultaneously improving effectiveness, is to create a naming convention for the files you manage and share. Naming conventions are commonly used in science, such as those for naming chemical compounds or different species, and such approaches are easily transferrable to file naming. These conventions serve to both specify what something is as well as delineate it from similar items.

Such conventions also allow us to use abbreviations and shortcuts that are still easily understood, once the convention is defined and shared. These abbreviations may undermine the desire to make the file names intuitive, so this must be done with caution. If in doubt, error on the side of ease of use.

The appropriate naming scheme varies according to the work function, how teams are organized, the document content type, the communication medium, and many other factors, so no specific recommendations are provided here, other than to suggest that you test whatever approach you choose on the audiences who will be accessing this information.

Glossary

While Chapter 7 extols the virtue of eliminating acronyms and jargon, sometimes they are difficult if not impossible to avoid. In such cases, create a team glossary that can be made available to everyone for reference.

Maintenance

Regardless of the pull system you use, maintain it properly. Add new material, update existing material quickly and delete or prune outdated information on a regular basis. A beautiful system with outdated or erroneous information is not much better than an ugly system. You may want to establish a schedule (e.g., first of the week, first of the month, whatever is appropriate for the type of material you are managing) and hold yourself to it.

Presentation Aesthetics

Public speaking presents a challenge for people across society, and as a result, there is no shortage of experts offering assistance: books, seminars, and personal coaching. There are even those who provide specialized assistance for technical professionals, as Joey Asher has in his book *Even a Geek Can Speak*.

Ideally, you have someone who can help you with this, as it is very difficult to assess yourself in this area. Look for someone who has a good ear for articulation, tone and tempo, a good command of the language in general, and preferably someone who is a compelling presenter. Through a series of practice presentations, feedback and corrections, most people can make significant improvements rather quickly.

If you do not have someone who can help you, a fallback approach is to record your practice presentations and review the results yourself for:

- Articulation – Are your words pronounced accurately and clearly?

- Volume – Is the volume of your voice loud enough to be heard well (or possibly too loud)? Is it consistent, i.e., does it drop off at the end of the sentence?

- Modulation – Do you alter the volume as a way of stressing certain points and making it sound more interesting?

- Tempo – Do you go too fast or too slow? Do you vary tempo and use pauses effectively?

Again, it is hard to assess your own speech; so a way to facilitate this is to model your speech after a skilled professional. Many news organizations allow you to access past broadcasts as well as transcripts of the broadcasts. Hence, you can record yourself presenting the same material and then compare your results to the professionals. Listen alternately to yourself and the professional and consider how you compare on articulation, volume, modulation, and tempo. Then try again, and continue to do so, until you think you are closer to the professional. Compare your first recording to your last. Do you notice much of a difference?

Then repeat this using different professional presenters. The point is not to imitate the style of one professional, but to learn how to use the best practices from a variety of professionals so that you can develop a new and better style of your own.

Of course, you do not have to use news broadcasts. The same approach could be done for political speeches, and symposium presentations, though accessing the recordings and/or transcripts might not be so convenient. The more you mix it up, the more likely you will find approaches that work for your personal style.

Then, when it is time to make an actual presentation, markup your presentation notes to help you deliver what you have learned. For example, you might want to insert a note "pause" at certain points, to let your audience digest what you have just said, or underline certain words to remind you to emphasize them. If you have a tendency to speak too softly, you might want to write "volume" in the margins at several different places so that you do not start off strong and then drift softer.

Vocal Aesthetics

One thing you are likely to notice if you compare your recordings to those of professionals, is the sound of your voice. Alternatively, if someone is assisting you, maybe they will mention this to you (encourage them to be candid with you). The question is whether you have a neutral voice or one that might undermine others' perceptions of you (very high pitched, nasally, raspy, hoarse, etc.). If it is among the latter, how bad is it? Imagine having to sit through a presentation by Fran Drescher – actress best known for the sitcom *The Nanny*. There is very little she could do in terms of articulation, volume, modulation and tempo to make that voice palatable to me for a 20-minute presentation.

Delivery Aesthetics

Along with the verbal aspects of presentations, your visual aesthetics are also important. Do you gesture or stand motionless? Do you appear rigid or relaxed? Do you stare at your notes or engage your audience?

As with the verbal part of the presentation, having someone watch and provide feedback is invaluable, but if that is not possible you can do a variation of the voice recording technique just discussed. Videotape yourself making a presentation and then compare that with videos of skilled presenters (many are available on YouTube). Have the volume turned all the way down as you analyze the presentation, for it is easier to focus on the visuals if you are not distracted by the sound. Make sure to select a variety of speakers for the comparison. Some can be very good with minimal gestures and body movement while others are very animated and move all over the stage. Try different techniques until your practice videos demonstrate an engaging and confident you.

Personal Aesthetics

When it comes to how you look, dress, and groom yourself, my advice is simply to be appropriate to the situation. We do not need to achieve some aesthetic ideal, only avoid the things that would call negative attention to us. Unfortunately, what is appropriate and what calls negative attention is relative.

In the late 1990's I worked at a large, conservative corporation on their first major e-commerce initiative. This was still in the frontier days of e-business and management was concerned as to whether the existing IT team had the "right stuff" to succeed in this new era. "We need some people in here with ponytails and earrings," said the marketing executive who had overall responsibility for the initiative. Sure enough, those who fit that description were hired even as hardworking and well-intentioned existing developers – whose sole offense was not looking the part – were assigned to areas that were largely being phased out. This is an example of the power of surface credibility, which will be discussed further in the next chapter.

I am not suggesting that the existing developers should have grown out their hair and had their ears pierced – such affectations would have been ridiculous and done more harm than good. If, however, they could have only updated their appearance so that they did not look so "main-frame," they might have avoided that fate in the first place.

While what looks appropriate will vary by a number of factors, individuals should pay attention to relevant norms and best practices in their organization and field. Once again, this is one area where the input and feedback of others is especially valuable.

How to:
Avoid Inappropriate Aesthetics

1. **Perform an audit of the various communication tools and channels you use to share information with others.**

   ☐ Assemble a broad, representative sample of communication pieces you create.

   ☐ Make a list of the various pull communication channels (SharePoint, intranet, shared system drive, database, etc.) you use to share information.

   Note: depending on your organization, positions, or tenure, there may be many of these or very few. If your sample is small, you may wish to consider communication pieces or channels from previous positions you have held. The intent is to gather information that will help identify your natural abilities and inclinations.

2. **Perform an assessment of your existing personal user interface (the sum of all the ways others interface with you, your communications, etc.). Write down your responses.**

   ☐ How do my push communications (those I actively distribute to others) look?

   ✓ Are they generally attractive (appropriate formatting, organization, and overall feel)?

   ✓ Are they properly calibrated to the needs and tastes of different audiences receiving them (assuming that there are disparate audiences)?

   ✓ Is there some consistency between pieces, and if so is that beneficial? Or are they very independent from one to another, and if so is that beneficial?

   ✓ Does their appearance comply with common practices of my organization?

   ✓ If they do not conform, how are they different? And do they appear to be superior or inferior?

   ✓ Are the channels typically used to share those the most appropriate for their respective audiences?

☐ How well are my pull communication channels organized?

  ✓ Can those wishing to access the information find it easily and quickly?

  ✓ Is accessing them easier, harder, or the same as compared to the way others in my organization share information?

  ✓ Are they well maintained (latest updates added quickly and outdated information pruned)?

☐ What does my personal appearance say about me?

  ✓ Would someone make distinct inferences of me based on my dress, voice, or mannerisms, etc.? If so, what would those likely be?

  ✓ Would someone meeting me for the first time likely see me as more credible, less credible, or the same based on the way I look and how I present myself?

3. **Seek external feedback. Consult with one or more people who know you, your work, and ideally are well familiar with the audiences you most need to influence, and ask them to assess the same items as in Step 2.**

  ☐ Assemble representative samples of a broad range of your communication pieces for them to review.

  ☐ Write down their responses to the questions.

4. **Compare their responses to your self-analysis.**

  ☐ If there is consensus that your push and pull communications, as well as your personal appearance, are not out of line in any particular way, you may skip to the next chapter, though I suggest reading through the following items anyway, and considering whether such items may be of assistance to you.

  ☐ If this analysis determines there are certain areas of your personal user interface that need adjusting, read the following steps, with special focus on the things identified for change.

5. **Simplify and standardize your standing communications.**

☐ Take stock of all the communication pieces you create on a regular or semi-regular basis (i.e., reports, newsletters, anything where the same type of information is shared on a reoccurring basis).

☐ Create a design approach for each, starting with those that are most important or shared most often. The goal here is to create an approach for each that is most effective for the particular use, saves you time because you are not starting from scratch each time, and provides a level of continuity that makes it easier for your audience to consume your communications.

✓ Does your organization offer graphic standards (guidelines for how certain documents should look, trademarks used, etc.) or templates you can use as a starting point? If so, follow them.

✓ Beyond that, seek out the best practices and examples from within or outside your organization and adapt them in whole or in part.

Note: Best means appropriate and effective, not necessarily what has the most flair or complicated design.

✓ Consider using/modifying the document templates included in most document-creation software.

✓ To the extent that these do not exist or are inadequate for your needs, create your own. Following is a list of things that may need to be considered, however it does not mean that every piece will require all these elements. The design should be appropriate for the usage; generally, the simpler, the better.

  o *How information will be organized and presented?*
  o *Which typefaces and font sizes will be used for various elements?*
  o *What colors will be used and for what?*
  o *A plan for the consistent use of graphic elements.*
  o *A plan for the consistent use of illustrations and photographs.*

✓ If possible, share your proposed design approaches with others and get their feedback before adopting.

☐ Once you have defined a personal design approach, follow it consistently.

✓ It is okay to fine-tune them, but fight the urge to change them for change's sake.

6. **Organize each of the pull communication systems you manage so they are easier to use.**

    ☐ Consider how your audiences are most likely to search for and use the information you share, and then reorganize your material in the most intuitive way possible for them.

       ✓ Seek input and feedback from representatives of your target audience, those similar to your target audience, or those who are familiar with their preferences and ways of doing things.

    ☐ For all audiences, minimize the amount of information they must process in order to find what they are likely to need.

    ☐ Use terminology and labels they will easily understand.

       ✓ Consider creating a naming methodology that will help others anticipate what is contained in a given document, and to distinguish it from other similar documents.

    ☐ Regularly review the content so that the most recent information is included, and outdated or redundant information is pruned.

       ✓ Depending on the amount and complexity of information you manage, you may want to establish a specific timeline for checking and updating information.

7. **Address aspects of your personal appearance, voice, or mannerisms that may be undermining your ability to excel in the workplace.**

    ☐ Identify someone who can objectively assess your personal characteristics and provide you a candid and honest opinion on which may diminish others' perceptions of you. In particular, ask:

       ✓ Are there aspects of my dress, hairstyle, etc., that draw negative attention to me?

       ✓ Does my vocal delivery (voice, inflection, modulation, pace, etc.) undermine the content of my comments?

       ✓ Do I have mannerisms, gestures, or ticks that may distract or bother my audiences?

✓ Is there anything beyond these things that may negatively affect my ability to communicate and connect with essential audiences?

☐ Create a plan for mitigating or eliminating personal aesthetic detractions.

✓ Prioritize the list by its importance to your effectiveness (i.e., the extent to which it is holding you back now).

✓ Determine which corrections can be made quickly or which will require prolonged effort.

✓ Designate each as to whether it is something you can manage yourself, with the assistance of a colleague, friend or loved one, or if you will need professional assistance.

✓ Calculate the order of attack that provides the best effort to improvement ratio.

✓ Continue working on these until you believe the indentified issues have been adequately addressed.

✓ Monitor and refocus activities as necessary.

Note: The goal is not to become someone else. In fact, efforts to affect a different persona are likely to be transparent and could potentially make matters worse. The goal here should be simply to avoid the things that unwittingly undermine your credibility and communication effectiveness.

Summary – Chapter 12
Style AND Substance

Matters of *Style* – aesthetics – are not irrelevant to those in STEM professions. In fact, they can be essential, as is exemplified by Apple. Apple's emphasis on the aesthetics of the user interface has been key to its rise to the apex in personal computing, portable music, and smart phones.

Each of us presents a personal user interface: a series of characteristics that determine whether it is easy, appealing, and rewarding for others to work with us. Those who present a poor interface can fail, despite all other advantages, while others with an agreeable interface can succeed, despite more modest attributes.

By becoming more accepting, empathetic, uncomplicated, concise, and results oriented, you have already improved your personal user interface. But you also need to take into account how you look, sound and dress, as well as how you create, organize, and share information.

When formatting materials for others, keep things simple and follow the best practices of your organization. If possible, use graphics, but they should be appropriate, pleasing to your audience, and support the communication efforts, not just be an effect.

The information you share through central repositories should be well organized and intuitive for your audiences to find and use. A new mantra to adopt is, *If they can't find it, it doesn't exist.*

Your personal aesthetics – how you, look, sound, etc. – can also influence what you can achieve in the workplace. Ideally, what you project should reflect how you want others to perceive you. At the very least, you want to avoid things that attract negative attention to yourself.

Monitor, Assess, and Log ...

- When your communications do not conform to organizational norms and/or best practices (if in doubt, they probably do not).

- How much of the information you share remains difficult for others to find and use intuitively (if in doubt, it probably is)?

- The aspects of your personal presentation (what you can change) that may still undermine your professional objectives.

You Will Know You Are Overcoming This When ...

- You note fewer complaints about the readability of your communications.

- There are fewer requests for changes from those with whom you collaborate on communications.

- You have fewer requests to find or provide information that is already located in a shared location.

- You, yourself, find it easier to locate and maintain information.

- Others respond more favorably to your presentations.

- In general, you find that you are better received than your peers, who have not made efforts to be aesthetically neutral.

– Chapter 13 –

It Takes a Team

Those disputing, contradicting, and confuting people
are generally unfortunate in their affairs.
They get victory, sometimes, but they never get good will,
which would be of more use to them.
– Benjamin Franklin

Foible: Collaboration (deficient)
Precept: Be a valued team player

Keith was brilliant. If there was one thing everyone in his department agreed upon, it was that. He had an extremely quick mind and an extraordinary breadth of knowledge. If brains equaled athletics, he would have been the first one picked when divvying up sports teams as a child. But he was as an adult and was usually the last person someone wanted on their work team.

Colleagues considered him to be arrogant, uncooperative, and untrustworthy. He cast a pall upon every meeting he attended. He rarely had anything positive to say and would pepper conversations with personal gibes and condescending remarks. It was not enough for him to prevail based on his own merits; he needed to undermine those around him.

He was unyielding to the goals and the actions of the team and generally did only the things he wanted to. He rationalized that he knew better and it was not in the organization's best interests for him to defer to the opinions of others, regardless of their level in the organization.

It is not that he blatantly defied them. His trick was to foster and exploit ambiguity within the team. He would cherry pick the parts of meetings that he could use to justify his own agenda and conveniently forget or ignore those that contradicted them. And if that failed, he would work the corridors and offices behind the scenes to derail team plans and undercut his opposition. Even when he was aligned with the team direction, he failed to share important information or update others on his work. Despite his great potential, he was perceived as a net negative when trying to get things done within a team.

William Shockley, the Almost Household Name

Unlike Keith, whose *Peter Principle* was reached relatively early, William Shockley is an example of someone who experienced prominent success, but who was destined to have achieved so much more if not for the way he interacted with others.

Like Alan Turing, he is credited with making great contributions to the Allied war effort in World War II, however, the greatest part of Shockley's fame came after the war. Shockley was part of the Bell Labs team credited with inventing the transistor and he shared the 1956 Nobel Prize for physics as a result.

While it has been suggested that some do not achieve great power or wealth simply because they are not seeking it (the work itself is what is most important to them), that does not seem to be the case with Shockley. He was apparently very eager for executive promotion at Bell Labs, but was passed over because of his abrasive management style. Seeking the power and profit he felt he was being denied, he left Bell Labs in 1955 and established Shockley Semiconductor Laboratory, within Beckman Instruments.

After his departure, he attempted to lure some former colleagues from Bell Labs to join him, but despite Shockley's prestige and Beckman's financial strength, he was unsuccessful, assumedly due to their past experiences with him. As a result, he took the opposite approach, seeking out the greatest minds among newly-minted graduates from the country's top universities. This way, it is assumed, he could mold them to his way of doing things. He was tremendously successful in attracting brilliant minds and by all accounts this should be the story of the founding of one of the world's greatest companies; he had everything: leading expertise in one of the most important inventions in history; an exceptional team to support him; and ample capitol to develop, execute and implement.

Shockley, however, could not escape his own foibles. He created an intolerable work environment and in 1957, after less than two years, eight key team members, labeled the Traitorous Eight, left simultaneously to form Fairchild Semiconductor.

Fairchild quickly eclipsed Shockley in the semiconductor development. Then, over the next 20 years, those eight would go on to be involved in starting 65 new enterprises including Intel, National Semiconductor and AMD, dwarfing Shockley in terms of the power and profit he so desired. In *Broken Genius: The Rise and Fall of William Shockley, Creator of the Electronic Age* author Joel N. Shurkin writes, "In truth, he had no idea how to manage … One physicist swore that Shockley could actually see electrons [but] he had trouble seeing people."

Of course, this is a rather selective examination of the man, and he was a far more complex person, both for the better and worse. But what if he could have seen people a little better. Keep in mind that at the time this event occurred, the norm was for employees to remain with their employers for life. It took a lot to push the Traitorous Eight away. So, what if Shockley could have softened his edges, acting a little less autocratic and a little more collaborative, at least enough to keep that dream team aligned with his genius for a little longer. He may have far exceeded even the greatest of the industry titans and technology billionaires who followed him.

The Team Interface

The previous chapter discussed the topic of our personal user interface in terms of various aesthetics: of the communications we create, the information we share, and even our appearance, voice, etc., but our personal user interface is also heavily determined by the way we collaborate and team with others. Keith and Shockley had poor personal user interfaces and, though few could match their extremes, they are not alone. Recall that Teamwork was found to be the fifth most important thing to hiring managers in the ABET study referenced in Chapter 1.

Executive Recruiter Gary Erickson says that, "A lot of technical people have gone through the years thinking they were the smartest person around because they got the best grades in the toughest subjects, but intelligence is not just about doing a math problem. The best things come out of group efforts, as opposed to individual efforts, and that can be a tough transition for someone who has been highly dependent on their brain to get them where they wanted to go."

*Un*teamwork

The ability to collaborate effectively is a key determinant of whether someone will thrive professionally or not. When executives meet to discuss succession planning, among the primary things they discuss are leadership and people skills. Intelligence, hard work, and other attributes are just the admission to the discussion. Fundamentally, what they want to know is who will contribute to a greater team output. So important is this attribute that someone may escape complicity with all eight other foibles listed in this book, yet be severely hindered in their careers because of this single dynamic.

Of course, it is not really a single dynamic. It is the end result of many characteristics, attitudes and tendencies, some major, some minor. In my experience, there have been four major streams that feed into this river, though not all are present in all occasions, and for some, none at all.

1. Introversion or a preference to work alone.
2. Innate personality characteristics that run counter to good team participation.
3. A clash of thinking styles with those they are expected to team.
4. A tendency for passive aggressiveness.

Introverts and Loners

According to analysis of data extracted from hundreds of thousands of Myers Brigg Type Indictor (MBTI) personality assessments, those in technical professions are more likely to be introverted. The average is 53% introverted across 44 STEM professions analyzed, versus 50% for the general public. While a small difference, keep in mind that the extent to which one is introverted or extraverted is not captured in this data, and I suspect that the frequency of "extremely introverted" people – introversion that significantly hampers one's ability to interact effectively with others – is much greater among those in STEM professions.

Introvert or not, there are some people who just prefer to work by themselves. The following is a post on collegeconfidential.com (a web site for sharing information related to colleges):

> *I was just wondering is there an engineering major that consists mostly of independent work? I've read engineers need to constantly work with people but I really work best independently. Could you rank (best guess) which engineering majors require the least amount of interpersonal skills 1 requiring least 10 the most?*

The ability to succeed as an individual performer may be more common in technical professions than others (many organizations have special job classification tracks that allow for higher relative compensation for strong technical performers without promoting them into management), but it is not absolute. Even those in the most isolated of work environments will likely have to team with others at times, and need to do so increasingly as they progress through the ranks. Those who cannot collaborate adequately will pay a price, and for some that price will be dear. One brilliant information technologists rose all the way to the chief information officer position in a large organization, but only because he had a strong ally in the top leadership. Unfortunately, he was unable to work effectively with others in the organization, and when his protector retired, he was soon fired.

Innate Personality Characteristics

As mentioned in Chapter 3, the most common MBTI type among STEM professionals is ISTJ (Introversion, Sensing, Thinking, and Judging), followed by its sibling, ESTJ (Extraversion, Sensing, Thinking, and Judging). Nearly one third of people in STEM professions are either of these two types. Following are some characteristics commonly associated with ISTJs or ESTJs.

- Have a strong need to control and are extremely leery of others controlling them.

- Have a tendency to believe that they're always right.

- Lack of interest in other people, or in relating to them.

- Maintain general selfish "look after oneself" tendencies.

- May judge others rather than themselves.

- May look at external ideas and people with the primary purpose of finding fault.

- May become a slave to their routine and "by the book" ways of doing things, to the point that any deviation is completely unacceptable.

- Value for structure may seem rigid to others.

- May inadvertently hurt others with insensitive language.

- Generally are uncomfortable with change and moving into new territories.

Some of these characteristics are shared by ENTJs and INTJs, which have the highest SSR ratio among those in STEM professions (see page 113 for an explanation of SSR).

Benjamin Franklin seems to be describing aspects of this when he wrote in his autobiography about one of the original members of the Junto – an organization he formed when he was 21 that was dedicated to the exploration and sharing of scholarly material.

Thomas Godfrey, a self-taught mathematician, great in his way, and afterwards inventor of what is now call'd Hadley's Quadrant. But he knew little out of his way, and was not a pleasing companion, as like most great mathematicians I have met with, he expected unusual precision in every thing said, or was forever denying or distinguishing upon trifles, to the disturbance of all conversation. He soon left us.

And consider what happens when you team two or more such people (who have a strong need to control and are extremely leery of being controlled by others; have tendency to believe that they're always right; judge others rather than themselves; and who are preoccupied in finding fault in others) together. You are bound to have conflicts.

Inherent Friction

If there is one thing that unites dysfunctional teams, it is their disdain for those outside their group. "Those damn users," I once heard a CIO refer to his internal clients.

It should not be surprising that if ISTJ represents the most common type among technical professions, its opposite type, ENFP, is most common among "creative types." The ensuing clash of these is often satirized in the *Dilbert* comic strip through the ongoing battles between Dilbert's team and the marketers.

In one example, Dilbert is providing complex information to a marketer, who interrupts to say, "Do you engineers have a secret pact to withhold all useful information …?" In the next panel, Dilbert is back in his office and his colleague Wally asks, "We hear you are giving information to Marketing." Dilbert responds, "Just the time of day. He would have found that out anyway!"

This acrimony, though, is not just the result of conflicting personality preferences. It is a clash of opposing thinking styles: left-brain versus right-brain, linear thinking versus lateral thinking.

Linear vs. Lateral Thinkers

Linear thinking, also referred to as convergent thinking (which is most associated with those in technical professions), can be described as a logical approach that attempts to achieve the desired result by approaching problems in sequential steps, methodically working through each one towards the result, like a Slinky descending a set of stairs.

Lateral thinking, also referred to as divergent thinking (which is most associated with creative types), is characterized by patterns that are more unstructured, resembling a pinball game, with thoughts bouncing around, but then scoring in random ways.

A story of the creation of Nike's iconic *Just do it* slogan, retold by Jonah Lehrer in *Imagine: How Creativity Works* – is a good illustration of the latter.

> *The slogan was the creative child of Dan Wieden of the firm Wieden+Kennedy. He was trying to create a shared slogan for seven videos his firm had just created, but was coming up dry. At some point shortly before his epiphany, someone mentioned Norman Mailer in another context, but Mailer remained in the back of his head. It's near midnight, his deadline is approaching, and he is really, really frustrated because he can't come up with this damn slogan. And then suddenly he thinks of Norman Mailer. He remembers Norman Mailer's book, The Executioner's Song, about Gary Gilmore. And he remembers Gary Gilmore's last words right before he's executed by a firing squad in Utah: 'Let's do it.' That phrase resonated with him, but it wasn't quite right, so he tweaked it to get 'Just Do It.' This circuitous route led to one of the most influential advertising slogans of the second half of the 20th century.*

The contrast of linear and lateral thinking styles helps explains why engineering and IT have traditionally had such an adversarial relationship with marketing, or similar functions. Both thinking styles have their advantages and disadvantages, each conversely relating to the other. Linear thinking is efficient and dependable. Because of its focus on disciplined thinking and logic, time is not wasted on the superfluous. Furthermore, different linear-thinkers working independently will likely come up the same or similar answers. Linear thinkers tend to abhor lateral thinkers and their chaotic approach and dismiss any solution that cannot be justified by linear logic.

Lateral thinking, however, opens up vast new possibilities of solutions or even ways of defining the problem. There are certain ideas and solutions that will simply not be found by a linear thinker. Lateral thinkers view linear thinkers as intellectually rigid, unimaginative and … boring.

It is no wonder that when contrasting groups are forced to work together, a gap is evident. This is the geek gap described in Bill Pfleging and Minda Zetlin's book of the same name. The technical professionals find their counterparts in other functions have difficulty understanding and appreciating what they do, and they, in turn, do not appreciate the work of their counterparts. Even when technical and non-technical functional teams are rather integrated and cooperate extensively, a "we"/ "they" dichotomy (or "geeks" and "suits" as they are referred to in the *Geek Gap*) often prevails. It is common to hear IT and engineering people use such terms as the "business side" or "business partners," when talking of their functional peers. "You don't hear finance talking about business partners," says Robert Scott, a former P&G vice president, and technical professionals are "the worst conspirators in this situation."

Passive Aggressive

With so much discordance, the uninitiated may envision a rather animated and combative workplace, but in my experience that is rarely the case. In fact, probably the most common sign of a dysfunctional technical team is when they are unusually quiet. Rather than openly confront each other, they will retreat, but stealthily continue the fight: lobbying behind the scenes, withholding necessary support, undermining their opponents, failing to share information, all while on the surface seeming to cooperate. In short, they are unwilling to subordinate their wills to that of the team, but their means of doing so makes it difficult to call out. Keith was a master of passive aggressiveness.

Not Invented Here Syndrome

A related behavior is the "not invented here syndrome," a tendency to discount any idea that is not internally generated. Like passive aggressiveness, it is not directly expressed; people do not say, "I don't like it because it was not my idea," but its behavioral pattern is so common that it became the inspiration of a comic strip, *Not Invented Here,* set in the software development industry.

Passive aggressiveness, not invented here syndrome, and other similar behaviors are extremely counterproductive and an important underlying reason so many large technical projects fail, are delayed, or go over budget. Even if the right internal resources are in place, the team may not be aligned in the same direction, and if the right resources are not available, the team may be reluctant to accept them from the outside.

It is Not Enough to Be Right

One of the reasons some technologists face challenges when collaborating with others is because they *know* they are right. "They have thought out all the details involved in the strategy or systems change and are bursting with a need to tell everyone how exactly to do it," says Abbie Lundberg, business technology analyst and adviser, and former Editor-in-Chief of *CIO Magazine.* "They are thinking 'okay, I have nailed this and I am going to tell you how this is going to go' versus really engaging with people." If in the process they are challenged, they may become frustrated, intransigent or even outright antagonistic, and feel justified in being so because, 'they are right.'

As Gary Erickson explains it, rather than say, "'I hear what you are saying and let me respond to that,' they say 'you're wrong, you just don't get it.'"

"The test of a first-rate intelligence is the ability to hold two opposing ideas in mind at the same time and still retain the ability to function," said

F. Scott Fitzgerald, though he may as well have said, "first-rate *social* intelligence," because that is what is needed when STEM professionals find themselves at loggerheads with those outside their area of expertise. Two people looking at the same thing but from different perspectives can see different things and both still be right.

Remedies:
Collaboration

… let his air, his manner, and behaviour, be easy, courteous and affable, void of every thing haughty or assuming; his words few, express'd with modesty, and a respect for those he talks to. Be he ever ready to hear what others say; let him interrupt no body, nor intrude with his advice unask'd. Let him never trouble other people about his own affairs, nor concern himself with theirs. Let him avoid disputes; and when he dissents from others propose his reasons with calmness and complaisance. Be his wit ever guided by discretion and good nature, nor let him sacrifice a friend to raise a laugh. Let him not censure others, nor expose their failings, but kindly excuse or hide them. Let him neither raise nor propagate a story to the prejudice of any body. In short, be his study to command his own temper, to learn the humours of mankind, and to conform himself accordingly.

On Conversation

Benjamin Franklin – printed in *The Pennsylvania Gazette*, October 15, 1730.

The most common image people have of Benjamin Franklin is that of a wise, witty, jovial grandfatherly-type individual. In many ways, that description is apt, but Franklin was also a man of some glaring contradictions. Franklin's surviving correspondences demonstrate his many deep and lasting friendships, but he was also emotionally distant with his own family. He preached such things as diligence, dietary restraint, and temperance, but later in life he awoke late, suffered gout due to dietary excesses and was known to enjoy his drink (alcohol is "constant proof that God loves us and loves to see us happy"). And against long odds he was able to persuade France to support the American Revolution, yet he could not persuade his own son.

I believe that these various contradictions can be explained, at least partially, by saying that while he exhibited many virtues, he may not have been naturally inclined to all of them. Certainly this is suggested by his youthful quest to master virtuous living. After all, would a naturally virtuous man have taken the trouble to create such an elaborate methodology to achieve this? Not likely. Instead his effort suggests an ambitious and practical man (both unquestioned characteristics of Franklin) recognizing his own weaknesses and their negative implications for his prospects. He did this because he wanted to increase his odds for success. And if this is the case, then the antonyms of the virtues he strove to master paint the picture of a less than pleasing person. For example:

- Silence – Speak not but what may benefit others or our self; avoid trifling conversation.

- Sincerity – Use no hurtful deceit; think innocently and justly, and, if you speak, speak accordingly.

- Justice – Wrong none by doing injuries or omitting the benefits that are your duty.

- Moderation – Avoid extremes; forbear resenting injuries so much as you think they deserve.

- Tranquility – Be not disturbed at trifles, or at accidents common or unavoidable.

- Humility – Imitate Jesus and Socrates.

If we flip these we can image a man who may have been more than a little boisterous and argumentative, self-centered, conniving, hotheaded, and arrogant. Consider what he wrote in his autobiography regarding the virtue of humility.

> *My list of virtues contain'd at first but twelve: But a Quaker friend having kindly inform'd me that I was generally thought proud; that my pride show'd itself frequently in conversation; that I was not content with being in the right when discussing any point, but was overbearing and rather insolent; of which he convinc'd me by mentioning several instances; I determined endeavouring to cure myself if I could of this vice or folly among the rest, and I added humility to my list, giving an extensive meaning to the word. I cannot boast of much success in acquiring the reality of this virtue; but I had a good deal with regard to the appearance of it*

He later added:

> *In reality there is perhaps no one of our natural passions so hard to subdue as pride. Disguise it, struggle with it, beat it down, stifle it, mortify it as much as one pleases, it is still alive, and will every now and then peep out and show itself. You will see it perhaps often in this history* [his autobiography]. *For even if I could conceive that I had compleatly overcome it, I should probably be proud of my humility.*

Franklins efforts to achieve these virtues, or at least "the appearance" of them, may explain how he could succeed so well in some measures, yet fail in others when his natural inclinations "peeped out and showed themselves." For the most part, though, he succeeded because he had the ability to recognize and accept his weaknesses, the practical sense to realize how these impaired his success, and the willpower to change.

Preeminently, he appreciated that to get ahead you must get along, and according to Walter Isaacson in his biography of Franklin, "He adopted a style based on self-deprecating humor, unpretentious demeanor, and unaggressive conversation. When discussing contentious issues, he avoided direct confrontation in favor of a more diplomatic indirectness, often utilizing suggestions and Socratic questions that permitted other people to discover for themselves the weaknesses of their reasoning." Notice Isaacson did not say he *had* a style ..., but instead *adopted* a style .... Just as Franklin's inventions were the result of his problem solving instincts and gifts, so too was the persona he presented to others.

Be a Teammate
Author, artist and philosopher Elbert Hubbard said, "If you want a friend, you must be a friend." If we want the benefits that come from collaboration and teamwork, or avoid the repercussions of the lack of either, then we should first be good teammates. And even if we are not naturally great collaborators, we should *adopt the style* of great collaborators.

Obviously our ability to contribute to the achievement of the team goal is of preeminent importance, but how we contribute is also crucially important. Consider, which you would predict to win a tug-of-war competition: a team of football linemen pulling in different directions or an equal number of 98-pound weaklings all pulling in the same direction? What constitutes adequate teamwork may vary by one's environment, but there are certain basic characteristics that I have found to be particularly relevant to this discussion.

- Transparency
- Openness
- Flexibility
- Tolerance
- Supportiveness
- Dependability
- Positivity
- Sincerity

Transparency
It is frequently said that the greatest fear in the world is the fear of the unknown. When we do not know something, our imaginations can go wild filling the void with worst-case scenarios. And so it is in our personal relations. When others do not appear to be forthright with us, we assume they do not have our interests at heart, especially if there are past incidents that might substantiate that. Likewise, if we are opaque in our dealings with others, they may assume the worst of us, regardless of the reality.

Transparency is an antidote to distrust. If we can avoid perceptions that we are not being forthright – better yet, exude a sense that we are happy to share anything – we build trust, which is an essential element for collaboration. Even when we disagree or dissent, it is important that we do so in a forthright manner. As such we should abstain from all behind-the-back criticisms or lobbying. Few things undermine our reputation more than being caught in skullduggery.

Openness and Flexibility

Being seen as transparent, as a straight shooter, is a good start. However, for us to influence others we may need to demonstrate our own openness to being influenced first. Recall the MBTI traits associated with STJs: if both sides believe they are always right and are resistant to being controlled by others, the result may be intransigence on both sides.

One way of achieving the appearance of flexibility, while remaining true to our beliefs and convictions, is to avoid all wording that would suggest a direct contradiction. That is what Franklin found and used to great effect throughout his life. In fact, this may be one of his greatest legacies. He wrote:

I made it a rule to forbear all direct contradiction to the sentiments of others, and all positive assertion of my own. I even forbid myself, agreeably to the old laws of our Junto, the use of every word or expression in the language that imported a fixed opinion, such as certainly, undoubtedly, etc., and I adopted, instead of them, I conceive, I apprehend, or I imagine a thing to be so or so, or it so appears to me at present. When another asserted something that I thought an error, I denied myself the pleasure of contradicting him abruptly and of showing immediately some absurdity in his proposition; and in answering, I began by observing that in certain cases or circumstances his opinion would be right, but in the present case there appeared or seemed to me some difference, etc. I soon found the advantage of this charge in my manner; the conversations I engaged in went on more pleasantly.

The modest way in which I proposed my opinions procured them a readier reception and less contradiction; I had less mortification when I was found to be in the wrong, and I more easily prevailed with others to give up their mistakes and join with me when I happened to be in the right.

Such techniques can go a long way toward avoiding the downward spiral of mass intransigence.

Probably nowhere did he express this sentiment more effectively than in the speech he gave to the U.S. Constitutional Convention the morning of the draft constitution vote in September of 1787. In short, he said that over his many years he had encountered numerous times when he found he had been wrong regarding things upon which previously he had been absolutely sure, and that this had caused him to be more apt to doubt his own opinions and pay more respect to the judgment of others. The full text can be found at *www.brainiacparadox.com*.

While the successful vote later that day cannot be directly attributed to this speech, it is safe to say that the admission of fallibility from a man commonly acknowledged to be among the very greatest minds of his day must have caused even the most intransigent delegates to reconsider their position. All of us, no matter how smart, how experienced, how certain we may be in our own minds, must leave room for the possibility of being wrong. To the extent we are able to demonstrate that, so may others who disagree with us.

If some of these most recent points sound familiar, it could be because they are among the key points of Dale Carnegie's *How to Win Friends and Influence People*. Carnegie credited Franklin for many of the concepts in his books and seminars.

Tolerance

At times we must work with people we would prefer not to: maybe we question their intelligence, or character, or maybe they just rub us the wrong way. It may be hard not to betray our contempt by words or deeds, but doing so can be costly.

First, any enmity conveyed is likely to be returned, and probably escalated, jeopardizing our own agenda as well as the effectiveness of the team. Second, it is worth considering that a common reason others rub us the wrong way is because they are so different from ourselves, but that from such incongruous pairings often come the best results. Recall how Pixar organized their headquarters to encourage interaction between those who probably would not have otherwise. Perhaps the person who most aggravates us may also be the person who is key to our success.

Supportiveness

Because of the predominantly competitive nature of work, people assume that "if you are not for them, you are against them," and they, then, will be against you. Conversely, if you demonstrate that you support others they are much more likely to support you.

For those of us who share the previously mentioned trait of a strong need to control and equally strong aversion to being controlled by others, being fully supportive of others can be a vexing challenge. Even if we rationally attempt to defer to others, our instincts kick in and we try to take charge, or resist the lead of others. As with the other items in this section, the more we give, the more we get. Franklin was keenly aware of this phenomenon and wrote about it in his autobiography. He found, for example, that he could get much more done by making his proposals appear to be the ideas of others or by letting others take the lead (the antidote to the *not invented here syndrome*). He was willing to sacrifice his due credit in order to achieve his goals. Interestingly, in most cases the credit was ultimately attributed to him anyway.

Dependability
The characteristic of dependability may be too obvious to include here, but is too important to be left off this list. The whole point of collaboration is to achieve more or better through combined effort. Anyone who establishes a reputation for undependability will become the pariah of the team. Say what you will do, and do what you say.

Positivity
It would be easy to overlook, or underestimate the importance of this characteristic, but it can be crucial. First off, people naturally prefer to work with those who are positive, and avoid those who are negative. But more important, moods are contagious. If we are downbeat and negative, the mood of our team will likely shift in that direction, and everything will be more difficult. If we are happy and positive, the mood of the team is likely to follow and everything will be easier. If we make others feel affirmed and appreciated, they are more likely to do the same for us.

A project manager I know is a remarkably positive person. He juggles multiple projects at any given time and thus cannot make it to every project-related meeting. People often tell him that they hate it when he is not there, because everyone fights. It is not that he actively squelches the fights when he is present, but that his demeanor sets the tone for others in the room.

Sincerity – Say It Till It's True

As conceded earlier, the underlying attitudes associated with this foible may be the most stubborn of the nine, but they too can bend to the force of repetition. In other words, if we fake it long enough we begin to actually live it. Franklin wrote:

And this mode, which I at first put on with some violence to natural inclination, became at length so easy, and so habitual to me, that perhaps for these fifty years past no one has ever heard a dogmatical expression escape me. And to this habit (after my character of integrity) I think it principally owing that I had early so much weight with my fellow-citizens when I proposed new institutions, or alterations in the old, and so much influence in public councils when I became a member; for I was but a bad speaker, never eloquent, subject to much hesitation in my choice of words, hardly correct in language, and yet I generally carried my points.

Hope for All

In Chapter 1, I noted that Thomas Jefferson was a poor speaker and to the left we read Benjamin Franklin admitting the same thing. Most will be surprised. We assume that public figures will be gifted speakers, especially those with the reputations of Franklin and Jefferson. This should give heart to all who struggle with their verbal delivery, and serve to reinforce the idea that effective communication is about more than just good communication mechanics.

Though he acknowledges the failure to master all the virtues he set out to, his efforts likely rewired his brain so that he was fundamentally inclined towards certain behaviors. Thus not only was he able to improve his interactions with others, but he was able to do it with sincerity.

Building Rapport

The previous items provide a foundation for successful teamwork, but a truly powerful team is one whose members share a strong rapport. Rapport can be said to exist when people genuinely enjoy working together and perform better as a result. It depends on members investing a bit of their personal selves into professional relationships. With rapport comes much more power to influence others, both directly, and indirectly through the networks rapport often breeds.

Pick Your Battles

Despite our best efforts, there will be times when we must make an unpopular stand, even those that may threaten some of the collaboration, teamwork, and rapport we have been struggling to cultivate. When faced with such decisions, though, recall that discretion is the better part of valor.

As said earlier in this book, "It is not enough to be right." If the belief that we are right, or someone else is wrong, is the sole criterion by which we choose to engage, then we are likely to be in a constant state of conflict – such is the nature of opinions and the capriciousness of facts – and in so doing we are likely to dilute the effectiveness of our assertions.

People respect those who fight for their convictions, but abhor those who are *constantly* fighting for their convictions. Recall what Franklin said of Thomas Godfrey, "He expected unusual precision in everything said, or was forever denying or distinguishing upon trifles, to the disturbance of all conversation. He soon left us."

Like an old fashioned pull chain toilet, intermittent pulls of the chain invoke rushes of water that create compelling force, while frequent pulls (before the reservoir has refilled) have little useful affect and instead only annoy others with the droning sound of running water.

As such, it is important for us to pick our battles. Is the issue *absolutely* relevant to the work at hand and is the disagreement of significant magnitude? If yes to both, also consider timing and tactics. What is the most effective approach and does it have to be "now?"

Forewarned is Forearmed

Your efforts of transparency, openness, tolerance, supportiveness, forbearance and the others above should be returned in-kind from those you team with, but sadly there are some who will instead take advantage of such magnanimousness for personal gain. These organizational politicians not only sour teamwork, but also encourage others to retaliate, which leads the group towards a morass – "In the land of an eye for an eye, everyone is blind."

While I certainly do not recommend fighting such deeds with more of the same, I do believe that understanding the practices of such miscreants can help us confound or mitigate their efforts. Machiavelli's *The Prince* is the granddaddy of works that focus on the acquisition, maintenance, and manipulation of power. A recent book, *The 48 Laws of Power*, by Robert Greene, addresses the same topic in a more contemporary manner. While some of the "laws" are as contemptible as one might expect (Law 6: Court attention at all cost; Law 7: Get others to do the work for you, but always take the credit), others are legitimates pieces of self-defense. Law 1, for example, is *Never Outshine The Master*. To illustrate, the author tells the story of Nicolos Fouqut, the finance minister to Frances' Louis XIV who hosted the most spectacular party in the King's honor. Rather than ingratiating himself to the king, as hoped, he was arrested the next day for stealing from the treasury – though the only stealing he had done was on the king's behalf and with his full knowledge. Instead, the immensely proud king could not tolerate being outdone by an inferior.

So what do you do when you encounter the ill-intended work of others? Do not stoop to their level. Even if you were to succeed, you become suspect by others around you (Machiavelli talks of this). Instead, just remember that sunshine is the best disinfectant. Those who are guilty of such practices are usually found out eventually. If there are some modest ways you can speed up the process by shining a little light on their activities, fine, but in the mean time focus on understanding how you can avoid being made a victim of their malevolence.

More importantly, study such texts and scour your behaviors to identify cases where, as with the Nicolos Fouqut's example, you may be unwittingly administering self-inflicted wounds.

The combination of adopting basic collaborative characteristics, along with a fundamental understanding of how to prevent others from subverting your efforts, should provide you with the ability to succeed in your collaborative endeavors.

How to:
Be a Better Collaborator

1. **Perform a personal assessment of your collaborative characteristics.**

    ☐ First do a gut-check self-analysis. Off the top of your head, rate yourself on teaming, collaborating, and interpersonal relations at work. Capture this information and set it aside.

    ✓ Are you transparent in your ideas and actions?

    ✓ Are you readily open to alternative ideas?

    ✓ Are you flexible enough to compromise and alter plans as necessary?

    ✓ Can others depend on you to do what you say you are going to do or what you are assigned to do?

    ✓ Are you willing to defer your agenda to those of others?

    ✓ Do you support others' success, even if it involves personal costs?

    ✓ How well do you tolerate those who you do not like?

    ☐ Ask two or more people with whom you work what they see as your areas of strengths and opportunities for improvements in terms of collaboration. Ask them their opinions about you in relation to the questions addressed in the preceding self-analysis.

    ☐ Review the various feedback material you assembled earlier (performance appraisals, 360-degree reviews, etc.), noting any comments that may be related to elements of collaboration.

    ☐ Compare your gut check analysis with the previous two feedback sources.

    ✓ If the consensus is that there are no significant challenges, you may skip onto the next chapter, though I suggest reading through the following items anyway, considering whether such items may be of assistance to you.

    ✓ If it is apparent that there are areas for improvement, work through the following steps.

☐ Identify a personal coach from among colleagues, friends, or a spouse.

Note: As you pursue personal behavioral and/or attitudinal change, consider creating a communication plan – using the tool on page 318 – to change others' perceptions of you as it relates to these.

2. **Work to master individual characteristics that contribute to a good collaborative environment, which in turn will make you a more desirable teammate and leader.**

☐ Transparency
   ✓ Be forthright, clear, and concise in conveying your ideas and beliefs to others.
   ✓ Do not say things to individuals in private that you are not saying to the entire group in public.
   ✓ When in doubt about whether to inform or update others, error on the side of disclosure.
   ✓ Help the group drive towards clear decisions.

☐ Openness
   ✓ Carefully listen to others before responding.
   ✓ In matters of opinion, avoid dogmatic statements, and direction contradictions.
      o Rather than *certainly* or *undoubtedly*, try something like *I believe*, or *it appears*.
      o Rather than *no*, or *you're wrong*, try something like *while that may be true to an extent, in this case it would seem ...*
   ✓ In disagreements of fact that are resolved in your favor, accept your victory with humility.

☐ Flexibility
   ✓ In cases where your position does not prevail, seek out a way to compromise.
   ✓ When the team's course diverges from the direction you favored, be willing to change course with it.

☐ Tolerance

- ✓ Work with those you dislike in the same way you would work with those you like.
- ✓ Think twice before speaking when what you say might be taken negatively.

☐ Supportiveness

- ✓ Once the team has set a direction, support it regardless of your apprehensions or disagreements.
- ✓ Help others on the team succeed, even when it disadvantages you.
- ✓ Be willing to share, or even shift, credit for your contributions if it will further the team's progress.

☐ Dependability

- ✓ Faithfully participate in group meetings and activities.
- ✓ If you agree to or are assigned a task, deliver as specified.

☐ Positivity

- ✓ Be pleasant and upbeat.
  - o Start every interaction with a warm and sincere smile.
- ✓ At times of great stress or aggravation, keep your cool.
  - o Take a deep breath and focus on a positive.
- ✓ Integrate a degree of humor and levity into interactions as appropriate.
  - o Example: Start a presentation with a joke, a humorous cartoon, or show a funny and relevant YouTube video.
- ✓ Work to make others feel liked and appreciated.

☐ Sincerity

- ✓ Do not just "adopt the appearance" of the preceding characteristics, but endeavor to internalize them. *Say it till it's true.*

3. **Build rapport with a diverse set of colleagues.**

☐ "People don't care how much you know until they know how much you care" so make sure to integrate some personal interactions along with your professional interactions.

   ✓ Allow for a judicious amount of personal exchanges in formal professional gatherings.

      o At a meeting, use the time before everyone has arrived, to exchange pleasantries with those present. Use this opportunity to reach out to those you do not know as well, as well as those you do: "Any interesting plans for the weekend?" or, "Did you read the story this morning about...?"

      o Consider using time at the end of the meeting as well. Follow-up questions may work better here: "How did that _____ go last weekend?" or, "did you try that restaurant I told you about?"

      Note: Everything in moderation. Do not let personal talk crowd out professional work.

   ✓ Attempt to know at least a little bit about the personal lives of those with whom you work (their family situation, their personal interests, where they live, and where they grew up).

   ✓ When meeting someone new, also attempt to learn a little about him or her personally. Look for similar backgrounds, interests, mutual friends, etc.

☐ If not already, learn to be a proficient small talker.

   ✓ Get others to talk about themselves.

   ✓ Ask open-ended questions. Possible topics:

      o Their families
      o What they do for fun outside of work
      o How they got into their field
      o Where they went to school
      o Where they lived before

   ✓ Pay attention and respond is such a way that demonstrates you are listening.

      o Comment positively on what they have told you.
      o Ask follow-up questions.

- ✓ If you have trouble getting them to talk about themselves, try asking more neutral questions.
  - o If they have read a particular book (one that you really liked and feel that they might also like). Or it could be a movie, or music.
  - o If you have been to a certain place (that you think they may like).
  - o If they have tried a certain restaurant.
  - o Alternatively, ask if there are any books, movies, music, or travel places they would recommend to you.

    Note: Small talk does not have to stay small talk; as you come to better understand the person with whom you are speaking, you are likely to find opportunities to migrate the discussion to more meaningful topics.

- ✓ Search for commonalities; things you can both speak of with equal interest.
- ✓ Avoid hot-button topics (tread very lightly with regards to religion, politics, and anything that – based on context – you think may challenge their deeply-held beliefs … or they yours).

☐ Seek out opportunities for deeper personal relationships with a broad set of workmates.

- ✓ Participate in organizational recreational teams or community volunteer work.
- ✓ Arrange to have lunch with a variety of workmates.
- ✓ Organize or participate in social activities outside of work.

4. **Build networks. Even as you work to develop rapport with diverse groups of people, look for relationships that can provide you strategic advantages.**

   ☐ Identify the groups or individuals among whom a good rapport would be most important.

   ☐ Identify and target people who are *connectors*: people who naturally build large relationship networks.

   ☐ Identify and target the *mavens* within these groups: people whose knowledge or opinions are held in high regard, and who others seek out for advice.

   ☐ Identify and target the *salesmen*: people who have a natural charisma and great persuasive powers.

5. **Study organizational politics. Those who understand it can anticipate, recognize, and thwart it, without actually stooping to it themselves.**

   ☐ Study its foundation in human nature.
   - ✓ Read books, articles, or online content. *The 48 Laws of Power*, for instance, provides an excellent insight.
   - ✓ Closely observe those around you. Who is honorable, dependable, and sincere and who is not?

   ☐ Study your organization.
   - ✓ What characteristics and qualities does the organization appear to value (as opposed to official value statements)?
   - ✓ What behavior is rewarded and what is punished?
   - ✓ What types of people succeed and what types languish?

Summary – Chapter 13
It Takes a Team

Collaboration and teamwork are essential ingredients to professional success in all fields and yet they are weak points for some technical professionals. Four contributing factors are:

1. Introversion or a preference among some to work alone.
2. Innate personality characteristics that may run counter to good team participation.
3. A clash of thinking styles with those they are expected to collaborate.
4. A tendency for passive aggressiveness.

Often accompanying these is a strong underlying belief that "I am right." Whether we are right or not, if we cannot get along we will not get ahead.

Franklin himself appears to have exhibited counter-collaborative characteristics in his early years, but he recognized how these would impair his prospects and he worked to overcome, or at least mask, them as he entered early adulthood.

For us, overcoming this foible is best achieved by focusing on individual contributory characteristics such as: transparency, openness, flexibility, tolerance, supportiveness, dependability, positivity, and sincerity.

If we practice these, others are more likely to practice them with us. If we follow with efforts to connect more personally with others, we can create a genuine rapport, and from that sprouts relationships and personal networks, which can avail us to great opportunities.

However, we must stay vigilant against those who undermine honest efforts. It is helpful to also understand the workings of power and politics, not so that we too can use them, but so we can prevent becoming victims of them.

Monitor, Assess, and Log ...

- When you use contradictive language and dogmatic assertions.

- When once having formed an opinion, you shut down consideration of others' viewpoints.

- When you criticize or lobby against consensus decisions behind the scenes.

- When you say or do things that undermine others.

You Will Know You Are Overcoming This When

- You sense less tension in your interpersonal interactions.

- You can appreciate the advantages of working with those of different opinions, attitudes, and approaches (who previously would have aggravated you).

- You notice others appear more open to your views.

- You find yourself achieving unexpected and remarkable results.

- You not only are invited to be on more teams, but to lead them.

– Chapter 14 –

The Communicator
Is the Message

He that composes himself is wiser than he that composes a book.
—Benjamin Franklin

Foible: Credibility (mismanaged)

Precept: Establish and maintain the credibility necessary to
garner others' support

*P*eople, *now a days, are unwilling either to commend or dispraise what they read,
until they are in some measure informed who or what the author of it is,
whether he be poor or rich, old or young, a schollar or a leather apron man, &c. and
give their opinion of the performance, according to the knowledge which they have of
the author's circumstances.*

These are among the opening lines of Benjamin Franklin's first published
work – an April 2, 1722 letter to the editor of *The New-England Courant*
secretly submitted under the pseudonym Silence Dogood. At 15, this eager
student of human nature already grasped the seminal importance of
credibility as well as its fickle nature.

Franklin's autobiography and other writings reveal a man unusually
aware of how he was perceived by others and intent on managing those
perceptions to his benefit. The natural assumption is that he was driven by
more than a healthy ego, something Franklin admitted to having – but there
is good reason to believe that it may have more to do with Franklin's

practical nature. Just as Franklin was curious about how most physical things worked, using that knowledge for practical applications (e.g., the lightning rod), he was also curious about the inner workings of people, and of using that knowledge for practical purposes. Like few others, he was able to see himself through others' eyes, and thus able to manage his conduct in ways that would enhance his effectiveness in society.

Unlike his later peer John Adams, a great intellect and patriot but also blunt and uncompromising, Franklin operated on the principle that words and ideas were not enough, no matter what their merit; what people thought of a speaker greatly influenced what was communicated and how people were influenced. In 1964 Marshall McLuhan famously said, "The medium is the message," proposing that how a message is delivered is more important than the message itself. Franklin, more than 200 years earlier, knew that the *communicator* was the message. As such, rather than dismissing Franklin's many contrivances as shameful self-promotion, we should give this brilliant man the benefit of the doubt and consider that he may have merely been using all the tools at his disposal, tapping into the societal shorthand that is credibility.

Credibility

While the human mind can do extraordinary things – ponder the meaning of life, create great music and art, or woo a lover – much of the time it is a basic decision-making machine. Each day we make countless decisions: some micro – what stories to read in the morning paper; some small – what route to take to work; some medium – which person to work with on a project; some large – when to make a career move. Each decision, even small ones, can involve many variables and many possible choices. Considering such complexity, it is remarkable that we are able to function and interact so fluidly.

We navigate these decisions based primarily on the knowledge we have accumulated throughout our lives (emotions, instinct, and reflexes also play a part). Some of that knowledge is obtained firsthand through our experiences, but there are limits to what can be obtained this way, so the far greater portion of that knowledge is accumulated secondhand. This presents a dilemma, though, because we know that not all secondhand information is equally reliable. Some sources are incompetent, some benignly incorrect, others distort information, and finally some outright deceive. Therefore, when we face decisions, especially those that involve risk, we take into account the trustworthiness, i.e., the credibility, of the source. There are some sources we believe no matter what they say and others just the opposite. Credibility is allotted to sources based on four factors.

Experience: Track record with a source.

Repute: Trust conferred on one entity by a respected third party. This is the "9 out of 10 doctors recommend" technique used by advertisers.

Presumption: Trust we assign based on situational assumptions, often related to perceived motives. For example, juries will assess a witness' credibility based on what the witness has to gain or lose, i.e., their motive; those who testify in exchange for reduced sentences are less credible than those with nothing to gain.

Surface: This refers to an assessment we make based on superficial considerations: her physical appearance, his clothing, her accent, and so on.

Philosopher Patrick Wilson, author of *Second-hand Knowledge*, coined the term *cognitive authority* to explain the kind of authority based on the integrity of information. Those who are able to command considerable credibility, those who are deemed to "know what they are talking about," are said to be cognitive authorities. Cognitive authority differs from administrative authority – authority based on organizational hierarchy and power. Cognitive authority enables persuasion and influence, and is one of the things that provides a true leader his or her power.

Obviously, the more credible we can become, the more authority we will possess. That, in turn, allows us to achieve other things that can make us more credible still. It is similar to the saying that it takes money to make money; it takes credibility to build credibility. In fact, there are many aspects of credibility that parallel currency and which can facilitate its better understanding.

Just as currency is a proxy for wealth, credibility is a proxy for authority. Like currency, credibility can be earned and spent, won and lost, banked and loaned. We earn it with actions and behaviors that suggest we are trustworthy, competent, and dependable, and we spend it when we ask others to support us. It can be won when luck provides us successes, and lost when we do not deliver as expected. We bank it when we accumulate more than we spend, and we loan or invest it when we use our credibility to support people or programs outside our realm of control (if they succeed, we are more credible, if not, we are less).

High Tech Equals High Credibility Cost
Some things are more expensive than others in terms of credibility. In the free marketplace, financial costs are determined by the intersection of the supply and demand variables. Credibility costs can be said to be determined by an intersection of knowledge and risk variables. If the risks associated

with a decision are small and the decision maker has firsthand knowledge of the subject, the credibility cost is low. In other words, it does not really matter who makes the proposal, the decision maker will make the call based on his or her own experience. Conversely, if the risks associated with a decision are high in terms of funds, resources or possible negative outcomes, and the decision maker has inadequate knowledge to evaluate the merits of the proposal himself, the credibility costs will be high; it absolutely matters who is proposing it.

The types of work in which many technical professionals are involved often equate to high credibility costs: high financial or other risks, and decision-makers who must depend upon the expertise of others. Too few fully appreciate this, though. With a bias towards objective analysis, technical professionals may easily recognize and focus on the merits of the fact, idea or thing they are proposing and believe others should as well. They tend to overlook the fact that those they are communicating with may have inadequate knowledge or experience to make their own confident assessment. The failure of decision-makers to see the glaring benefits of certain proposals is a common complaint.

It may help us empathize with non-technical people, however, if we consider what it would be like if the tables were turned, and we were asked to make a major decision in an area outside our own expertise. Let's say that – for some implausible reason – the CEO of an organization was to entrust a member of her R&D team with the responsibility of purchasing some expensive modern art for her office. Assuming that modern art is not his area of expertise, and that failure to do a good job would negatively affect his career, it would be very important for him to learn as much, if not more, about the art broker with whom he would work, than about the art itself. After all, even if he studied and researched art extensively, he still might not be able to tell the difference between a masterpiece and a high school freshman art project, while to the art expert, it may be glaringly obvious. In the end, he needs to rely on the art broker's expertise and honesty, i.e., his credibility.

The same is true for many business managers asked to commit resources on things they do not fully understand. Sure, it may sound like a great idea, but are the estimates correct and will it deliver as promised? Ultimately it comes down to the credibility of those involved.

Building Bankable Credibility

As organizations have become more complex, and the functions within them more specialized, individual or team credibility has become increasingly necessary to offset the leaps of faith decision makers must take when they lack the mastery of the subject with which they are dealing. This represents a kind of credibility inflation. As such, it behooves us to understand and manage our credibility: to amass enough to provide us the authority necessary to do the things we want to do; to guard against unnecessary expenditures (of our credibility) big and small; and to invest it in ways that provide additional leverage.

Few people, however, consciously and actively manage their credibility. Sure, we may undertake general activities that will enhance it and guard against others that would diminish it, but how many actively focus on this, stepping back to take an objective look and then purposefully acting in ways that will most effectively build credibility the way Franklin did? Fortunately, those who have followed the methodology thus far should already be more credible than when they started the book. Acceptance, simplicity, empathy, concision, results orientation, teamwork, and aesthetics all contribute to one's credibility. However, there are additional things that can be done that will yield even greater returns.

Remedies:
Credibility

Managing Expectations

The basic place to start is with managing expectations. Direct experience is the most influential factor driving credibility, and fortunately it can be influenced because it is relative. In other words, the very same achievement may be perceived as positive, neutral or negative, depending upon on what was originally expected. The four-minute mile was considered one of the greatest human achievements, but it is now routine. If a shipping company promises to get a package to us in four days and gets it to us in five, we may be irked. But if they had promised it in six days and they delivered it in five, we would likely be pleased. All things being equal, it is our expectations that govern how a given event is perceived. It is essential to our credibility that we manage others' expectations so that we are sure to meet or exceed them.

Advice espousing the management of expectations is hardly anything new or surprising, but what is surprising is how infrequently people practice it. Whether excessive optimism or pressure to promise more, faster and cheaper, we are often undercut by unrealistic expectations. I am confident you have had more than one occasion when you delivered what, by objective criteria, would be considered a success, but were criticized because relatively minor items were not as expected.

In the realm of IT, unfortunately, this has almost become the norm. Repeated overruns, delays, deficient products, and outright failures have become a hallmark and serve to demonstrate what happens when a credibility deficit is amassed for an entire discipline. CEOs trade IT nightmare stories. It does not matter that such problems are often the result of clients who do not know what they want, do not commit the resources necessary to support the project, or make changes all the way up to the 11th hour: what is noted is that IT rarely delivers on expectations. Those in other fields may face their own versions of this.

We need to get ahead of this and manage expectations strategically. A brilliant example of this comes from Jerry, a New York apartment remodeler. He primarily works with high-end clients and over the years has experienced a tendency for some to try to finagle things out of him. They will assert that certain design elements or features were in the original agreement (but were not) and insist he include them, or they will claim damage occurred to other parts of their residence during the remodeling, which now require renovation. The logical, linear mind may see the solution to this problem is to have tighter agreements and to carefully document conditions beforehand, so there can be little room for disputes later. He, though, being an intuitive, lateral thinker, came up with a better solution. He learned to expect such behavior, and to bake it into his estimates. That way, when the client inevitably makes their claims, he may feign protest, but eventually he relents, delighting the client who feels they are getting something for nothing. These clients then rave about his work to their friends. Even though his approach results in his estimates being moderately higher than his competitors, the difference is easily offset by the strong recommendations he receives. His only promotion is word-of-mouth and yet he is always busy. That is not just managing expectations, but orchestrating them, and is just the type of thing Franklin might have done.

Einstein said that the definition of insanity is "doing the same thing over and over again and expecting different results," and yet time and time again, we undertake work based on the same erroneous assumptions. When IT leaders encounter project delays and overruns caused by client indecision, changes, and scope creep, their reactions are to demand ever-more detailed agreements and requirement definitions in future projects, rather than just realizing that certain clients will not know what they want until they see it. If they would only factor that in, and respond accordingly, as Jerry does with his remodeling clients, they could deliver the desired results within the expected parameters and simultaneously delight their clients with their flexibility and client-service orientation.

Say-Do Alignment

One of the most insidious impacts on our credibility comes when our actions do not match our words: when we talk the talk, but do not walk the walk. Saying one thing and doing another does not just detract from our credibility, it makes others cynical of us and hampers our ability to build credibility in the future. Typically, this is a top-down problem: executive leadership espouses the need to take more risks, but then punishes the first risks taken that do not pay off; a boss who stresses the need for honesty and integrity in her team, but who favors those who demonstrate neither. In both cases, leadership will damage its ability to influence those same audiences in the future.

This is not just a leadership problem, though. We are all likely to exhibit this behavior at times. The more we can avoid it, the better off we will be.

Two-Sidedness

Another important phenomenon of human nature and credibility – and one that may be counterintuitive to the logical thinker – is "Two-Sidedness." Researchers have found that individuals who present evidence that appears contrary to their own interests are perceived as being more credible. It is the converse of the logic, "If it seems too good to be true, it usually is," but in this case, "If they are honest about their deficiencies, then they must also be honest about their claims."

Alan L. Heill Jr., author of *Voice of America,* tells the story of policy makers in Washington who, during the early days of World War II, attempted to squelch a planned broadcast that included a quote from General Joseph Stilwell saying, "The Japanese gave us a hell of a beating in Burma." However, the broadcast staff prevailed and it was later learned from interrogations of Japanese that it was that quote that made them really believe Voice of America.

Even a source that is already perceived as very credible will be more so if they admit points that are perceived to be contrary to their self-interests.

Here too, Franklin was a master. Woven throughout his autobiography are admissions of his own shortcomings. He even questions his own objectivity and motives in the telling of his life's story. In admitting such things, Franklin made other claims more credible. Not only that, but his charming admissions make him so much more appealing to the reader: we *want* to believe the positive things.

When advocating an idea, product or service, proponents instinctively focus only on the positive attributes (one-sided communication). If you can offer or admit to a perspective that includes one or two things that are clearly contrary to your self-interest – of course you will want to avoid deal-breakers – you can overcome even a skeptical audience. Unfortunately, few are willing to take this advice. If they are already facing an uphill battle in trying to get approval on something, "Why would I admit something that would give them an excuse to turn me down?"

Objective Third Party Endorsements

A few years back I was working with the Information Technology department of a major corporation. Industry competition was putting extraordinary pressure on the organization to make a series of technology investments, some very large. Top corporate leadership, however, was hesitant. They acknowledged that something had to be done, but seemed reluctant to trust IT's recommendation on such a huge expenditure and commitment. A series of underperforming projects had depleted IT's credibility and undermined their ability to sell their solutions.

In this case, I worked with the leaders to reestablish broad-based credibility. We chose to segment the department's audiences into three groups: IT employees, the rest of the organization, and external trade organizations and publications. For the IT team, we undertook programs that improved overall communication, and in particular, efforts that fostered communication upward in the team, not just downward; the mere act of listening improved the credibility of management among employees.

For the rest of the organization, we cleaned up communication, ensuring that those emanating from the team were clear, concise, consistent and easily understood. Finally, we made efforts to attract industry awards, improve our standing in industry rankings, increase media coverage of our IT activities, and place IT executives in public forums. We called this last strategy, "selling from the outside in."

All our efforts were soon paying dividends, but it was particularly noticeable how the external coverage improved credibility. We attracted attention from a premiere industry periodical, which did a several-page feature story on the IT team. We also received some prominent industry awards and accolades.

Before long, internal technology leaders were noting the difference in interactions with corporate leadership. They more readily approved proposals and with fewer questions and discussion. Nothing else had changed, but these leaders obviously found the entire function more credible.

What we had done was leverage aspects of reputed and presumed credibility. These trade publications were seen as cognitive authorities. They covered technology developments and trends closely and had exposure to the best operations in the field, i.e., "they knew what they were talking about." Plus, they had no perceived vested interest that would bring their support into question. The executive leadership's attitude evolved from, "These guys are not as good as they claim" to, "If these publications say they are good, they must be good." The media reported on the same things the team had been saying to corporate leadership for some time, but those previous attempts were undercut by presumed IT team motives.

Attracting Media Attention

As the previous example illustrates, coverage by well-respected organizations can make you or your team more credible. It could be a story focused on some of your work, or simply quoting you.

How does one attract such media interviews or quotes? It can be hard to break into, because journalists often go back to a pool of sources they have used in the past. The good news is that once you are in that pool, they will check back with you from time to time. Here are some things you can do to attract attention.

Press releases are the most traditional way to attract media attention. Normally these are provided to appropriate print, radio, and TV organizations by the public relations department in conjunction with major developments. However, the role and importance of press releases has changed along with the evolution in news delivery channels. They still have their place, but it is foolish to make these the full extent of publicity efforts.

A great and underutilized approach to attracting media attention is services such as ProfNet.com, HelpAReporter.com, and others that allow you to offer yourself as an expert source. You simply register and post the appropriate information and either wait to be contacted (*www.profnet.com*), or respond to journalist queries (*www.helpareporter.com*).

Another way to spur coverage is to reach out to writers and editors personally. You could identify those who would seem relevant to what you have to offer and call or email them, or you could meet them at major conferences, symposiums, and other events related to your field; writers from industry publications sometimes attend these. Seek them out for a conversation, build some rapport and exchange business cards. If all goes well, there is a good chance they will contact you at some point when they have a relevant story topic. It does not hurt if you display knowledge on a hot topic and demonstrate reasonable eloquence (use the key messages you developed in Chapter 7 or create special new ones for this specific purpose).

Another approach is to monitor industry publication editorial calendars, which are listings of the topics a publication plans to cover in future issues. They allow companies to plan their advertisements to coincide with relevant story topics. For example, if there is going to be a story about cloud computing, vendors that provide that service will probably want to advertise in that issue, especially since they can expect that most of their competitors will. For our purposes, though, they also provide a heads-up for those who want story coverage. If your organization is doing some groundbreaking work in a certain area, the publication may

Not for Everyone

While anyone *can* court media attention, not everyone *should*. Generally, media organizations are looking for people who are uniquely qualified to speak on a topic, whether because of their specific expertise, the team they lead, a special project they are working on, or the organization they represent.

Though this may only be applicable to a small portion of those reading this, the accompanying information is provided anyway because the media can be such a potent tool to the right individual. Even if that is you, keep in mind that most organizations require any interaction with the media be pre-approved.

Do not engage with the mass media (or blogs and other new media) unless you have the proper authority to do so. Chapter 15 provides advice on working constructively with corporate communications (or its equivalent in your organization).

be interested in featuring, interviewing, or quoting you. If it is a visual topic, they may even want to take pictures. To participate, contact the publication, asking to talk to the applicable editor or the assigned writer. Unfortunately, only a few publications post their editorial calendars online, but they are very useful when available.

Getting Published

Writing something that is published is another avenue to enhancing credibility. Regardless of what you say and in what format (article, column or book), merely being entrusted with a mass-media outlet endows you with presumed credibility.

Self Perpetuating

Something to keep in mind regarding media coverage is that it often becomes self-perpetuating; once you have recognition in these areas, you are more likely to be interviewed for other stories. I have seen people reinvent themselves this way. This assumes one does a good job the first time. That is why key messages, Q&A's and sound bites are so important.

Unfortunately, getting published is not always easy and the strategies for achieving this are far too involved to cover adequately here. If you decide to follow this route, there are many books and other sources that can help guide you. There are times, however, when you get lucky and they come to you. If you receive a significant award or demonstrate leadership in a selected area, publications may request that you write an article or a guest column. However, you must consider that this type of platform carries risks, as well as rewards:

- Make sure you can deliver a quality product in the time allotted.

- Choose your topic carefully – both for appropriateness and for your ability to address it competently.

- Commit to your best effort when planning and executing.

- Seek support and feedback: have peers read for content accuracy and relevance; communication professionals review it for style and technique; and individuals who are representative of your audience for overall acceptability.

- Have a fresh set of eyes read the final draft.

Based on either time available or confidence levels, this is another case where seeking external expertise, even a ghostwriter, may be an excellent investment.

Awards and Recognition – Instant Credibility
Third-party endorsements come in many forms, some explicit and some implicit. Many industry organizations and publications sponsor awards programs and have designations used to spotlight leaders in the field. And though many of these designations result from an entirely internal process, and thus are difficult to influence, others are based on external suggestions and submissions. As in the preceding example, these can be a surprisingly effective way to get an instant boost of credibility.

Those who are familiar with the selection process for these may ridicule them as less than objective or rigorous – sometimes more resembling a beauty pageant – but that does not matter. They can still positively influence leaders in your organization and external audiences. For example, employers find it easier to recruit scarce talent when their organization receives such recognition.

Regardless of your technical specialty, there are probably several awards, industry rankings or other recognition opportunities associated with your field. They do not have to be a Noble Prize to confer some credibility, but obviously the more respected, prominent and independent the organization that bestows these the better. You can probably already think of a couple, and more can be found with a little research. Once you have taken inventory, make a strategic decision as to which to pursue. Then make a concerted effort with your application.

As you receive awards, make others aware of these. For example, post awards, plaques, certificates or copies of articles on the wall near the entrance of your office. Reference these on a department intranet site or (subtly and judiciously) in presentations.

New/Social Media
An increasingly popular and easy way to get published is through blogs, podcasts, inclusion in social networking sites, or any of the countless new-media forums. These can be a good way to achieve exposure but by themselves do not necessarily build credibility. After all, it is the barrier to traditional media that creates its reputed credibility value. Anyone can participate in the countless online venues and many do. However, if you find a new and creative approach, hit upon a niche market or are just very good at this, building a huge following, it can be very effective.

You can also piggyback on the success of others. Some bloggers, digital publications, podcasts, etc., have accumulated quite a following and may be interested in talking about you, your organization, or product. Here again, though, the value may be limited. Even the most prominent bloggers, for example, may only be known among a fairly narrow audience segment; your management or others may not appreciate the value of these. Then again, representatives of major publications often follow these. Hence, coverage in a niche online outlet could lead to coverage in large, traditional publications.

Professional Organizations

Though something many professionals do anyway, it is worth stating that affiliation with one or more professional organizations provides an opportunity to enhance credibility. This is particularly the case if you get more deeply involved by joining committees or holding offices. Even if you do not receive the type of industry awards and designations mentioned above, leadership positions in industry organizations suggests that you must be held in fairly high esteem among your peers.

If the organization offers special certification or accreditation designations, strongly consider pursuing them. Initials after your name convey a sense of credibility, even if, as in some cases, others do not know what they mean.

Academic Affiliations

Beyond pursuing additional degrees, affiliations with colleges and universities can enhance how others see you. Assuming you do not already work for a university, teaching as an adjunct professor or a guest lecturer is one method. There may also be a way to serve as an industry advisor within a department related to your field.

Speaking Engagements

Being invited by an external group to speak or participate in a panel discussion is similar in effect to getting published. If invitations do not come, consider offering to speak for certain groups, join a speakers bureau, or add your name to one of many online lists of experts that are available to speak on a specific topic.

Take note, however, that public speaking carries considerably more risk than most other avenues proposed. When you submit something in writing, there is the time to reflect, rewrite, and receive others' input. However, when you are presenting, there are so many more things that can go wrong … horribly wrong. Even if you are simply reading a carefully prepared and vetted speech, your presentation skills can fail you. In addition, misstatements, or being shown up on a panel, can diminish your credibility.

If you are interested in pursuing this path, or are already receiving invitations, you may want to consider getting some expert help, either in preparation or in reviewing and editing. You should practice and test presentations in front of others who are willing to give you candid and constructive feedback. In the end, despite speaking engagements' potential value, you are better off avoiding them unless you are sure you can do them reasonably well. Remember the saying: better to keep your mouth shut and be thought a fool, then to open it and remove all doubt.

Benchmarking

A different approach to objective third-party endorsements is benchmarking. You should not have benchmarking done just to enhance your credibility, but when done for the right reasons, it can still have that effect. Results that indicate you, or your team, are the best, most efficient, leading innovators, etc., can be leveraged to elevate your standing.

Generally, this is not a preferred approach. First, this will not be an option for many of those reading this book (because of the nature of their work). Second, not all benchmarks are known or respected enough for the results to carry much weight. Finally, there is always the risk the results will cast your team in a less than favorable light.

For some, though, this is a good option. There are four basic routes to doing this, which I have delineated based on funding.

Fund Internally

You can internally fund and conduct benchmarking, but the results will likely not serve the desired purpose. Those conducting the work will not be seen as objective nor as skilled as an external organization that specializes in this. The exception: some large organizations have internal teams that do this for various functions.

Pay External

Hire consultants to evaluate your operations according to your personal specifications – you pay the entire cost. The act of buying a service, however, automatically brings into question the objectivity of the results, though some benchmarking organizations have more credibility than others. Choosing the right one (it is more important that your audience trusts them than you do) may mitigate this issue.

Share

Collaborate with other organizations to have benchmarking performed. This has several advantages. It will be cheaper because the costs will be shared. It will likely be viewed as more objective. In addition, it may produce more accurate results because the participating organizations are likely to be more careful to provide good data when they have a financial stake.

Participate

You can also participate in omnibus research, funded by the research organization, or someone else; usually they share the results with you in return for your participation. In addition to being the cheapest approach (you still have to invest time), it may also be the most valuable, because the lack of a financial expenditure diminishes the potential of a perceived conflict of interest. On the other hand, you only get measured by what they want to measure. Also, other participants might not be as thorough in collecting and sharing information if they are not paying for it.

Other Endorsements

The previous options are some of the more common sources for third-party endorsements, but depending on your specific field and circumstances, there may be others. Are there especially respected institutions or individuals that can endorse you in some way?

Communication Mapping

Chapter 10 discussed the communication noise that bombards us and overwhelms our ability to absorb information. This noise is partly the result of the way the vast majority of people deal with their organizational communication responsibilities, which is reactively: in other words, there is a triggering event and then they communicate to various audiences accordingly: "Next month we start implementation of …," "last month we completed …," "performance is up …." The problem with this approach is that the flow of information is usually erratic and disharmonious. Sometimes there is much to report, other times there is nothing. Sometimes information is important, other times it is trivial. Sometimes the messages are all positive, and other times they are all negative. While there are a few cases, such as with project plans, where there is some tangible forethought and planning of communications, even then they are not considered in the broader context of what else is going on and being communicated. In short, even when our communications are targeted, concise, and easy to understand, we likely create communication noise. Now consider that music is just noise that is organized into a rhythm and pleasing harmony.

Communication Mapping is a unique technique that organizes formal communications into a harmonious flow, optimizing it for operational and psychological effects. The following explanation discusses it in terms of team communications, but the tool is completely scalable. It can be used by an individual to manage their regular communications with managers, peers, and others, and by entire organization to manage communications with various constituents, internal and external.

Communication Mapping could be called *Strategic Story Telling* because it seeks to forecast and organize sporadic communications into those that tell a story or paint a picture. For those familiar with lean manufacturing techniques, it has similarities to level scheduling (a method of production scheduling designed to reduce excess inventory and waiting periods by *leveling* each stage of the manufacturing process).

All organizations have standing communication tools and channels that members may – and often are expected to – feed with relevant information. These may be status reports, leadership presentations, newsletters, web pages, reports to the board of directors, and so on. In communication mapping, these represent the demand variable. The production variables are the communication items (news) related to our teams or us. These could be project updates, performance numbers, team accomplishments, and third-party endorsements.

Both the demand and production of these can be forecasted and planned, and while some items must follow rigid timing, others are more flexible. For example, demand items like organizational reports, newsletters, and the like, generally follow a set schedule, and others, such as web site updates, and email distributions are more ad hoc. On the news side of the equation, project milestones, status results and third-party recognition are more time-sensitive communication production elements, while the timing is more flexible on awareness-building communications.

To support a level and coherent flow of the information entails forecasting both communication demand and production along a set of intervals, and then adjusting the variable items to achieve a smooth harmonious flow of information. A sample of a tool to support communication mapping, as well as instructions for using it, is on page 326.

Whether for an entire organization or individual, communication mapping is a relatively easy and amazingly effective way to manage communications to their greatest affect in building credibility.

Although communication mapping may seem like a lot of additional work, it actually saves time; creating reports, memos, presentations or other communications, can consume a significant amount of our time and effort. Much of that time is used to figure out what we want to say and how. Communication mapping provides clarity of purpose that allows us to skip directly to production. It also provides other benefits: many organizations do not have tracking tools that provide a consolidated view of all projects and activities and as a result, conflicts and other problems are often not caught until too late. An unintended but useful benefit of communication mapping is that it provides a process and view that can help identify operational conflicts long in advance.

To pull it all together, communication mapping provides the mechanism to convert the random notes and percussions of reactive communication into a harmonic symphony of information that enhances our, or our team's, credibility.

How To:
Build and Manage Credibility

1. **Manage expectations – make commitments to others in such a way that you are always sure to exceed or at least meet expectations.**

   ☐ Time: Create a realistic assessment of how long it will take to perform a given task, add some time to that in order to deal with unforeseen difficulties, and promise the most conservative delivery time. If others set the deadline, and they are not conservative enough, warn them at the onset, or as soon as possible, that you may not be able to comply.

   ☐ Costs: Create a realistic estimate of the cost range for something, add enough to deal with unforeseen difficulties, and do not promise to deliver for less.

   ☐ Benefits: Only claim the most assured benefits or features of each proposed project. If you must claim benefits you are less sure of, carefully couch your language: "there is a small possibility that we could ...." Note: Remind others of this along the way, as some are likely to forget the "small possibility" part of the statement.

   ☐ Quality: Deliver quality.

   ☐ Tradeoffs: If you are forced to commit to elements of time, cost, benefits or quality that you know are unrealistic, clearly convey the tradeoffs that will be necessary to deliver on those, and then strive mightily to avoid them.

   ☐ Anticipate: If certain constituencies have a history of "moving the bar," then factor that into future estimates (rather than call them to task for this).

   Note: Do not let conservative estimates and pads lull you into less than your best performance (the goal is to exceed, not just barely meet expectations).

2. **Practice two-sidedness – any claim is considered more credible if it is accompanied by some admission that would seem to be contrary to your self-interests.**

   ☐ Do not provide only the positives of any given topic. If there are some downsides, risks, offsetting features, etc., acknowledge them.

   ☐ Do not overdo. This requires finesse.

3. **Establish and build a portfolio of third party endorsements. These can come in the form of explicit or implicit endorsements (the endorsement is inferred due to your involvement in or leadership with respected bodies).**

   ☐ Attract media coverage.

      ✓ This is best done in conjunction with a PR professional, and most organizations have rules about working with the media (read Not for Everyone on page 260).

      ✓ Identify and list mass media communicators that may be interested in you or your work.

         o Science, technology or other *beat* reporters at local newspaper, radio or TV outlets.

         o Bloggers, popular tweeters, or other social media leaders.

         o Trade publications or other media outlets that specialize in your area of expertise.

      ✓ Research and rank those on the previous list.

         o Read the prior work of those on the list (if you have not done so already), and familiarize yourself with the range of their interests, their style, their competency, etc.

         o Consider what you may have to offer that fits into the scope of their work.

         o Estimate the value of their coverage as well as the likelihood of their response to you. The most valuable are likely to be difficult to reach, and the easiest to reach are likely to be the least valuable.

         o Rank these according to fit, value and likelihood of attracting coverage.

      ✓ Reach out to the top few from the list above.

- o Call and introduce yourself, provide a brief background, and let them know you would be available as a source if they need expertise similar to that of your own.
- o Alternatively, email them. Consider including a CV.

    Note: There might be those tempted to skip the above step of trying to identify the appropriate target media (where there will be true value for both parties), and instead just spam indiscriminately. Doing so, however, is short sighted.

✓ Issue a press release if you have a significant announcement (use the news elements tool on page 314 to help determine what may be of interest to an outside audience).

- o Send to the identified media outlets or others that may be interested in a given topic (i.e., if you have a major advancement in battery technology, business reporters – not just your science and technology contacts – may also be interested).

✓ Subscribe to expert source services, which seek to provide reporters with expert sources for stories (either you list the topics upon which you can provide expertise, or you monitor a regularly-published list of story topics for which writers are seeking sources).

- o Helpareporter.com
- o Profnet.com

✓ Review the editorial calendars of major periodicals (those who publish them) and contact an editor or writer at that publication if you have something special to contribute to that topic.

- o These are aimed at giving advertisers advanced notice of the issues in which they may wish to purchase ads, but can also alert you when a publication is going to do stories that may be relevant to the expertise or experience you offer.

☐ Create something for publication.

  ✓ Write a story, column, editorial, etc., for newspapers, magazines or online tools (e.g., blog).

    o Conducting the *attracting the media* activities from the previous section may lead to an invitation to do these.

    o You may also offer to do an opposing editorial (op-ed) to respond to a story published by a news organization.

  ✓ Create an electronic presentation, podcast, video, etc., that may be viewed (for example on YouTube) by a large audience.

  ✓ Write a book.

    o Traditional.

    o eBook.

☐ Seek awards, rankings or other recognition of preeminent performance.

  ✓ Scour industry organizations and publications for relevant awards, rankings, etc., opportunities.

  ✓ Also consider awards and recognition that are outside your field, but that still may be relevant: innovation, environmental stewardship, human resources (best places to work), etc.

  ✓ Research those you believe may be worth targeting: what criteria do they use? Who makes the decision? What organizations/topics have been successful in the past?

  ✓ Rank according to value and the likelihood of success.

  ✓ Use the successful submission strategy information (available on *www.brainiacparadox.com*).

☐ Join or participate with relevant professional organizations.

  ✓ Create a list of potential organizations.

  ✓ Research, evaluate, and rank. Consider:

    o Relevancy to you and your work.

    o Value of programs offered.

    o Availability and value of any professional designations (e.g., accreditation) the organization may offer.

    o Current leadership and membership.

    o Potential for leadership positions.

- ✓ Affiliate with one or more organizations that offer the best payoff.
    - o Actively participate.
    - o Take on leadership roles or positions.
    - o Pursue any professional designations offered.

- ☐ Get involved in academia (if not already an educator).
    - ✓ Possible opportunities:
        - o Offer to speak as a visiting lecturer or participate in special class activities.
        - o Pursue opportunities to teach as an adjunct professor.
        - o Participate in an advisory board or other expert leadership support roles.
    - ✓ Ways to approach this:
        - o Express willingness to educators with whom you already have relationships.
        - o Seek out educators at industry forums.
        - o Email or call department heads at relevant schools and express your willingness and interest in participating.

- ☐ Pursue speaking engagements at industry events.
    - ✓ Possible opportunities:
        - o Symposiums sponsored by industry publications.
        - o Executive leadership events.
        - o Industry expos.
    - ✓ Ways to approach this:
        - o Usually they are staffed by invitation only, but those may come after some of the previous activities (industry awards, press coverage, published work) puts you on the organizer's radar screen.

- ☐ If you are a leader of a department that has substantial achievements or a great story to tell, but are not successful in using the previous techniques to showcase its success, you could consider participating in benchmarking or research studies.
    - ✓ Possible opportunities:

- o Most industry associations will do intermittent research.
- o Gartner, Forrester, or IDC in technology fields.
- o National Science Foundation for Best Practices studies in engineering and science.
- o Doing a search on past research related to your area can provide you clues as to who may be doing it in the future.

- ✓ Ways to approach this:
  - o Most independent researchers are eager to find groups willing to give them the time and access to necessary information, but you must fit the profile of the organizations they are studying. If you already contract with/subscribe to these services, relay your willingness to participate and ask about current and future projects.
  - o If necessary, you can contract with consultants to do some benchmarking for you.

- ☐ Consider other respected individuals or organizations, with whom an association would enhance your credibility.

4. Forecast and map out your communication activities (communication mapping).

- ☐ Start with the communication mapping tool (downloadable from *www.brainiacparadox.com*) and modify according to your personal/organization activities, audiences, and communication channels.
  - ✓ This will likely require a trial and error approach: adding, deleting, and modifying fields, adding respective information, and then modifying again as better approaches become apparent.

- ☐ Refer to page 326 for detailed instructions for creating and using the communication mapping tool.

- ☐ If relevant, create additional communication maps for different facets of your professional life.
  - ✓ If you have leadership responsibilities, one map could be for your team and the other for you personally.

Summary – Chapter 14
The Communicator Is the Message

The concept of credibility stems from the fact that it is impossible for anyone to know or do all things. We depend on others for knowledge or actions, but not everyone delivers equally. The practice of assessing and assigning credibility provides a means of minimizing risk, or enhancing potential outcomes. Hence, the more credibility one processes, the greater their potential influence.

The importance of credibility is even more acute when both the stakes are high and the decision-maker is particularly deficient in their understanding of the item they must evaluate (e.g., company president making decision on a big-ticket, cutting-edge technology project). As both factors are frequently found in the realm of technical professions, it is particularly important that those in these fields carefully build and maintain credibility in order to succeed.

Our audiences assign us credibility based on actual knowledge and experience as well as on certain assumptions. Obviously, performing well is the best way to build credibility, but performance is often relative. It is more important to meet or exceed expectations than it is to perform well by objective measures. Hence managing the expectations of various aspects of our performance is our first and most important goal: focus on delivering what we promise ... and promising only what we can deliver. Doing so provides a sound foundation in *experiential credibility*.

We need also to optimize our *surface credibility*. We need to look, sound, and interact in ways consistent with what our audience would expect of a respected person in our field.

Next, develop and execute a strategy that addresses *reputed credibility*. These can include awards, press coverage, speaking engagements at respected events – anything that suggests that we are well regarded by knowledgeable and objective third parties. These can do amazing things to enhance our credibility.

Likewise, we need to consider *presumptive credibility*. One way is to practice two-sidedness. When proposing something, or dealing with a problem, we should acknowledge things that seem to run counter to our self-interests; it makes our other claims more credible.

Finally, we should use communication mapping to orchestrate our communication activities. It will facilitate strong, consistent, and compounding messages that will enhance our credibility among various audiences. Anyone who takes the time to establish and maintain a communication map will greatly increase his or her credibility.

Monitor, Assess, and Log …

- When your performance – on small items as well as large – miss expectations.

- When you fail to provide both sides on something related to your self-interests.

- When you do other things that erode your credibility.

- When you fail to do other things that would build your credibility.

You Will Know You Are Overcoming This When …

- You find your requests are approved with far less scrutiny.

- Others increasingly look to you for input or feedback.

- You shift from competing for challenging and rewarding work, to having too much.

– Chapter 15 –

Sell Is Not a Four-Letter Word

The best idea in the world is worthless unless it can be 'sold' to others.
Samuel G. Florman – *The Civilized Engineer*

Foible: Selling (aversion to)
Precept: Leverage your abilities and credibility

The "right stuff," as defined by Tom Wolfe in his book of the same name, is a set of difficult-to-define qualities necessary for acceptance into a mythical fraternity of elite pilots. And among all the pilots Wolfe profiled in his book (about the early manned-rocket program of the United States), no one had more of the right stuff than Chuck Yeager. Yeager was a prickly World War II flying ace, the first man to break the sound barrier, and recipient of numerous other aeronautic records. He was a flyer's flyer, the best of the best. He sat, as Wolfe put it, at "the top of the pyramid," yet he is far less known than fliers further down on the pyramid. This historical slighting is a major subtheme of the screen adaptation of the book, and serves as a cautionary tale for anyone who is reluctant to sell their work.

This premise is foreshadowed in a scene set at the Happy Bottom Riding Club, a dusty, ramshackle pilot hangout located in the isolated desert near Edwards Air Force Base. Yeager sits at a corner table, having drinks with a U.S. Air Force press liaison officer. "You need more than speed in this day and age, you need [press] coverage," the man tells Yeager, as well as three pilots at a nearby table. "You know what really makes your rocket ships go up? Funding. No bucks, no Buck Rogers. Whoever gets the funding gets the technology. Whoever gets the technology stays on top."

Yeager, however, detested the press: "fruit flies, who always hovered, eager for the juice ... and invariably got the facts screwed up." However, the press liaison officer's message was not lost on the pilots at the next table: Gordon Cooper, Gus Grissom, and Deke Slayton. Not only would they learn to tolerate the press, but embrace it. As among America's first astronauts, they would go on to be household names and the idols of a generation while, if not for *The Right Stuff*, few would even know of or remember Yeager.

It is not enough to be great, even the best at what we do. The ability to sell our ideas and ourselves, to play the game if you will, can be a critical factor in determining our professional trajectory. Too many in STEM fields either fail to appreciate this or lack certain requisite abilities.

"I did have a lot of difficulty in business initially," says Bruce Burton, "because I prided myself with the belief that I was a great engineer. But I soon realized that it was not enough. I had to reinvent myself to become a salesman, which I thought was kind of a demeaning thing." Burton went on to create several successful businesses.

You've Got to Know the Territory

Ask any salesperson what is the key to their success and they will include, "understanding the customer" among their top items. But those who have challenges with empathy are at a distinct disadvantage in this regard. In addition, technical professionals skew towards introversion and while that does not preclude someone from being an effective promoter, it surely does not help. Similarly, many are modest and reluctant to draw attention to themselves.

Others have a disabling fear of public speaking. This can be true of extroverts as well as introverts. While selling does not necessarily require speaking in front of large groups, it likely will include occasional presentations in front of teams, committees, boards, or other groups large enough to evoke that fear. This can be a major barrier and, in fact, public speaking is at the top of most lists of people's greatest fears.

Some just do not see the need. To them the benefits of their offerings are so obvious that the need to sell does not even occur to them. It is enough, they believe, just to show others the better mousetrap.

One executive lamented her lessons learned on this topic: "I have always had a problem of thinking, 'obviously they are going to recognize my work. I am working so hard. Can't they tell?' 'What do you mean I didn't get that raise?' or, 'Why didn't you consider me for this position?'" She recalled a program manager from earlier in her career telling her, "'I know you are doing a great job. But you need to let others know. You don't sell yourself enough.'" Then she confessed, "I still don't. We believe it is like taking a test; it's objective; it's facts and data. 'I am going to get the good grade and be recognized for it.'"

Still others just overlook selling. They are so focused on their work, or stretched by various demands, that the added task of selling does not enter their minds, or they just never get around to it.

Finally, for some it is a matter of a conscious choice. They may see the act of selling as a sullied pursuit that tarnishes their noble work. They recoil from the idea of employing the same practices as the office politicians.

The Other Steve

When we think of Apple Corporation, we usually think of Steve Jobs. Apple and Jobs are so intrinsically linked that when Jobs announced that he had pancreatic cancer in 2004, stock analysts began monitoring his health more closely than the company's financial performance. Despite this, it is the other co-founder named Steve, to whom Apple owes its very existence.

It was Steve Wozniak who designed the electronics of the first Apple computers and the software to drive them. And it was not just that he created the computer, but that in the process he introduced numerous breakthrough innovations that would eventually make personal computers more desirable and affordable to the masses. He could be said to do for personal computing circuitry design what Henry Ford's assembly line did for the automotive industry.

However, if left to his own inclinations, Wozniak would not have exploited those innovations. In his autobiography, *iWOZ*, he talks about being so incredibly introverted that he was afraid to speak up at Homebrew Club meetings (ground zero for the earlier personal computer enthusiasts in Silicon Valley).

> *I was never the kind of person who had the courage to raise his hand during the Homebrew main meeting and say, 'Hey, look at this great computer advance I've made.' No, I could never have said that in front of a whole garage full of people. But after the main meeting every other Wednesday, I would set up my stuff on a table and answer questions people asked … I was so proud of my design – and I so believed in the club's mission to further computing – that I Xeroxed maybe a hundred copies of my complete design (including the monitor program) and gave it to anyone who wanted it. I hoped they'd be able to build their own computers from my design.*

Rather than connecting with people so he could share his solutions, he was sharing his solutions so that he could connect with people.

While Wozniak says he would have been satisfied with building computers for fun and sharing his innovations for free with other PC hobbyist, Jobs recognized the potential and was anxious to exploit it. Beyond his aesthetic flair, Jobs possessed another valuable attribute: the salesmanship instincts of a nineteenth century snake oil salesman. Job's salesmanship was another key ingredient in Apple's success.

A Dirty Job, but Someone Has to Do It

West Virginia University Engineering Professor James E. Smith understands the essential role selling plays in a technical career and his students' aversion to it.

He tells new students that they have to provide information in writing and orally, in multiple formats, over and over. He even has guest professionals sit in and critically evaluate their presentations because, "that is how the world works."

When students ask him what they are supposed to convey, he responds that it is not about what they are conveying, it is about selling who they are (reinforcing the importance of credibility covered in the previous chapter). "The moment I say sell, they get offended. 'We are not sales people, they protest.'" He counters that, "As an engineer you are going to need to sell your position, your project, your something, but more importantly, you are going to sell who you are, and that you can backup what you are representing. If you can't do that, the only chance you have is to find someone who can, and you work for them!"

Just as denial needed to be the first foible – because nothing could be achieved unless that was overcome – an aversion to selling needs to be the last, because the benefits of overcoming the others are not fully achieved without it.

Fortunately, success does not require becoming a great salesperson – though it surely does not hurt. We just need to avoid the traits of a poor one. In *The 25 Most Common Sales Mistakes and How to Avoid Them*, Stephan Schiffman lists what could be otherwise described as the top foibles of sales professionals. A review of the list will demonstrate many that are similar to the foibles addressed in this book. This is a subset of his list, with the name of this book's corresponding chapter in parenthesizes:

#2. Not listening to the prospect (Chapter 8: *Audience-Oriented Communication*)

#3. Not empathizing with the prospect (Chapter 8: *Audience-Oriented Communication*)

#4. Seeing the prospect as an adversary (Chapter 13: *It Takes a Team*)

#5.   Getting distracted (Chapter 10: *Less is More*)

#10.   Not looking your best (Chapter 12: *Substance AND Style*)

#12.   Not taking the prospect's point of view (Chapter 8: *Audience-Oriented Communication*)

#18.   Not using people proof (Chapter 9: *So your Grandparents Could Understand*)

#20.   Being fooled by "sure things" (Chapter 11: *It's Not the Journey, It's the Destination*)

#21.   Taking rejection personally (Chapter 13: *It Takes a Team*)

#28.   Not getting enough information (Chapter 8: *Audience-Oriented Communication*)

#29.   Not knowing when to stop talking (Chapter 10: *Less is More*)

Success in mitigating the previous Brainiac Paradox foibles provides a foundation for effective selling.

- You better understand and respond to your audience.
- You communicate based on what they need to hear.
- Your communications are concise, clear and user friendly.
- Others perceive you to be a good collaborator.
- You have proactively banked credibility … and now can spend it.

Remedies:
Selling

Prior to a presentation to the executive committee for a new project, Mitch was an almost invisible midlevel manager. The executives knew him to varying degrees, but they did not think much about him. At most, they just considered him a competent but otherwise unremarkable employee. By the end of the meeting, that all changed.

He strode into the meeting with a confident smile, and after a couple niceties, he got to work, enthusiastically making his case. His presentation was concise, well organized, and he moved through it at an appropriately quick pace, although with some strategic short pauses to allow the audience to consider certain points. He also interjected a little levity here and there. When he finished, he answered the committee's question with equal adeptness. Upon leaving the meeting, the executives looked back and forth at each other in astonishment, remarking on the unexpected feat.

What only one of them (his manager) knew was that I had worked with him prior to the presentation. His manager had known that Mitch had potential to move up but could not convince the other executives when they did succession planning. Well, Mitch was invisible no longer.

So, what magic did I work to help him deliver such a great sales performance? Actually, not that much, but more about that later. First, some remedies.

Resolve to Sell

To overcome the first foible of denial, you needed to internalize the mantra: *If they haven't heard it, I haven't said it.* Later, there was, *If they can't find it, it doesn't exist.* For this foible, the mantra is, *If I don't sell it, they won't buy it.* Whatever your current prospects – based on talent, knowledge, and effort – selling is a key determinant to your success.

Effective Communication = Selling

If effective communication, as this book proposes, is constructively influencing others perceptions and behaviors, then selling is just effective communication with a specific behavior in mind: to get someone to buy. As such, the communication planning tool provided in Chapter 11 offers a step-by-step process for planning and executing your sales plan. Any time you really need something from someone, you should use the communication planning tool on page 318.

Leverage Rapport

Great salesmanship is often built on great relationships. Whether selling a product or an idea, the relationship between you and the person to whom you are selling will likely have a major affect on the outcome. It is said that, "All things equal, people buy from people they like," and "All things *not* being equal, people buy from people they like."

Building a rapport among key audiences was discussed in Chapter 13 as a way to build more collaborative relationships. Now, you should be able to reap the fruits of your rapport-building efforts.

Lay the Groundwork

Nemawashi is a Japanese word (literal translation: going around the roots) that involves quietly building consensus for a decision prior to the actual decision-making event. The idea is to ensure success. As one Japanese colleague described it to me:

> *Let's say I have a proposal that I want a management team to approve. I will determine who will be involved with the decision process and meet with each individually beforehand to discuss the proposal. I will start with the most influential person, seeking their feedback and suggestions. I incorporate any necessary changes and then meet with the next most influential person. Again I will explain the proposal and seek their feedback and suggestions, but also share that I have the support of the previous person. In most cases they will go along, but if they have serious objections, I will confer again with the previous person and mention the new objections. Depending upon their feedback, I will again modify the proposal, or continue with the previous version. I continue this approach until I know how everyone is going to respond when the actual decision is made. In this way, the decision itself is mostly a formality.*

While this approach may not translate directly to western work cultures, adapting aspects of this and laying the proper groundwork can be useful. The audience-oriented communication approach stresses an understanding and anticipation of our audiences as a way of improving effectiveness, but an even greater likelihood of success can be attained by engaging and gauging our audience prior to an actual decision.

Adapt the Proper Demeanor

The stereotype of a successful salesperson is that of a great manipulator: they lie, distort, talk fast, pressure, and pester the buyer until the customer relents. But truly great salespeople are very different than that, according to Malcolm Gladwell in *The Tipping Point*. Rather than characteristics that irritate and repel us, great salespeople have characteristics that make others want to agree with them.

When asked about the personality qualities desired, potential employers, romantic partners, and coaches use very similar descriptors: confident, but not cocky; accomplished, but modest; ambitious, but not ruthless; and fun loving, but not irresponsible. Consider consensus heroes from business, politics, sports, and entertainment and they likely share these characteristics, all of which could be said to fall under the umbrella of *balanced optimism*.

When people with positive characteristics engage with us, we naturally feel better, more confident and more optimistic ourselves. These are the people others like to be around. They are the ones who can achieve great things *with* others, rather than *at the expense of* others. These are the kind of people in which others are willing to invest.

When we need to sell, whether it is to get a project approved, to receive funding, or to be hired for a particular position, this is the demeanor we want to project.

Smile and the World Smiles with You

The smile is probably the most underestimated communication tool we possess. In fact, few people consciously consider it at all. It is just one of many things we do reflexively (yawn, frown, sigh) and take for granted. However, the more researchers study the human smile, the clearer is its complexity and power.

I have a family photograph I prize. It shows me holding two of my sons, one in each arm, on a beautiful summer day. Behind me is a gorgeous lake surrounded by undulating hills and capped by a deep blue sky. However, it is not the setting that captivates me. What distinguishes this picture from all the others are the smiles on my sons faces. In this particular picture the smiles communicate a combination of happiness, contentedness, and security. In other pictures they appear happier, others more content, others more secure, etc., but this is the only picture where their smiles somehow communicate all three so completely and simultaneously. Every time I look at that picture I feel a deep warmth well up within me – every time. All that from their smiles.

Depending on how they are parsed, experts have identified three – felt, false, and miserable – to eighteen or more smile types. Smiles are part of a larger basket of facial expressions that are crucial to non-verbal communications. Nevertheless, what is germane to our discussion is how effective smiles are in altering the mood of those we encounter.

The brain prefers happy faces to other emotional expressions and recognizes them more quickly than negative expressions. This phenomenon has been named the Happy Face Advantage. What's more, smiles are contagious: "Smile and the world smiles with you." For example, when researchers used functional magnetic resonance imaging (fMRI) to measure brain activity of participants observing the smiling face of another person, they found that the pattern of brain activity of the participant corresponded to those of the person being observed.

This is an unconscious social reflex that delivers tangible results. In one piece of research, individuals who had normally-functioning eyes, but blockage of the signal to the occipital cortex, were exposed to images of people with fearful and happy expressions. Though they could not consciously see anything, they were able to sense the expression displayed in the picture. This is because the visuals of the facial expressions were still transmitted through a separate circuit that ran to the amygdale (the part of the brain associated with emotions). Participants reported feeling happier when the smiling face was placed in front of their eyes even though they had no idea why.

Another remarkable thing about smiles is that not only does a sense of happiness cause us to smile, but the physical act of replicating a smile makes *us* feel happier. Try it. Force as big a smile as you can for five seconds. Do you feel it? The facial expression and the emotional state have a type of two-way linkage.

Taking this a step further, there are those who organize group laughter therapy (laughter yoga) sessions. Participants are instructed to stand close together in a circle and to laugh. While originally the laughing is manufactured, it soon turns to true laughter. Both laughing and watching others laugh is a catalyst for sincere laughter, which in turn triggers even greater laughter for others. The amplification cycle continues until the group finally fatigues and the participants part, drenched in a sense of happiness and well-being.

An interesting thing about these laughter sessions is that if you observe the people gathering for these, they already have huge smiles on their faces. The mere thought of laughing starts the process. It is like the child who knows they are going to be tickled, and starts laughing in anticipation.

These principles of positive-emotion contagions can be extended to help us influence key audiences. If we prime our interaction with a sincere and appropriate emotional state, we will trigger an equivalent response in our audience that, ultimately, will increase the likelihood of their support.

There is, however, an operative word in that sentence: sincere. Just as our brains are sensitive to smiles, they are also quite effective in deciphering both the meaning of the smile (the eighteen different types referenced above) and, more importantly, its authenticity. An insincere or misplaced smile triggers just the opposite emotion, sometimes powerfully. Think of the most evil characters from film; they are most terrifying when they smile or laugh. Maybe that is why some people are afraid of clowns; the painted on smile may trigger a creepy suspicion rather than the smile reflex it is designed to elicit.

If you fake a smile, smile the incorrect way or at an inappropriate time, you may invoke a similar response. Laughter therapy only works because the original fake laughter is just a primer to get the authentic laughter engine going.

Hence, in order to make use of this advantage, you must generate an authentic sense of happiness and/or humor. For example, I used to drive my sons to school in the morning, and around mid-terms and final exams, they were quite anxious. They sat in silence during the drive. I would tune into one of the comedy stations on satellite radio and soon they were laughing. By the end of the 10-minute drive they were relaxed, smiling and able to attack their tests without the anxiety that just minutes ago held them emotionally hostage.

Sincerity

It is not just with a smile that sincerity is important. If we try to establish a personal connection, but our audience senses that we do not sincerely care about them; if we flatter them but they sense it is contrived; or if we attempt to demonstrate our knowledge, but it is seen as only superficial: we attract the scorn of our audience.

So, what do you do when you are dealing with an audience you do not like or respect? If you try to pretend otherwise, they will likely sense something is askew. Even if they do not know what you are thinking, they may *feel* it. But now consider there are usually *some* things about almost anyone that you can find to appreciate. Think of someone of whom you do not think favorably. Are their aspects of their personal lives that you share in common (family, schools, hobbies, etc.)? Are there aspects of their life's experience that you truly find interesting? Put aside what you do not like, and focus on these things and you will be able to exhibit a sincerely positive attitude towards them … even if only temporarily.

Present Competently

Not all selling is done verbally, but when that is what is required, those who are introverted or fear public speaking, will be at a distinct disadvantage. These characteristics can be difficult to overcome, especially the latter. I know from experience. Count me among those who, as Jerry Seinfeld joked, "would rather be the person in the casket [at a funeral], than the person eulogizing them." Fortunately, I discovered a way to cope with this at a young age.

When in fifth grade I was assigned a role in a school play. I was petrified. However, I soon found that the more I memorized my lines, the more my anxiety waned. By the day of our first performance, I knew my lines backwards and forwards and the anxiety had disappeared! It seems that my primary fear was that of forgetting my lines in front of my peers and embarrassing myself. But, because I had so thoroughly memorized the material, I was completely confident that I would deliver without error. As such, I could focus my attention on how I delivered my lines rather than on just recalling them.

Although I still have an aversion to speaking publicly, I thoroughly prepare what I am going to say and find I am able to marshal through it.

If you are shy and introverted, or have a fear of public speaking, this may work for you as well. In addition, the key messages developed in Chapter 7 may give you a head start. Gaining command of your key messages can give you the confidence you need to face any audience.

The Answer Is the Question

Asking questions – good ones – is an incredibly powerful and versatile sales technique. Most obviously, questions provide a way of tuning into the audience's problems, needs, and wants, but they can do so much more.

- Questions can help you connect with others personally. Ask questions that demonstrate you are interested in and care about them.

- Probing questions can reveal audience attitudes, biases, or beliefs that can significantly affect the landscape of your efforts. For example, you may discover that they had a previous bad experience with something similar to what you are proposing. Asking questions allows you to focus on the right things, and avoid the wrong things.

- Asking questions can create a halo effect. Market researchers have found that individuals usually have a more favorable attitude (or less negative) towards something after they are questioned about it. Merely seeking someone's opinion on a topic can improve their opinion of that very thing. Some organizations conduct research in a bid for this effect as much as with the intent of collecting audience opinions.

- Questions allow us to shape the discussion. A skillfully worded and placed series of questions can guide your audience to your topic or viewpoint, without them realizing it. Franklin used this technique to lead his audiences to his way of thinking without the direct contradiction and dogmatic statements that he had sworn off.

- Questions can also be very useful in demonstrating your knowledge and competence. Have you ever had someone outside your field ask you a question related to your work that surprised and impressed you? You think better of them, do you not? Likewise, you can cast yourself in a more favorable light by asking questions that demonstrate your interest, and a little of your knowledge, in your audience's domain. Be careful, though. You have also probably experienced people who use this as a pretext for showing off what they know (or think they know). If done poorly, or excessively, the audience will think less of you.

- Questions can be a more subtle way of complimenting and appealing to the ego of your audience. Ask questions that inspires a very positive response from others. If they feel good about themselves, they are more likely to feel good about you.

Hype

Even if the word *sell* does not have a four-letter-word connotation, the word *hype* may for some. The word suggests deception or excessive exaggeration. Now consider that some common traits of technical professionals include a respect for rules, order, honesty, and integrity (based on the MBTI traits of Thinking and Judging, which account for approximately 50% of those in STEM fields). Hype also smacks of desperation; it is only necessary for something that has no merits on its own. Hence, to hype something is to admit inadequacy. But if you truly believe in something, is it really unseemly to hype it?

Consider the old advertising adage, *You don't sell the bacon, you sell the sizzle.* Even though many people love bacon, it is hard to appeal to them directly: "Come on, you know you love bacon, now buy it." However, by selling the sizzle, it is possible to do an end run around the cerebral cortex and appeal to consumers' visceral love for bacon. The *sizzle* triggers positive feelings: the sound as it cooks on a sunny weekend morning and the smell that fills the house, the texture of crisp bacon and the taste that overwhelms the mouth. Selling the sizzle is just another way of leveraging the perceptions others already posses.

Benjamin Franklin was not above a little hype. He proudly notes in his autobiography, that as a young printer just starting out, "I sometimes brought home the paper I purchased at the stores through the streets on a wheelbarrow," conveying the idea he was both hardworking and already successful.

Franklin capitalized on such practices throughout his life, but probably never more artfully than when sent to France to enlist its support for the colonies during the Revolutionary War. When he arrived in Paris in late

1776, he was already among the most renowned scientists in the Western Hemisphere, and nowhere was he more celebrated than in France. Despite this, he knew his physical presence may not live up to his reputation, when contrasted with the sophisticated dress, style, and manners of the French elite – those whom he needed to influence. Since he could not hope to match them, he instead played the role of "noble savage," dressing in a relatively plain suit and fur hat. This persona enchanted the French, created a sensation, and soon he rose to be one of the city's most popular people (even today, there are statues of Benjamin Franklin scattered across Paris).

There was nothing dishonest about wheeling the paper conspicuously through the town or adopting the noble savage persona. He was simply leveraging the assumptions others already possessed, a kind of psychological jujutsu. Franklin biographer, Walters Isaacson, calls him "America's first great publicist," but notes that our images of him have been sustained because they are rooted in reality. Whatever one thinks of his methods, they delivered results.

Sometimes hype may be needed for more than just conveying the benefits of our offerings; we may need it to outcompete those vying for the same thing. It could be other qualified candidates for a position; another department for organizational funding; or peers for limited department resources. Consider the joke about the two campers who discover a ferocious bear just outside of their tent. One gets up to run, but notices the other one putting on his shoes. "Why are you bothering? Those won't help you outrun a bear," he says. "I don't have to outrun the bear," the other responds, "I only have to outrun you."

For some, hype comes naturally and there is no need to explain it. For others it does not, and a mere explanation would be insufficient because the best hype is not intrinsically logical. The examples attributed to Franklin are examples of lateral rather than linear thinking (Franklin has been widely estimated to be type ENTP, with the N (Intuition) more closely associated with lateral thinking). Its opposite, S (Sensing), is more prominent among those in technical fields.

If this tactic presents some difficulties for you, consider recruiting the assistance of someone to whom this comes naturally, as there are risks in doing it poorly (recall the perceptions that anything that is hyped must be unworthy). There are however, a handful of little things anyone can do to sell the sizzle.

- Include one or more wow factors: information that will surprise and amaze your audience.
- Use superlatives (recall the news element of prominence). When you have a *first*, *biggest*, or *most advanced*, make sure to highlight it.

- Use stronger verbs like: ... *exceeds standards*, rather than ... *meets standards*.

- Use stronger adjectives: *innovative* is more powerful than *new*.

- Use emotionally charged words: my *strategy* as opposed to someone else's *scheme*.

- Use language and imagery that evoke positive emotions. Make sure this is based on what works for your audience. If you are trying to sell bacon to someone who has never had it before, selling the sizzle will not work.

- Use catchy words or phrases.

- Use a Gimmick. At its launch, the Apple Macintosh introduced itself, "Hello, my name is Macintosh. It sure is great to get out of that bag!" Apple could simply have listed voice synthesizing as one of the many groundbreaking features introduced in the Mac, and the audience would have been impressed, but this gimmick did so much more. It was humorous and memorable, and is still referenced to this day (as I am doing now).

Whatever you do, do so sparingly. If your promotional efforts are clumsy, obvious, and overdone, they can have just the opposite effect, discrediting you or your initiative.

Do Not Forget to Ask!
One of the last sales mistakes on Schiffman's list is, "Not asking for the sale." It seems almost too obvious to mention, but I cannot count the number of times I have seen people make otherwise great presentations, but then end without ever stating what specifically they were requesting. If you do not make a clear, concise request, you are not likely to get what you desired or possibly not get anything at all.

Deliver
Once they have bought into your idea, funding proposal, product, service, etc. ... deliver! If you do, you will have the additional credibility necessary for your next request; if you do not, future support will be more difficult to attain.

And Mitch ...

So what made the difference for Mitch?

- I had him use the communication planning tool to prepare for the presentation. That helped him think through his audience's dynamics and develop a message strategy that would have a high probability of success.

- He prepared a series of key messages and Q&A's.

- After he prepared his presentation, I helped him edit and fine-tune it.

- He practiced. I had him present it to me and a female colleague (who was preparing for a different presentation in front of the executive committee that day). Afterwards, we critiqued it, then she presented and Mitch and I critiqued her. We had three different practice sessions – they did some on their own in between.

- I had him listen to a favorite comedy recording – in his case Bill Cosby's *Chicken Heart* – shortly before the session. This provided all the benefits associated with laughter and allowed him to enter the room relaxed with a sincere smile on his face.

The time I invested with Mitch was not as much as it may appear. The practice sessions took the most time, and I intentionally had the other presenter provide most of the feedback. I only stepped in for the things she missed. I provided him with only a handful of tools he could stitch together for a great performance. Everyone can hope to achieve similar results if they do the adequate preparation and adopt the proper demeanor.

How to:
Sell Better

1. **Accept the reality that you must *sell* in order to further your ideas, projects and career.**

   ☐ Internalize the mantra, *If I don't sell it, they won't buy it,* by saying it repeatedly to yourself.

2. **Develop a strategic approach to your selling.**

   ☐ Use the communication-planning tool on page 318 to assist you in creating the most effective approach to selling. Recall that effective communication is defined in this book as *the ability to influence others' perceptions and behaviors constructively*, and that selling is merely effective communication with a specific behavior in mind: support a project, fund a program, approve a promotion, etc.

3. **Use the concept of Nemawashi (described on page 283) to vet your proposals.**

   ☐ Before important or complex proposals are decided upon, meet personally with as many of the people who will be involved with the decision as possible, starting with the most influential person first.

   ☐ Once you have support from the first person, use it to leverage the next person.

   ☐ Incorporate feedback and continue to socialize your proposal until adequate support is assured.

4. **Leverage rapport. This is where earlier work to diversify those you have a rapport with can pay off.**

   ☐ Outside of the actual decision makers (among whom you may be practicing Nemawashi), there are those who can influence the decision makers. If there are some among them with whom you have built a relationship, request their assistance.

5. **Present competently.**

   ☐ Master your material: study your key messages, updating them as needed, until you can make your case forcefully.

   ☐ Make sure your Q&A's cover the most likely and difficult objections others may have.

   ☐ When the stakes are high, practice in front of others and have them critique all aspects of your delivery.

   ☐ If your selling is not verbal, but written, the same is true: prepare your material carefully and have others review and critique it.

6. **Present a demeanor that will predispose your audience to support you.**

   ☐ Before any sales pitch, psyche yourself up.

   ✓ Confidence: You want to exude great comfort in what you are proposing (practicing your material as outlined above will help you do that).

   ✓ Positivity: Smile and be upbeat. Emotions are contagious and – all things equal – people are more likely to respond affirmatively if they are in a positive mood.

   ✓ Sincerity: If you are not sincere, others are likely to get a whiff of that, and as soon as they do, they are likely to discount what you propose.

7. **Use questions strategically. Questions can do much more than just solicit a response.**

   ☐ Ask thoughtful questions (those that demonstrate you are listening and attuned to others' perspectives) and demonstrate that you care.

   ☐ Use questions to explore your audience's true thoughts, beliefs, and concerns.

   ☐ Ask questions that covertly lead your audience to raise the topics you wish to discuss. People are more likely to heed topics they initiate, or at least think they initiated.

    ☐   Ask questions that indirectly stroke your audience's egos. Others are likely to be more generous when they feel good about themselves.

8.   **Consider ways you might incorporate a little hype.**

    ☐   Include one or more wow factors – pieces of information that will astound your audience.

    ☐   Use superlatives – facts relating to your proposal that are the best, biggest, first, most effective, etc.

    ☐   Use stronger verbs – e.g., … *exceeds standards*, rather than just, … *meets standards."*

    ☐   Use stronger adjectives – *innovative* is better than *new*, and *leading edge* is better than *innovative*.

    ☐   Use emotionally charged words – my *strategy* as opposed to someone else's *scheme*.

    ☐   Use language and imagery that evokes positive emotions.

    ☐   Use catchy words or phrases (i.e., sound bites).

    ☐   Use a presentation gimmick.

    Note: Just because a little hype might be helpful, does not mean more is better. Be judicious.

9.   **Ask**
    ☐   Always include a clear and specific request in your pitch. Always!

Summary – Chapter 15
Sell Is Not a Four-Letter Word

Regardless of the career one pursues, most will need to do some selling. Those who do not will almost certainly fail to achieve their full potential – let alone their aspirations – and ultimately remain at the mercy of those who can sell. Successful selling, however, may require addressing some traits that tend to be more common among technical professionals: empathy deficiencies (difficulty anticipating what the customer wants), introversion, fear of public speaking, and a general aversion to the unseemly characteristics associated with selling.

Anyone who has mitigated the previous eight foibles will already possess a strong base upon which to develop their selling abilities. They will have tamed certain behaviors, attitudes, and habits that hampered their interactions with others. In addition, they will have command of the communication planning process, from which they can create a sales strategy; and key messages, from which they can create the pitch. In addition, they will be able to leverage the additional relationships they have fostered and the credibility they have accumulated.

The key missing ingredient is the understanding and belief that it is necessary to sell. It starts with the internalization of the concept, *if I don't sell it, they won't buy it.*" After that, effective selling is facilitated by an appropriate demeanor, presenting competently, using questions strategically, incorporating a little hype if appropriate and, most of all, completing the pitch with a clear and specific request of the audience.

Monitor, Assess, and Log …

- When you fail to advocate for what you need.
- When you do not advocate competently.
- When you fail to make a specific *ask* to your audience.

You Will Know You Are Overcoming This When …

- You feel unnecessary obstacles and frustrations lifted.
- You no longer feel that matters of communication and interpersonal interactions are standing in the way of you making your full contribution.

- When your career trajectory is greater than that of your competitors.

Section IV

The Alternative

This short section provides an alternative for those who, despite their best efforts, cannot seem to mitigate one or more of the foibles. More than that, though, it provides strategies that can help all readers supplement efforts to achieve their full potential.

— Chapter 16 —

If You Can't *Be* Them, Join Them

A single man has not nearly the value he would have in a state of union.
He is an incomplete animal. He resembles the odd half of a pair of scissors.
Benjamin Franklin

I can think of no better example of serendipity than the collaboration of Steve Wozniak and Steve Jobs. When they met in 1969, each was eminently gifted, yet poignantly flawed. Separately they were destined for middling careers within the ubiquitous California tech industry. Together they sparked a revolution in personal computing.

Wozniak had extraordinary gifts for electronics design and optimization, but lacked the inclination and the ability to exploit them. Jobs had the seeds of a great vision, but possessed personality traits that most would not tolerate unless forced to (the archetype asshole according to Robert I. Sutton in his book, *The No Asshole Rule*). Jobs provided Wozniak the zeal and style that would take advantage of his innovations, and Wozniak provided Jobs a groundbreaking product upon which he could build a movement. Their chance meeting "changed the world."

There are two foundational premises of this book: first, the aptitudes that contribute to success in STEM fields, seem to be at odds with those that contribute to effective communication; and second, the problems associated with the latter can be minimized by methodically working to address a selection of nine foibles. For most, modest progress in addressing these foibles will be enough to lubricate the gears of their innovation and solution engine, and possibly more important, to reduce the contentious issues that may have denied them recognition and enjoyment in the workplace.

Unfortunately, there will be those who cannot overcome all their foibles. Perhaps some characteristics are just too deeply rooted or they lack an environment conducive to change.

A reading of Wozniak's autobiography, *iWoz*, and the authorized biography of Jobs by Walter Isaacson, suggest that if they had not found each other, neither would have been good candidates for tackling their particular foibles on their own. Wozniak talks of being painfully shy and awkward. Frankly, he was just too nice of a person (nice is good as long as it does not prevent you from selling your work and yourself). On multiple occasions he said, "I could never do that," either in regards to aspects of his own personal foibles or when discussing characteristics of his partner, Jobs.

It is unfeasible to think Jobs could have changed. There were many occasions when he was under immense pressure to do so, yet did not. He, himself, lamented to his biographer the many personal and professional prices he paid for his personality, but none was motivation enough to drive change. Even age and terminal illness seemed not to mellow him much.

There will be those who cannot muster the necessary will to change, or others who work diligently to address the various foibles that hinder them, and yet continue to feel the sting of their effects. If either of these scenarios pertains to you, then it is probably time to consider Plan B: if you cannot be the person you want to be, join with someone who is.

Plan B is an extension of what you should have already been doing, seeking the assistance and feedback of trusted individuals, but it takes that further: either seeking a full synergetic collaborator or identifying and working with individuals who can provide assistance on an ongoing basis.

Some of the great accomplishments in history are the result of collaborations of two or more complimentary individuals.

Partnering

Your quest for a great partnership should start with a determination of what assistance would be of most use to you. Assuming you are having troubles with more than one foible, rank each foible on three factors:

- How difficult it will be to overcome.
- How much time it will take.
- To what extent you believe it impedes your success.

Next create an overall ranking, with the foibles that most hamper you and are most persistent on the top, and those least persistent or impactful on the bottom.

Hopefully, you will only have one or two problematic foibles at the top of your list. If you do, the process of indentifying collaborators should be relatively straightforward. If there are several, however, you may need to find more than one collaborator to shore up significant holes.

With Whom to Collaborate

Now consider who around you may have gifts that compliment your own, and you theirs.

- Direct peers – Consider colleagues within your department or organizational function.

- Indirect peers – Consider individuals with similar positions, but who are in other departments, functions or possibly even organizations.

- Different disciplines – After all, those who most complement your abilities are likely to be in different types of positions and/or in different functions (e.g., an engineer partnering with a marketer).

- Superiors – Many leaders are open to taking on mentees, especially if they feel they can make a significant impact.

- Subordinates – Collaborations do not have to be equal partnerships, though they should be mutually beneficial. Do not let your pride necessarily stop you from teaming up with someone at a lower level in your organization.

- Internal professionals – Depending on the need, professionals in corporate communications or human resources may provide important assistance.

- External professionals – Sometimes the only place to find the necessary expertise is outside your organization (e.g., consultants who specialize in presentation training).

- Loved one – Maybe a spouse, sibling or cousin is the perfect Yin for your Yang.

- Virtual – The web and social media provide entirely new ways for people to collaborate. The perfect collaborators can be found among total strangers (an artist may assist an IT manager create some attractive communication templates in exchange for some computer expertise).

Make a list of potential collaborators. As counterintuitive as it sounds, do not outright exclude an otherwise good synergetic partner, just because the two of you are not on the best of terms. In fact, you might want to seek them out. In his autobiography, Franklin told of running for the post of Clerk to the Philadelphia General Assembly. For his first term he ran unopposed, but in his bid for a second term, an influential member of the General Assembly gave a long speech against Franklin and in favor of another candidate. Franklin won, but he was troubled by this member's opposition; surely this would continue to cause problems down the road. Franklin's solution was another example of the power of lateral thinking.

> *Having heard that he had in his library a certain very scarce and curious book, I wrote a note to him, expressing my desire of perusing that book, and requesting he would do me the favour of lending it to me for a few days. He sent it immediately, and I return'd it in about a week with another note, expressing strongly my sense of the favour. When we next met in the House, he spoke to me (which he had never done before), and with great civility; and he ever after manifested a readiness to serve me on all occasions, so that we became great friends, and our friendship continued to his death.*

This phenomenon has been dubbed the Ben Franklin Effect.

Now, create a short list of candidates. Consider their potential value to you, your potential value to them, and how well you think you could work together (e.g., personal chemistry, demeanors). Also consider any relevant miscellaneous factors – things beyond the first three that could bode well or ill for the success of your collaboration (e.g., organizational dynamics, logistics).

How to Arrange

There are multitudes of ways you can initiate the collaboration, and the best way for you will depend on many factors (structure and size of your organization, current relationship with the person with whom you wish to collaborate, the extent of assistance needed, etc.). Following are various potential approaches to consider:

- Directly approach the person with whom you seek to collaborate, explaining how he or she could be of assistance to you and you to him or her. Provide a proposal for how such a collaboration could work (addressing details up front can avoid misunderstandings and problems down the road).
- Build the relationship slowly: look for small things you can collaborate on – or build on earlier work done together – and continuously nurture and expand the extent of collaboration. In this scenario, the idea of forming a relationship need never be explicitly mentioned and instead the collaboration can evolve naturally.

- Matchmaking: ask the assistance of a person who can broker the collaboration (e.g., someone you and your target collaborator report to). Explain the synergetic value of such a collaboration. They may even be aware of potential partners that you did not consider. Besides, their participation may facilitate the effectiveness of the relationship.

Also consider:

- Asking help of internal experts: depending on your area of need, your organization's communications or human resources teams may have individuals to assist you. Likely there is someone who would be eager to help, though the amount of the time that person can provide might be limited. The result would not be a full partnership, but it could still provide you a very valuable ongoing collaborative source.
- Contracting with external consultants: there are consultants who specialize in just about any area of need. You can search for them on the Internet or find them through recommendations from your HR department, colleagues, or business network.
- Working through a freelancer organization: depending on your need, you may find assistance from professional freelance services like Elance, Guru or Odesk (*www.elance.com, www.guru.com* and *www.odesk.com* respectively). These allow you to evaluate potential specialists based on clearly stated qualifications and recommendations from previous users. While typically this work is done on a piecemeal basis, it appears that many people develop a long-term relationship with freelancers with whom they have good experiences.

It's All Good

While I have discussed different resources for different scenarios there is no need to limit yourself. You could develop a stable of people with whom you collaborate, while at the same time tapping into the corporate communications department at times, and an external expert for other reasons.

More importantly, such collaborations are not just for those who have trouble addressing one or more of the foibles. They can be very beneficial to anyone. Even if you have worked through the various foibles successfully, you are likely to increase your effectiveness if you can tap into the expertise of others. Keep in mind that beyond the increased capabilities, you will benefit from the alliances you foster in the process. After all, the old adage that two heads are better than one remains incredibly popular because it is so often true.

Similarly, if you skipped directly to this chapter because you are convinced that you cannot overcome some of the foibles, reconsider the opportunity. Even minimal progress in addressing the foibles may go a long way in greasing the skids of your career success. Besides, even if you do find some great resources with which to work, they may not always be available. Finally, the more that can be brought to bear … the more that can be brought to bear.

– Chapter 17 –

It Ain't Over Till It's Over

An ounce of prevention is worth a pound of cure.
Benjamin Franklin

The first smallpox inoculation in America was performed in 1721. The process entailed taking tissue from the lesion of an infected person and inserting it under the skin of a healthy person. While this caused the recipient to become infected, it was typically with a much milder form of the disease. The recipient's body would respond by creating antibodies to the smallpox virus and in most cases the patient recovered with minimal or no harm. More importantly, their immune system was then primed to make those antibodies again if needed; hence, the recipient would have immunity to the devastating disease – killed one in four of those who contracted it in the typical fashion.

It was not long after hearing of the procedure and its demonstrated benefits that Benjamin Franklin became one of its greatest champions. Franklin advocated for it in numerous forums including his newspaper and autobiography. He even established the Society for Inoculating the Poor Gratis in 1774, to make the procedure available to everyone.

The process of inoculation could be used as a metaphor for the self-improvement methodology offered by Franklin in his autobiography and adopted in this book: the foibles represent the infection, drawn from the past troubles of others, which offer the secrets to avoidance in the future. One by one, you have been exposed to them and resultantly you have become more cognizant of their repercussions, much as the immune system learns to recognize a new pathogen. The remedies are like the antibodies. Whether the ones provided in this book, additional ones offered at *www.brainiacparadox.com*, those of your own discovery, or a combination, they overcome the foibles and their harmful effects. Moreover, because you have sensitized yourself to these foibles and have mastered the remedies, you should have immunity against these foibles returning in the future.

Denial

If denial was one of your foibles, the exposure laid bare the reality that it does not matter who is at fault for the communication or social interaction issues that impede your progress, because you likely pay the most significant price, regardless.

As a result, you claim ownership of your need to change and develop, and embrace the mantra, *if they haven't heard it, I haven't said it.*

Now, you find that many communication and collaboration issues are avoided, or quickly resolved. What's more, others admire you for the way you handle interpersonal adversity.

Empathy

If a lack of empathy was one of your foibles, the exposure has underscored the importance of the principle that for you to get what you want and need from others, it is necessary for you to meet the wants and needs of others. This does not mean that you defer your communication agenda to your audience; you simply achieve what you want from your audience by being responsive to them.

As a result of putting yourself in situations where you are exposed to those of different perspectives and thinking styles, by reading literary fiction, and by listening with more care to all with whom you interact, you have strengthened your "empathy muscle." And by developing a news sense and using audience analysis worksheets, you are able to read and anticipate audiences more effectively.

Now, your communications have more relevance and appeal to your target audiences, and your interactions go more smoothly.

Jargon, Acronyms, and Complexity

If jargon, acronyms, and complexity were among your foibles, the exposure has helped you tame them, not by outright elimination, but by limiting them to the appropriate audiences.

As a result, you have sensitized yourself and created a "mental early-warning system," allowing you to adjust your communications appropriately and on the fly. You have also started creating a library of key messages that provide you precisely crafted and practiced messages that you can deliver deftly to address most situations.

Now, your communications are more accessible and effective to a broader range of audiences.

Verbosity

If verbosity was one of your foibles, your exposure has helped you realize the corrosive effects of excessive content.

As a result, you continually strive to craft your messages so that they are focused, concise, and organized for maximize comprehension; you communicate more with less. You do this by limiting the scope of things you try to communicate at any given time, by trimming and boiling the messages to their most effective length, and by organizing them so that audiences are sure to receive the most important points first. Likewise, you use meeting best practices to wring the most out of such gatherings.

Now, your communications are more likely to be welcomed, accurately received, and retained by your audiences.

Process Bias

If a process bias was one of your foibles, the exposure has highlighted the problems created when one relies too much on fixed communication processes.

As a result, you have updated your approach to ensure they include accurate initial problem identification and goal setting on the front end, and the measurement mechanisms and flexibility in the later stages, to ensure you drive constantly towards your objectives.

Now, your communication efforts help deliver the perceptions and behaviors you desire.

Aesthetics

If aesthetics was one of your foibles, the exposure has helped you appreciate both the importance aesthetics plays in others' attitudes about working with you as well as the relatively large rewards that can be reaped from seemingly small changes.

As a result, you have tweaked any aspects of your overall personal user interface that may have undermined you in the past.

Now others interact with you more willingly, easily, and effectively.

Collaboration

If collaboration was one of your foibles, the exposure has helped you better appreciate the indispensible role it can play in your success and career satisfaction; without it, the current runs against you; with it, the current runs with you.

As a result, you consciously strive to counter any natural inclinations that would impair interactions with others. You avoid "direct confrontation in favor of a more diplomatic indirectness," and you relentlessly seek transparency, openness, flexibility, tolerance, supportiveness, dependability, positivity, and sincerity. You consciously attempt to build rapport with those you meet. However, you have also studied the "laws of power," not so you can use them against others, but so that you can blunt their use by others against you.

Now, you are a desirable and effective collaborator, your work progresses with greater ease, and your rarely find yourself the victim of others' misdeeds.

Credibility

If mismanaged credibility was one of your foibles, the exposure has helped you better appreciate the crucial role it plays in others' willingness to trust and take risks on you. You also better understand credibility's fickle nature.

As a result, you proactively address your credibility, managing expectations, leveraging the power of third-party endorsements, and orchestrating your communications so they paint a cohesive and consistently-positive picture of you and your work.

Now, others trust you and your ability to deliver.

Selling

If an aversion to selling was one of your foibles, the exposure has demonstrated that even patently-great ideas and work need to be sold.

As a result, you resolve to sell yourself and your work. You leverage your enhanced "value" – due to your progress with the previous eight foibles – and actively advocate on your own behalf.

Your ideas and aspirations are no longer unnecessarily thwarted.

General Immunity

However, in the process of overcoming the various foibles, you have also been practicing, repeating, and reinforcing the methodology itself. And just as each infection strengthens the overall immune system, each foible you have addressed has strengthened your ability to recognize and address new challenges. As such, you should be well positioned to use this methodology to achieve any desired change going forward.

Even if you have been successful in overcoming the nine foibles, there may still be others standing in the way of your full success. As stated at the beginning of this book, the nine foibles included here are just the most common and consequential. Beyond these are others I have observed among those I have worked with, such as a lack of business acumen. Even excessive niceness (e.g., Steve Wozniak) can be a foible at times if it allows others to impede or preempt your success.

Based on the self-assessment efforts you conducted earlier in this book, you may have encountered feedback from various sources consistently pointing to an issue that significantly hampers you and that is not addressed in this book. While I am not sure of the original author, my father used to quote "the definition of education is: all that is left when all that is learned is forgotten." It is applicable here because the work you have done thus far prepares you to identify your unique foibles, to research possible ways to address them, and to use the methodology to overcome them.

Back to the Beginning

Prior to launching on the quest to address these foibles, I suggested that you write down responses to the questions listed below. Without referencing your original responses, write a response for each again.

- What is your ideal work environment?
- What external (things you do not control) barriers do you feel are hindering your ability to succeed?
- What do you consider your communication and interpersonal strengths?
- What do you consider your communication and interpersonal weaknesses?
- Which communication and interpersonal challenges have had the greatest negative effect on your career?
- Which audiences (individuals and groups) are important to your ability to perform (rank by declining importance)?
- What do you know about these individuals/groups? In particular, summarize what you currently believe is important to working effectively with them.
- What is your desired relationship with them?
- How effective is your current relationship with them?

Now compare your new responses to those you wrote down before. I trust this exercise will demonstrate an improvement in your circumstances, but I also hope that you will find you have developed a greater awareness of yourself and of your environment, and that the path for your continued development and progress are now clearer to you.

Keep at it. Tackle those additional things that need addressing and revisit the original nine foibles from time to time as necessary; lubricate that solution and innovation machine. Also, visit *www.brainiacparadox.com* periodically to see updates and new offerings.

Considering the role Benjamin Franklin has played in the book, it seems only appropriate to give him the last word: "Be at war with your vices, at peace with your neighbors, and let every new year find you a better [person].

Appendix

The Toolbox

The toolbox contains detailed information and instructions for tools referenced previously in the book. These include:

Foible Tracking Worksheet

Modeled after the tracking tool Benjamin Franklin created in his workbook (see page 86 for a replica), this worksheet can be used to track foible breaches. A digital version can be downloaded at *www.brainiacparadox.com*, or you could create your own.

Foible Tracking Worksheet

	Mon	Tues	Wed	Thurs	Fri	Sat	Sun
Denial							
Empathy							
Jargon							
Verbosity							
Process Bias							
Aesthetics							
Collaboration							
Credibility							
Selling							

INSTRUCTIONS

- Use this tool in conjunction with chapters 7 through 15.
- Place a check in a box whenever you fail in terms of the targeted foible. The appropriate position is determined by the day of the week and the targeted foible.
- Tallying should be done as soon as possible after violations.
- Checks can also be assigned to other foible sections, but such tracking should be done at the end of the day, so as not to distract attention from the targeted foible.
- At the end of the week, start again with a new sheet.
- Continue with the targeted foible until no marks can be assigned for the period of several days, or until an alternate target is achieved (i.e., it may be impossible to achieve zero marks in some cases).
- Once the target has been achieved with one foible, move on to the next.
- When the last foible is addressed, start again at the beginning of the list and repeat the process.

- Continue with several series until there appears to be little difficulty maintaining a clean slate. Then return to this tool from time to time to ensure there is no backsliding.

News Elements Evaluation Tool

This tool is designed to help objectively evaluate which topics are of more interest to a general audience. Among other things, this can be used to:

- Vet a specific topic for applicability to a general audience.

- Determine which of a series of potential topics would be of the most interest.

- Choose which elements of a complex topic should be emphasized over others.

"Newsworthiness" Tool

Consequence	0	Topic little affects audience
	1	
	2	
	3	
	4	Implications of topic greatly affects audience
Prominence	0	Topic has little awareness or is small in magnitude
	1	
	2	
	3	
	4	Topic is widely known or is great in magnitude
Proximity	0	Not close geographically or personally to audience
	1	
	2	
	3	
	4	Very close to audience geographically or personally
Conflicts, Crises and Catastrophes	0	Topic has no element of conflict or misfortune
	1	
	2	
	3	
	4	Topic is very controversial or calamitous
Human Interest	0	Topic has no "Gee Whiz" factor
	1	
	2	
	3	
	4	Topic is very novel, surprising, humorous, heartwarming, etc.
Timeliness	0	Happened relatively long ago or will happen in the distant future
	1	
	2	
	3	
	4	Something that just happened or will happen shortly

INSTRUCTIONS

1. Evaluate your topic(s) against each of the six criteria based on your audience's likely perspective (go to page 131 for a more detailed explanation of these criteria).

2. Designate a number from 0 to 4 based on where the topic fits among the provided examples at each end of the spectrum.

3. Continue to evaluate your topic(s) against the rest of the criteria.

4. Add the individual scores for each topic.

5. Map the topic on the following chart using the above score for the X-axis and the importance of the topic to you on the Y-axis.

6. If vetting a single topic, you should likely communicate those that are located in the upper right corner, and reconsider wither to do so with those located in the lower left corner.

7. If comparing different topics or elements of a complex topic, use or emphasize those in the top right corner and ignore or deemphasize those in the bottom left corner.

While this will be cumbersome at first, if you use it on a regular basis, you will eventually develop a "news sense." Then, without even referencing this tool you will be able to select topics for maximum effectiveness for a general audience, whether it at a large speaking event or during small talk.

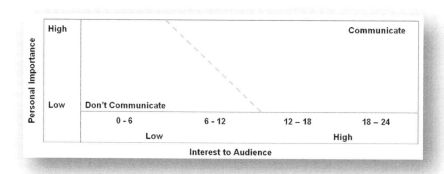

Note: This is an estimating tool for use with a general audience. This should be adjusted or overridden when relevant additional information is available for the audience. For example, a given topic concerning automobiles may score low on almost all the criteria provided, but may still warrant communication to an audience of "car people." The Audience Analysis Tool can assist you in targeting specific groups.

Audience Analysis Tool

Psychographics is the segmentation of audiences by shared preferences, values, behaviors, or other characteristics. This compares to traditional demographic segmentation, which uses such information as age, gender, geographic local, income, etc. (go to page 135 for a more detailed description). Just as marketers use psychographics to more effectively sell products, we can use it to more effectively sell our ideas to key audiences within an organization. Psychographics can help:

- Select which audiences to target.

- Identify which messages will be most effective for our key audiences.

- Determine how best to package and deliver communications.

Audience	Nature of Job	Responsibilities (and relationship to me)	Values/ Drivers	Preferred Channels	Communication Implications
Board of Directors	- Corp. oversight - Part-time (hence limited focus and availability)	- Corporate governance - Represent shareholder interests	- Stock price - Shareholder satisfaction	- Board meeting presentations/ discussions - Reports and briefing documents	- Generally, only interested in big wins, big risks or items of interest to shareholders/public - Material should be summarized and extremely well organized
CEO	- High level direction setting and review - Looks to their team to digest and package information for them	- Establishes organizational priorities and sets tone for what's important - Set/approve budget - Monitors major program progress	- Impact on corporate objectives (leadership incentives) - ROI - Corporation's external reputation - Impact on employees	- Standing leadership meetings communication pieces - Specially requested reports or documents	- Provide big picture - Emphasize business language and concepts - Link info/messages to corporate strategies or objectives - Be specific about what you are requesting of them.
Other Executives beyond my group	- Both strategic and operational leadership - Satisfy top management - Ensure team performance	- Partners or clients or providers or rivals - Competing for top leadership support and limited resources - Need their cooperation and/or support	- Career ambitions - Organizational metrics that affect bonus calculations - Opportunities to impress the CEO or board of directors - Risk adverse	- Leadership meetings - Standing organizational communications - Special reports - Email	- Hard to reach (receive more info from above, below and peers than can be properly processed). - Info sent to them should be carefully vetted
Peers within department	- Responsibilities for fairly narrow scope of work	- Partner or collaborator on certain activities - Rivals for management support and limited resources	- Career ambition - Career insecurity - Opportunity for high-profile successes	- Varies per individual	- Wants to be kept in the loop, hence requires more regular and detailed communication
Base-level employees (outside my area)	- Have little control over their workday	- Varies per individual - May need their cooperation and/or support	- Work environment - Job security - Recognition - Advancement opportunities	- From their supervisors/managers - General corporate communication tools	- Work with their supervisors/managers to reach them. - Keep communications clear and uncomplicated - Be specific about what you need from them - Need to feel in the loop - Recognize and/or reward

You may want to create a series of psychographic charts for your various key audiences, and create new ones as needs arise. The chart included here is a generic example. As some of these audience assessments may be similar from one organization to another, it could also serve as a starting point for your usage. However, care must be given to ensure that proper audiences are included and that specific evaluations are accurate.

INSTRUCTIONS

1. You can download the sample chart (as a starting point) or a blank worksheet at *www.brainiacparadox.com*.

2. Create a list of your key audiences, segmenting them by shared psychographic traits, and list them in the rows down the left side of the chart.

3. Across the top of each column, list the common characteristics for these audiences. You can use the example provided (nature of their job, their responsibilities and how those relate to me, their values and drivers, and their preferred way to receive communications), edit them or replace them altogether depending on what makes sense for your particular situation.

4. Input information into the matrix according to the respective audience and characteristics.

    a. Start by entering the information you will likely know off-hand with great confidence.

    b. Next, enter information you can derive by additional research.

    c. For remaining informational holes, consult others who may know this audience better.

5. Next, analyze the sum of each audience's characteristics for their *communication implications* and summarize those in the right-hand column.

6. If possible, verify both the characteristics assigned to each audience as well as the communication implications with a trusted and knowledgeable source.

7. After each communication initiative where this tool is used, evaluate and adjust entries as necessary based on the experience.

As with the News Elements Evaluation Tool, repeated use will breed familiarity to the extent that you will eventually be able to calibrate communications for your various audiences intuitively and without referencing your charts.

Communication Planning Tool

Human communication is much more complicated than we typically realize. Even basic interchanges encompass an unimaginable number of variables and potential failure points. This helps explain why effective communications – that which influence others' perceptions and behaviors constructively – is so elusive. Communication planning can help us identify and factor for those many variables, but they are usually more cumbersome than most people are willing to endure. The following tool is a shortcut for doing much the same things. It also provides other advantages including:

- Scalable: can be used to drive effective communication whether for a single communication or a large and complex communication initiative.

- Fast and easy: just enter abbreviated information according to the respective row and column items.

- Facilitates linear planning: audiences can be listed from top to bottom, in order of importance; each audience can be analyzed progressively from left to right.

- Facilitates non-linear planning: what is known can be entered first and then used to help determine the unknowns.

- Easy to process: all information available at a glance.

- Facilitates collaboration: the entire tool can be projected on one page/slide – so a group can view and provide input simultaneously. Available for download at *www.brainiacparadox.com*.

Communication Planning Tool

Communication Goal:

Audiences/ Stakeholders	As Is Perceptions/ Behaviors	Desired Perceptions/ Behaviors	Issues/Potential Barriers	Communication Strategy	Key Messages	Communication Channels	Timing
–	–	–	–	–	–	–	–
–	–	–	–	–	–	–	–
–	–	–	–	–	–	–	–
–	–	–	–	–	–	–	–
–	–	–	–	–	–	–	–
–	–	–	–	–	–	–	–

INSTRUCTIONS
Gathering Requirements
The left hand side of the tool (non-shaded) is designed to capture the basic requirements for the communication initiative.

1. Establish your goal.
   a. See page 185 for a discussion of goal setting (and problem statements).
   b. Write your goal at the top of the worksheet.
2. Identify audiences.
   a. List audience that will be key to achieving your goal down the column labeled Audiences/Stakeholders.
   b. Also consider secondary audiences: those who need not be influenced in order to achieve your goal, but who will need or desire related communication. Even if they do not seem essential, they can become an obstacle if left out of the loop.

Communication Planning Tool

Communication Goal:

Audiences/ Stakeholders	As Is Perceptions/ Behaviors	Desired Perceptions/ Behaviors	Issues/Potential Barriers	Communication Strategy
—	—	—	—	—
—	—	—	—	—
—	—	—	—	—
—	—	—	—	—
—	—	—	—	—
—	—	—	—	—
—	—	—	—	—

3. **To Be**: In the third column, list the perceptions/behaviors that are needed for each audience in order to achieve the communication goal.
   a. Validate: ask yourself and/or others, "If I achieve these perceptions/behaviors with these audiences, am I confident my

problem will be resolved or my opportunity seized?" If not, revise until you have confidence in your stated Audience and Desired Perceptions and Behaviors.

Note: The desired perceptions and behaviors can be different for all audiences, the same for all, or mixture of each.

4. **As Is:** List your assessment of the audiences current perceptions/behaviors in the second column.

5. **Barriers:** For each audience, list the issues/potential barriers that may impede the respective audience's transition from the *As Is* to the *To Be* in the fourth column.

    a. Consult the Audience Analysis Tool entry for this audience, if you have created one.

Identifying the Solution

With the basic requirements identified, the right-hand part of the tool (shaded) is designed to capture the main elements of the solution.

6. Review the information in the four columns to the left and consider a communication strategy (see page 187 for a definition) that would most effectively achieve the desired perception/behavior for that audience.

    a. Review the audience analysis tool on page 316 for information that will help shape your strategy (if you have not yet performed an analysis of this audience, do so now and add it to your psychographic chart).

    b. Even if considering all these factors does not lead you directly to a specific strategy, it can help you narrow down the possibilities.

Note: If unsure what to enter in this, or any other cell on the right (shaded) side of the tool, skip that cell and move on to the next. This missing information may come to you when viewed later in relation to other information in the tool.

Communication Planning Tool

Issues/Potential Barriers	Communication Strategy	Key Messages	Communication Channels	Timing
—	—	—	—	—
	—	—	—	—
	—	—	—	—
	—	—	—	—
	—	—	—	—
	—	—	—	—
	—	—	—	—

7. In the Key Messages column, summarize the messages that are necessary to support your strategy.
   a. If possible, draw from the Key Messages you previously created.

8. In the Communication Channel column, list the means of communication this audience prefers or that make the most sense based on other aspects of the plan.

9. Next, enter the timing information in the following column.
   a. This might include timing of periodic communications, a specific time/date, or relative times (e.g., "just before project launch").

10. Enter the same information for each subsequent audience listed, focusing on what is best for each specific audience.

11. When you have completed this process for all audiences, return to enter information into any cells that may have been left blank before and try again.

   a. If still having trouble, review entries down or across from the cell in question, to see if there are any insights.

   b. If still unsure, enter your best estimate.

Consolidation

Now examine the whole of the solution to see if the entire plan can be optimized, recalling the Lean Communication mantra, "Less is More." Consider whether you can replace two or more communication elements (strategies, messages, etc.) that are perfect for their respective audiences with one that will be very good for both. In many ways, this is like trimming and boiling. What you might lose in precision you can more than make up in an improved effort-to-outcome ratio.

12. Review the Communication Strategy column to determine if two or more audience strategies can be shared.

13. Review the Key Messages Column.

    a. Look for opportunities to consolidate any of the Key Messages.

    b. Examine whether any messages conflict or contradict each other. If so, edit or replace them.

14. Review the Communication Channels and Timing columns for consolidation opportunities.

Timeline Worksheet

More complex communication initiatives – those involving numerous audiences and activities over time – will benefit from a tool that translates the communication activities to a timeline.

Communication Timeline Tool										
Goal:										
					Time Period					
Audience		2	3	4	5	6	7	8	9	10

INSTRUCTIONS

1. Write your goal at the top of the page (keeps us from getting so focused on the execution that we lose sight of what we are trying to accomplish).

    a. If working with a digital version of this tool, you can simply copy this – and the audience list – from the first part of the tool.

2. List audiences down the left-most column.

3. Set a timeframe for the communication initiative.

    a. Establish a baseline: enter the date of the first communication activity in the column to the immediate right of the audience column.

    b. Determine whether your timeline will be in hours, days, weeks, months or will have specific dates for each column (necessary when the communications will not follow a regular time pattern) and enter the notation H, D, W, M. Alternatively, you can list specific dates or times at the top of each column.

    c. Map the communication activities, milestones, etc., from the first section of the Communication Planning Tool to this tool.

    d. If you were able to successfully consolidate items in the previous step, some communications will be listed in multiple cells on this tool.

4. Create additional timelines (nested) if necessary.

    a. Large, complex communication plans may require different levels of detail at various stages of the plan, so it may be necessary to create finer-incremental timelines that relate to a single column in the main timeline. For example, if the main timeline is segmented by months, the nested timeline might have activities listed by weeks, days, hours, or even minutes.

    b. Create as many of these as will be needed to support the communication plan.

    c. Make a reference note of these additional timelines (e.g., see Timeline 2 for additional detail) in the respective columns of the main timeline.

5. Add assessment points to the timeline.

    a. These are intended to assure we do not get so lost in the details that we fail to notice that our efforts are not working or circumstances have changed.

    b. These can range from a personal gut check to a formal survey, but in most cases, this will entail getting verbal feedback from some well chosen individuals.

Responsibilities Worksheet

Complex communication projects may have several people contributing different elements of the plan. The following tool is provided to help ensure clarity as to who needs to do what by when.

Communication Assignments

Goal:

Communication Item	Content	Assigned To	When Due	Who Approves

INSTRUCTIONS

1. As with the other tools, start by inserting the communication goal at the top of the tool.
2. Create a list of all the communications that need to be prepared and list them in the left-most column.
3. Provide a brief description of the assignment in the Content column.
4. Enter the name of the person responsible for the task and when it is due in the next two columns.
5. If applicable, identify who is responsible for approving the item and list them in the right-most column.
    a. This column is optional, as there may not be someone in that role.
6. At this point, you may want to sort the list, by due date or assignment.

Communication Mapping Tool

Much of the information we share with key audiences is reactive: something has just happened, or is going to happen soon. Too often, the events we report occur somewhat chaotically and as a result, our key audiences receive a very discordant series of messages from us. However, if we forecast potential communication items and tweak their form and delivery, we can:

- deliver a more cohesive and compelling series of messages.

- time our communications for maximum impact.

- minimize the impact of sharing potentially damaging information.

- reduce the overall communication burden we place on our key audiences.

- improve our "user interface."

		February	March	April	May	June
Noteworthy Items	Projects					
	Misc.					
Team	All Team Meetings					
	Team NewsLetter					
Executives/ Board	Executive Committee Mtng					
	Board Report					
General Org.	Corp Intranet Site					
	IT Intranet Site					
External	Press Release					
	Presentations					
	Collaborations					
	Others					

Communication Mapping Tool (example)

The basic Communication Mapping Tool has three main elements:

1. The top row representing the time interval.
2. The next series of rows, which are labeled "Noteworthy Items."
3. The bottom series of rows, which represent both key audiences, and specific communication channels.

This is a generic example of the tool that will be used to show how to perform the communication mapping process. This version is available for download from *www.brainiacparadox.com*. You may be able to edit it to meet your specific needs or you might be better off starting from scratch. The starting point should be the three elements indentified above.

INSTRUCTIONS

Use of the tool follows a four-step process:

1. Mapping Tool editing/creation
2. Mapping
3. Balancing
4. Rebalancing

Tool Creation

1. Edit the existing Communication Mapping Tool, or create a new one, to meet your communication needs.

    a. Establish a timeline frequency (monthly, bi-weekly, weekly, etc.) that corresponds with the pace of your work or reporting needs.

    b. Categorize the likely sources of noteworthy items. It could be generic and basic (Activities and Misc. as in the example) or it could be highly categorized. The advantage of the latter is that having specific categories helps prompt your consideration of likely topics. To help you project what may be noteworthy in the future, review the types of information you have officially shared about yourself, your team, your work, etc., over the last 12 months.

    c. Categorize the audiences and communication channels in the bottom part of the tool. As above, review the previous 12 months activities to assist identifying necessary categories.

Mapping

1. Perform analysis to forecast potential Noteworthy Items on the horizon.

    a. The analysis of the previous year's communications should give you ideas of similar things you can forecast in the future.

    b. Review team and personal plans as far out as they exist with consideration for what could and/or should be communicated.

    c. Consider forecastable activities that may not be contained in a planning document (e.g., activities that occur or reoccur, regardless of discretionary plans) and that may provide Noteworthy Items for communicating.

    d. Consider things you can predict (or plan to make happen) but do not fall within the previous two categories. For example, is there external recognition you expect to receive?

        Note: Do not worry if any of the items are uncertain or are subject to change. Later steps in the process adjust for this. Also, do not be overwhelmed by the time required by this initial step; future additions take less time and eventually become almost automatic.

    e. Review what has been communicated by/about others in the past to prompt ideas about what may be applicable to you in the future.

    f. Review the list of news elements from the tool of the same name. This will both help you vet some of the items you have already identified, but more importantly, may spur your identification of potentially applicable items in the future.

2. Make a notation on the tool at the proper Category/Timeline intersection for each element identified.

    a. If an item – a project for example – generates numerous potential Noteworthy Items, note them all according to the time they occur (e.g., major milestones).

    b. As a memory aid, look back on what you have reported via various channels in the past, albeit reactively, and consider if similar items are expected in the future. Also, do not be afraid to note items that may occur, but are not guaranteed (e.g., an industry award).

3. After gathering all available forecastable information at this time, the next steps involve mapping the noteworthy items to the proper audience/channel below.

4. Examine each Noteworthy Item above for its communication implications. Who should know this and when? Review all the options in the audience/channel section and note the communication wherever applicable (i.e., the same item may, and often should, be communicated to several audiences or through several channels).

    Note: Not all communications will be located in the same column as respective notation in the upper half. A project launch, for example, may generate several communications prior to the actual launch date. Other items may generate communications after the fact, such as reporting the results following an implementation.

Continue to map all items above to the lower section.

Balancing

Upon completing this process, you are likely to find significant unevenness in your entries in the communications sections: sometimes you have too much, and other times too little. In this phase we attempt to balance the entries.

1. Identify areas where there is an excess of communication for either channel or audience.
2. Review the communications in these areas.
   a. Determine which may have flexibility in terms of communication timing and shift forward or backward on the timeline accordingly. For example, if you are planning a "heads up" communication to announce a project launch one month before commencement, maybe distributing it two months in advance would be okay.
   b. Also consider the noteworthy event. Maybe that can be altered.
3. Rearrange until there is no excessive communications at any given time.
4. Identify where there is a shortage of communications.
   a. Review communications in the adjoining time periods to determine if some communications (or their noteworthy items in the top section) can be changed to the period where there is a shortage.
   b. If there are still shortages, consider what "manufactured" events might be created during this time period. For example, if you have been meaning to do some awareness building about an important topic, but just have not yet done so, you may wish to add it to your plans for this time period.

Rebalancing

At this point, your planned communications should be relatively balanced quantitatively, but not necessarily qualitatively. In other words, you may have planned an optimal flow of information for your key audiences, but the sum effect of that content might not deliver the perceptions or behaviors you desire. The next step is to rebalance the communications so that they deliver a more cohesive and compelling message.

1. Starting with your most important audience, help calibrate to their perspective by reviewing the Audience Analysis Profile for this audience.
2. Now review the planned communications for that audience from left to right.
   a. What is the accumulating perception this audience is likely to have?
   b. Does the progression of communications paint the desired picture of your or your team's efforts?
   c. Are certain messages too front loaded or back loaded?
   d. Could the messages be rearranged or augmented for better affect?

3. Determine if the timing of noteworthy events or planned communications can be changed to optimize "the story" you are telling to your various audiences.

4. Are there events or communications that can be added or removed that would facilitate a more complete or harmonious story? For example, if you really want to drive a process improvement message, but find that absent in your communication map, scour your planned activities for process improvement items that could be included.

5. Do this for each key audience.

6. Continuing to rebalance your communication plans until you feel you have achieved an optimal balance of communication activities.

Note: Creating your first communication map may require a significant investment of time, but once it is complete, it should not take much time to maintain. Add new items as they arise and adjust other items as schedules change, which inevitably they will. Once you have updated the upper section, remap the lower communications and then balance and rebalance.

Customization

As you begin to customize, do not limit yourself to the example components provided. For example, one large organization wanted to emphasize its core values as it went through tremendous employee growth, so it focused on a specific value each month. In response, a row was added between the top and bottom sections. These provided an additional consideration when balancing communications for a given month.

	Organization Values	Collaboration	Innovation	Agility
	All-Team Meetings			
	Team Newsletter			

Whether used for an entire organization or an individual, communication mapping is a relatively easy and amazingly effective way to manage communications to their greatest affect towards building credibility.

Although communication mapping may seem like a lot of additional work, it actually saves time. Creating reports, memos, presentations or other communications, often consumes significant time and effort – much of that used figuring out what to say (as well as what not to say) and how. Communication mapping provides a clarity of purpose that streamlines that process.

It can also provide auxiliary benefits: many organizations do not have tracking tools that provide a consolidated view of all projects and activities, and as a result, conflicts and other problems are typically not caught until too late. An unintended but useful benefit of communication mapping is that it provides a process and view that can help identify operational conflicts long in advance. In short, communication mapping provides the mechanism to convert the random notes and percussions of reactive communication into a harmonic symphony of information, underscoring the credibility of you and/or your team.

— Acknowledgements —

Writing acknowledgments can be difficult when a project has germinated over as many years as this one has. So many individuals have helped inform and shape the content of this book – ranging from casual conversations to formal interviews – that a full list would be excessively long and bound to contain embarrassing omissions. As such, I start with a blanket thank you to everyone who has discussed this topic with me, answered my questions, or shared their stories.

Next I thank the colleagues and organizational leaders I have worked with over the years, both within the communication field and across various STEM disciplines. These include those who were consistently supportive of my efforts to address this issue as well as those who, at least at times, pushed back. The Brainiac Paradox is a titanic issue. Both the supporters and dissenters played essential roles in forging and tempering the ideas shared in this book.

Of course, I cannot forget the STEM professionals who provided the impetus for this book in the first place. They have awed me with their brilliance, even if they sometimes exasperated me with their foibles. Special among them in my thanks are the individuals and teams that served as guinea pigs for the development and refinement of the techniques offered in this book. It was the memory of their successes that propelled me forward at the times when the effort seemed too daunting.

Naturally, I owe a huge thanks to all those from Stein, Klauber & Company. They have been like a family to me.

Among those I specifically thank is a group of former colleagues who read various drafts of the manuscript along the way. First is Gary Robertson, who proved a valuable sounding board and cheerleader in the early stages of this effort. Next is Mark Cybulski, who more than anyone else seemed to really "get it." He was a goldmine for insights, ideas, and feedback. Then there was Janice Rydzon, who read several draft pieces and whom I could always depend upon for candid feedback. Finally, Twila Osborn: her diverse experience and thoughtful comments proved invaluable in the closing stages of this project.

I extend a special thanks to my friend Bruce Burton, not just for his valuable technical and business wisdom, but for his contagious enthusiasm for the project. I could always depend upon him to pump me up.

I save my final acknowledgements for those who deserve them most, my family. To my mother, Mary Jean, who I credit for anything *good* that I have ever done, and to my late father, Henry, who served as an ever-stalwart example of integrity, hard work and, most of all, generosity. I am likewise grateful to my late in-laws, Raymond and Prudence Bair, not only for raising an incredible daughter, but also for their own inspirational examples, intelligence and humor.

Thanks also to my siblings Dan, Tim, Kathy, Joe, Tom, Gary, Mary and Margaret, who made growing up a rich experience. Particular gratitude goes to my brother Tim, whose input, feedback and assistance were extremely helpful; to my sister Kathy for her extraordinary attention to our mother at a time when I was in the throes of finishing this work; and to my brother Joe who personifies the best of both my parents and serves as an ongoing example of how one should live and work.

Finally, and most of all, I thank my wife and children. Living with someone struggling through the creation of a book can be very difficult. My sons, Peter, William, and Charles have had to deal with an often preoccupied father, bear the many times I wove topics from the book into our family discussions, and endure my incessant quoting of the great Dr. Franklin. Then there is Elizabeth. No person could ask for a better partner in life and I will savage anyone who tries. Her beauty, positive attitude and sense of humor buoyed me through even the most difficult moments of this endeavor, even as her share of the family workload increased. Beyond that, she has a keen eye, an impressive intellect, and impeccable judgment; her input has been indispensible. Strangers will think these the obligatory superlatives of a grateful husband, but those who know her will insist I have understated the matter.

— Index —

Made in the USA
San Bernardino, CA
17 January 2014